Migrants, Regional Identities and Latin American Cities

Library of Congress Cataloging-in-Publication Data
Migrants, regional identities and Latin American cities / edited by Teófilo
    Altamirano and Lane Ryo Hirabayashi ; Xavier Albó . . . [et al.] ; foreword by
    Stephen D. Glazier.
    p.   cm. —(Society for Latin American Anthropology publication series ; v. 13)
    Includes bibliographical references.
    ISBN 0-913167-79-7
    1. Rural-urban migration—Latin America. 2. Migration, Internal—Latin America. 3.
Regionalism—Latin America. 4. Group identity—Latin America. 5. Ethnicity—Latin America.
6. Urbanization—Latin America. I. Altamirano. Teófilo. II. Hirabayashi, Lane Ryo. III. Albó,
Xavier, 1934—. IV. Series.

HB1990.5.A3M55   1997   97-3401
307.2'4'098—dc21   CIP

Migrants, Regional Identities and Latin American Cities

Edited by **Teófilo Altamirano and Lane Ryo Hirabayashi**

Xavier Albó
Teófilo Altamirano
Hernán Carrasco M.
Paul L. Doughty
Lane Ryo Hirabayashi
Michael Kearney
William P. Mitchell
Bryan Roberts

Foreword by Stephen D. Glazier

Volume 13:
Society for Latin American Anthropology Publication Series
Jeffrey David Ehrenreich, General Editor

A publication of
The Society for Latin American Anthropology
and The American Anthropological Association

1997

CONTENTS

Foreword
Stephen D. Glazier

Preface
Teófilo Altamirano and Lane Ryo Hirabayashi

Chapter 1:   **Introduction: Change and Regional Identities in Contemporary Latin American Cities**   1
Bryan Roberts

Chapter 2:   **The Constitution of Regional Identities in Urban Latin America**   7
Teófilo Altamirano and Lane Ryo Hirabayashi

Chapter 3:   **Pressures on Peasant Production and the Transformation of Regional and National Identities**   25
William P. Mitchell

Chapter 4:   **The Politicization of Regional Identity among Mountain Zapotec Migrants in Mexico City**   49
Lane Ryo Hirabayashi

Chapter 5:   **Life Goes on: Revisiting Lima's Migrant Associations**   67
Paul L. Doughty

Chapter 6:   **Indians of the Sierra in Quito and Guayaquil: Interethnic Relations and the Urbanization of Migrants**   97
Hernán Carrasco M.

Chapter 7:   **La Paz/Chukiyawu: The Two Faces of a City**   113
Xavier Albó

Chapter 8:   **Borders and Boundaries of State
and Self at the End of Empire**   **151**
Michael Kearney

Chapter 9:   **Conclusions**   **169**
Teófilo Altamirano and Lane Ryo Hirabayashi

Notes on Contributors   **181**

Cover Photo: Paul L. Doughty
Urban bound migrants leave Cuzco for the
coastal cities, aboard the truck "Agente 007."

FOREWORD

The various civilizational processes spawned by the Urban Revolution were able to consolidate the myriad of micro ethnos, each of which possessed its own language and culture, into a smaller number of entities equating with larger political units.
Darcy Ribeiro, *The Civilizational Process.*

It is a pleasure to present this volume to the membership of the Society for Latin American Anthropology and other readers interested in processes of urbanization and Latin American ethnology. *Migrants, Regional Identities and Latin American Cities* is the thirteenth in a distinguished series of volumes published jointly by the Society for Latin American Anthropology and the American Anthropological Association. The editors– Teófilo Altamirano and Lane Ryo Hirabayashi–have assembled here an outstanding group of well-integrated, highly focused essays dealing with common themes of Latin American regionalism, urbanization, and migration. Contributors include scholars from the United States, Peru, Bolivia, and Ecuador. Collectively, these contributors provide an abundance of hitherto unpublished ethnographic detail as well as addressing major theoretical issues in the study of regional identities in urban settings in Latin America and, by implication, elsewhere in the world.

Historically there have been two basic approaches to the study of urban life in the developing world (Breese 1966). The first approach examined cities as isolated, independent entities–each having an existence largely separate from its rural 'hinterlands.' The second approach stressed the interdependence of urban centers and rural areas. By the 1930s, it became readily apparent that the first approach was untenable since much of the evidence suggested a high degree of interaction between urban dwellers and rural dwellers. Social scientists began increasingly to recognize that what is urban must, in turn, be fashioned by and fashion what is rural and *vice versa.*

Contributors to this volume productively follow the second approach. By focusing on the complex and ever-changing flow of people, goods, and labor from rural areas to urban areas and back again, these essays go a long way toward demonstrating once and for all that neither rural dwellers nor urban dwellers are truly isolated one from the other. Theoretical models emphasizing dependence have given way to theoretical models focusing on interdependence. For many Latin American peoples, it is not so much a matter of living *within* a culture as *between* cultures. The concept of Latin American "regionalism"–as espoused by Bryan R. Roberts in 1974–gives apt voice and an accurate description of the ways in which Latin American peoples understand and articulate their own lives (see Joseph and Szuchman, 1996).

For many cities in the developing world it is unclear, as Steve Barnett so cogently observed in 1973, exactly what constitutes "urban behavior." There are any number of creative ways to deal with the process of urbanization, and many Latin American peoples–

through complex networks of kinship, politics, and affinity—are doing so on their own terms. It is not only that "politics makes strange bedfellows," but that "bedfellows also make strange politics" as well.

Some recent Latin American migrants may more resemble Herbert Gans's (1962) classic depiction of "urban villagers" than the alienated, uprooted "victims" of progress forced into larger political units anticipated by Darcy Ribeiro (1968:50). On the other hand, one can never underestimate the potential for isolation so inherent in urban life. Enrique del Acebo Ibañez illustrates this in his poignant portrayal of the life of Ivonne Rivero, an urban squatter from Uruguay in Buenos Aires:

> *Ivonne knows little or nothing about Buenos Aires. She almost never goes outside her neighborhood, except to work or to take her children to school. 'I am not interested in going out. Here I am in my place, in my house, with my things, with my bed'* (1987:291).

There are doubtless many more thoroughly-alienated urban migrants who are exceptions to Larissa Lomnitz and Rodrigo Diaz's (1992) findings concerning social networks and support groups in Latin American cities as well as the important findings of Paul L. Doughty and others (*intra*).

Contributors' findings also fly in the face of those theorists who would assert that social class always overrides ethnicity in an urban setting or that religious affiliation often serves as a substitute for kinship ties. Patterns of urban behavior are astonishingly irregular. In examining the papers in this collection, a social scientist might well throw up his/her hands in agreement with Steve Barnett (1973), proclaiming: "Urban is as urban does!"

A number of chapters carefully underscore economic changes brought about by migration and contrast sharply with the economic arrangements described for Caribbean and European migrants to North American cities in the early part of this century. In the North American case, distances and inaccessibility rendered reciprocal exchanges impractical. In the Latin American case, however, distances may hamper but by no means eliminate intense and protracted social, economic, religious, and political alliances. In short, the Urban Revolution anticipated by Darcy Ribeiro has never fully penetrated the Latin American city. Many Latin American cities remain a myriad of micro ethnos that have never been consolidated into the so-called civilizational process.

Migrants, Regional Identities, and Latin American Cities has been a long time in the making. The editors and authors are to be commended for their clear and accessible presentations and for their willingness to revise and update their respective essays. It has been an honor to have had a hand in such a high quality, well-integrated collection and a pleasure to work with everyone connected with the project. I thank Teófilo Altamirano and Lane Hirabayashi for their patience, their good humor, and for their unflagging dedication and determination that saw this special publication to completion. Last, I thank Jeffrey David Ehrenreich for so generously allowing me to serve as an associate editor for this volume.

Stephen D. Glazier
Kearney, Nebraska, June 1996

REFERENCES CITED

Barnett, Steve.
  1973   "Urban Is as Urban Does: Two Incidents On One Street in Madras City, South India." *Urban Anthropology* 2(2):129-160.
Beezley. William H. and Judith Ewell, editors
  1987   *The Human Tradition in Latin America: The Twentieth Century.* Wilmington, DE: Scholarly Resources Incorporated.
Breese, Gerald.
  1966   *Urbanization in Newly Developing Countries.* Englewood Cliffs, NJ: Prentice Hall.
Gans, Herbert.
  1962   *The Urban Villagers.* Glencoe, IL: Free Press
Ibañez, del Acebo, Enrique.
  1987   "Ivonne Rivero: Urban Squatter." In *The Human Tradition in Latin America: The Twentieth Century.* William H. Beezley and Judith Ewell, editors, pp. 283-293. Wilmington, DE: Scholarly Resources Incorporated.
Joseph, Gilbert M. and Mark D. Szuchman, editors.
  1996   *I Saw a City Invincible: Urban Portraits of Latin America.* Wilmington, DE: SR Books
Lomnitz, Larissa and Rodrigo Díaz.
  1992   "Cultural Grammar and Bureaucratic Rationalization in Latin America." In *Rethinking the Latin American City.* Robert M. Morse and Jorge E. Hardoy, editors, pp.179-192. Baltimore: Johns Hopkins University Press.
Ribeiro, Darcy
  1968   *The Civilizational Process.* Translated by Betty J. Meggers. New York: Harper and Row.

PREFACE

Why are regional identities created in Latin American urban settings among some populations, and why do they appear to persist? Teófilo Altamirano and Lane R. Hirabayashi began to correspond in the mid-1980s in the hope of organizing a research seminar to examine these questions. Two initial foci were, first, identifying the varied manifestations of regional identities among migrants in Latin American cities; second, explaining regional identities as a predominantly twentieth-century phenomenon, as well as exploring whether they would persist as an ongoing dimension of Latin American urban social organization into the twenty-first century.

The basic concepts and conceptual framework initially adopted for this seminar originated some twenty years ago with the project "Regional Structures and Entrepreneurial Activity in a Peruvian Valley." Co-directed by Norman Long and Bryan R. Roberts, then professors of the Social Science and Economics Faculty at the University of Manchester, the project was one of the first of its kind in Peru in terms of its subject and its methodology.[1] Although research focused primarily on entrepreneurs in the regional setting of the Mantaro Valley, a diachronic and multidisciplinary approach perforce led the team to consider out-migrants from the Mantaro Valley in Lima, as well as the evolution of dynamic networks that conjoined individuals and families in the points of origin and destination.

The major way that we could think of to express our recognition of the achievements of this project was to organize a seminar focusing on the analysis of regional identities in Latin American cities specifically in terms of conditions at both the provincial point(s) of origin *and* the urban center(s) of power and production–an analytic framework that Roberts and Long have utilized to good effect throughout their work on the social, economic, and political organization of the Mantaro Valley. In essence, we sought to demonstrate how and why the hypotheses Roberts and Long initially advanced, concerning the role regional identities have played in the economic strategies of indigenous peasant migrants in contemporary Latin American urban settings, have renewed analytic relevance today.

Organization of the workshop, where drafts of the chapters that appear here were first presented, began with the selection of appropriate scholars, each of whom had carried out original fieldwork in indigenous peasant communities at the point of origin, as well as fieldwork among migrants from such origins in a major urban point of destination. In order to generate a set of comparable cases to examine these issues, we decided to focus specifically on Mexico and the Andean states of Latin America. In part, this was because these countries have sizable migrant populations of both indigenous and peasant backgrounds who have moved to and live in urban centers. Although this is a limited sample, we are confident that we have formulated and presented our findings in such a way that they will have broad relevance for urban research in other cities of Latin America and beyond.

On this basis we invited the following anthropologists to develop presentations that, taken together, would provide a global perspective on the issue of the appearance and dynamics of regional identities. William P. Mitchell and Lane R. Hirabayashi were given the task of examining the rural bases and dynamics of regional identities, Mitchell by focusing on rural economic strategies and Hirabayashi via a consideration of impact of state-initiated development programs on both "home village" and out-migrant communities. Paul L. Doughty and Hernán Carrasco M. were invited to focus specifically on the urban manifestations of regional identities, Doughty by revisiting his work on urban migrants from Huaylas in Lima and Carrasco in terms of his research on out-migrants from Puesetus in two different Ecuadorian cities. Finally, Xavier Albó and Michael Kearney were invited to participate because both of their research projects document the play between regionally specific and broader ethnic manifestations of identity.[2]

The present anthology is a product of the scholars' workshop we organized, funded by a generous grant administered by the National Science Foundation–specifically, the U.S. Latin American Cooperative Science Program, then directed by Dr. David Kelland.[3] We are deeply grateful to the National Science Foundation, Dr. Kelland, and his staff for making the sessions possible. The workshop was convened from May 10 to May 12, 1990, at the Institute of Latin American Studies at the University of Texas at Austin. We wish to acknowledge and thank both Professor Richard N. Adams, then director of the institute, and Professor Bryan Roberts, then director of the Mexican Center of the Institute of Latin American Studies, for their support, both moral and financial. Ms. Selena N. Solis, also of the Mexican Center, provided us with logistical support that facilitated our sessions in a variety of ways.

Collegial interchange, following presentation of papers, owes much to the contributions of the following commentators, the first five of whom were faculty at the University of Texas, Austin. Henry Dietz, of the Department of Government, and Bryan Roberts, of the Department of Sociology, presented comments on the Peruvian cases. Alan Knight, of the History Department, commented on the Bolivian material. The Mexican cases were handled by Roberts, and by Henry Selby and Daniel Nugent, both of the Department of Anthropology. Teófilo Altamirano, of the Catholic University of Peru, commented on the Ecuadorian case. Norman Long, of the Agricultural University of Wageningen, Holland, provided concluding commentary on the workshop themes. Our thanks to each of these participants, who gave their time and effort–during final exams, no less–contributing greatly to the scholarly ambience of the seminar. We also could not have completed this project without the efforts of everyone involved in the Society for Latin American Anthropology Publication Series, especially Jeffrey David Ehrenreich and his staff at Cornell College: Cheryl Dake, Annelise Earley, and David Syring.

We wish to acknowledge and thank the universities and the programs that helped us organize and carry out this project: the Department of Social Sciences, and the Anthropology Major, at the Catholic University of Peru; the SFSU Foundation, and the School of Ethnic Studies, San Francisco State University; and the Center for Studies of Ethnicity and Race in America, at the University of Colorado, Boulder.[4] The Committee on University Scholarly Publications of the University of Colorado, Boulder, provided us with a generous grant to generate the maps and tables that appear below. Additional support that allowed Lane R. Hirabayashi to coordinate the completion of the manuscript came from the University of Colorado at Boulder's IMPART Program, whose director, Albert Ramirez, is greatfully acknowledged.[5] Finally, because we have shared equally in the work this project entailed, our names appear in alphabetical order throughout.

Teófilo Altamirano
Lima, Peru

Lane Ryo Hirabayashi
Boulder, May 1995

NOTES

1. The final outcome of this project is summarized in two anthologies, both of which were edited by Norman Long and Bryan Roberts (1978, 1984). The following books and theses also make up part of the project's output: Altamirano (1984), Grondín (1975), Laite (1981), Samaniego (1974), Smith (1989), and Solano (1975). Numerous articles presenting project data have also been published in specialized journals, both in English and Spanish.
2. We would like to acknowledge the support of the Mexican Center of the Institute of Latin American Studies, at the University of Texas at Austin, for enabling Michael Kearney to attend our sessions. Other scholars were invited but, in the end, could not be funded or were not able to attend the workshop. This resulted in what we believe is the main limitation of the database: we were not able to include papers focusing specifically on the role of women.
3. The material in this anthology is based upon work supported by the National Science Foundation under Grant No. INT-8912746.
4. We would like to thank Evelyn Hu-DeHart, director of CSERA, for her support and advice, and Karen Moreira for helping us to proofread the manuscript.
5. Needless to say, while we are most grateful to these institutions, as well as to the National Science Foundation, any opinions, findings, and conclusions or recommendations expressed in this anthology are those of the authors and do not necessarily reflect the views of any of the above-mentioned organizations.

REFERENCES CITED

Altamirano, Teófilo
    1984   *Presencia andina en Lima metropolitana: Estudio sobre migrantes y clubes de provincianos.* Lima: Pontificia Universidad Católica Del Perú.
Grondín, Marcelo
    1975   *Un caso de explotación calculada: La comunidad campesina de Muquiyauyo, Perú.* Ph.D. dissertation, Universidad Iberoamericana, Mexico City. [A published version is also available: *Comunidad andina: Explotación calculada.* Santo Domingo: Secretaría de Estado de Agricultura de la República Dominicana, 1978.]
Laite, Julian
    1981   *Industrial Development and Migrant Labor.* Manchester: Manchester University Press.
Long, Norman, and Bryan Roberts, editors
    1978   *Peasant Cooperation and Capitalist Expansion in Peru.* Austin: University of Texas Press.
    1984   *Peasants, Miners, and Entrepreneurs: Regional Development in the Central Highlands of Peru.* New York: Cambridge University Press.
Samaniego, Carlos
    1974   *Location, Social Differentiation and Peasant Movements in the Central Sierra of Peru.* Ph.D. dissertation, University of Manchester, England.
Smith, Gavin
    1989   *Livelihood and Resistance: Peasants and the Politics of Land in Peru.* Berkeley: University of California Press.
Solano Saez, Juan
    1975   *De hacienda a cooperativa: El caso de Pucara.* B.A. thesis, Universidad Nacional Del Centro, Perú.

CHAPTER ONE

Introduction: Change and Regional Identities in Contemporary Latin American Cities

Bryan Roberts
University of Texas, Austin

OVERVIEW

The themes of urban migration and migrant adaptation to the city are familiar ones in the literature on Latin American urbanization. Less attention has been paid to the significance of the regional identities that migrants bring and that not only help them cope with an unfamiliar environment but continue to shape urban life in the modern Latin American city. The issue is one of the bases on which urban identities are formed that orientate people in their individual and collective behavior. Due to their rapid and disordered growth and unevenly developed economies, Latin American cities have not been conducive to the formation of clear-cut class identities or to a politics in which power is disputed on the basis of parties reflecting class divisions. Recently, attention has been focused on other sources of urban identity and on the social movements that derive much of their strength from them, such as gender, neighborhood, or ethnicity. Our aim is to explore not only possible new directions in politics but changes in people's conceptions of social relationships brought about by the exigencies of daily life in urban Latin America (Jelin 1987:5-7). The present volume is primarily the result of the efforts of two people–Teófilo Altamirano and Lane Hirabayashi–whose researches in Peru and Mexico, respectively, constitute pioneering contributions to understanding the contemporary significance of urban ethnicity in Latin America. The perspective of this volume follows the emphasis in their work on understanding the construction of ethnic identities through the practices of everyday life.

It is an appropriate time to take stock of the significance of migration and regional identities for the shaping of urban life. The years of rapid urban growth in Latin America are drawing to a close. The natural rate of increase of the population in urban and rural areas is declining, and the contribution of rural migration to urban growth decreases as the rural component of the population becomes ever smaller–28 percent of the total in 1990, with 72 percent urban (United Nations 1987:Table 3). The theme is not only of historical significance since, as the chapters to follow will show, regional identities remain an important source of urban social relations even as internal migration diminishes, and become, as Kearney argues, the bases of transnational identities as international migration acquires increasing significance.

The impact of regional culture on Latin American cities is pervasive, but often overlooked. This volume deals with some striking cases of persistence of regional identities–the Andean countries and, to a lesser extent, Mexico. In the cities discussed–Lima, La Paz, Quito, Mexico City–differences in language, dress, and custom between migrants and the urban middle and upper classes can be pronounced, reflecting, in attenuated form, the legacy of an older dualism between urban-based Spanish colonial elites and rural-based indian populations. This legacy is described in Albó's account of the two cities in one: La Paz, the capital of official Bolivia, and its other face, Chukiyawu, the Aymara capital.

COPING WITH URBAN LIFE

Economic imbalance and social divisions associated with colonialism and subsequent neocolonial relations of external dependence are a general phenomenon of the Third World. As Hirabayashi and Altamirano make clear in the last chapter, cultural contrasts based on region of origin are widespread in Third World cities. Even in Latin American countries that lack a strong indigenous presence, regionalism is still an important organizing principle of urban life. One instance is the apparently ethnically homogeneous city of Buenos Aires, in which regional culture has had considerable influence on social and political life. An expression of this is a tradition of popular music that from the 1950s to the present has provided a source of identity to internal migrants and migrants from Bolivia and Paraguay, who have faced social and economic discrimination by the dominant "white" middle classes (Vila 1991).

Regional culture and identities are some of the strongest expressions of community-based ties that are basic means of coping with urban life in the unevenly developed cities of Latin America. Though it is only one among the multiple sources of identity present in the contemporary Latin American city–and often not the most important one–regional ties persist as a basis of identity. These have not been replaced by identities, such as those of economic class, that would appear to be more germane to the exigencies of urban life. The continuing importance of regional identities reveals a fundamental contradiction in urban development. As cities grow, modernize, and become more bureaucratic, so, too, the daily life of much of the population continues to depend on kinship and community relationships, including those based on common regional identity. These relationships, as Altamirano and Hirabayashi argue, can be seen as substitutes for formal urban institutions. This has happened in economic relations where the counterpart of the modern, formal economy in every Latin American city is a robust, and growing, informal economy based on personal, not contractual relations (Portes et al. 1989). The neighborhood and its social relationships have become a crucial element in welfare provision as well as in collective political action (Friedmann 1989).

THE INFORMAL ECONOMY

The continuing significance of regional identity is based in part, then, on the failure of the economic modernization project in Latin America to produce an even pattern of spatial and social development. Concentrating opportunities at the expense of smaller places, and attracting all classes of people, the large city has been unable to offer stable employment prospects for much of its population. Wage work and the cultures pertaining to different types of jobs are an insubstantial source of individual and collective identity. Job and social security, access to adequate housing, and the prospects of a stable urban career based on these, continue to be denied to a substantial section of the urban population. Indeed, in the period since the mid-1970s, the prospects for urban social mobility have substantially worsened in comparison with the "golden years" from the mid–1950s to the mid–1970s (CEPAL 1989a). The most dynamic recent sources of employment have been within the urban informal sector, which CEPAL (1989b:Table 1) estimates to have grown by 56 percent between 1980 and 1987, compared with a 25 percent growth in the economically active population.

There is a certain affinity between informal economics and regional identities. Albó's chapter contrasts the world of formal institutions, including formal business, with the world of the Aymara in La Paz, which thrives on the informal economy. The informal economy provides easy entry for migrants who can be incorporated into the enterprises of kin or fellow-villagers, as the chapters by Mitchell and Carrasco document for Lima and Quito. Ties with place of origin also serve as a continuing basis for trade. The informal economy is also a source of exploitation and thus is part of the poverty in which many migrants are trapped. While the informal economy creates entrepreneurial opportunities, especially for owners of small businesses, the vast majority of those who work within it are unpaid family member or workers who earn below the minimum wage. In the crisis years of the 1980s, the informal economy expanded through women and young children seeking any kind of work to supplement household incomes that had declined substantially in real terms.

MIGRATION AND RURAL-URBAN LINKAGES

The presence and strength of regional identities in Latin American cities also derive from the patterns of migration that have been characteristic of Latin American urbanization. Since at least 1940, the smallest urban places (those under 100,000 people) have been bypassed by the migrant flows, growing less rapidly than both intermediate cities and the large metropolis (Oliveira and Roberts 1989:Cuadro 1). As Doughty points out, migration to Lima has usually come directly from small as well as intermediate size places—hamlets, villages, small and large towns. The cultural "shock" of migration is not usually mediated by step migration whereby migrants move in one or more generations from remote villages to district centers, from there to provincial capitals, and on to the metropolis. Moving directly from place of origin, migrants need to rely on those who preceded them for initial shelter, help with finding work, and general orientation in an unfamiliar milieu. These networks have a persisting importance in the city, reinforcing regional identities because of the continuing importance of informal channels to jobs, housing, and welfare. Consequently, the heterogeneity of culture in the largest cities depends, as Hirabayashi and Altamirano argue, on a set of variables concerning both the diversity of the places of origin–differences in economy, customs, and, at times, language–and the ecology of the city, particularly the residential niches available to migrants that facilitate or not the concentration of people of common provincial origin.

One of the most interesting variations in the presence of regional identities is the degree to which they have a formal urban organization. The degree of organization present in Lima is rivaled only, and in a somewhat different way, by La Paz. Doughty documents the strength of regional associations in Lima over more than half a century, arguing that they serve not so much to facilitate migrant adaptation to the city as to strengthen rural-urban ties. Regional associations send significant amounts of aid back to the village and towns of origin and lobby government on behalf of regional interests. By these means urban residents keep up their ties with their places of origin, where they often still retain economic interests, and participate in national politics.

Hirabayashi's account of Zapotec migrants shows similar processes occurring in Mexico. This case, along with Kearney's account of Mixtec identity as a transnational phenomenon, adds a further dimension to the accounts of the political significance of regional identities provided for Peru and Bolivia. In the Mexican case, a key variable is the state's attempt to centralize in the face of a centrifugal regionalism. The state's intervention also stimulates regional identities and factionalism. Hirabayashi shows that the specific forms of regional identity in Mexico City are often the result of competition for resources, as villages and factions seek to take advantage of the extension of state services. People become conscious of regional identity and difference among local groups as they organize in the cities on behalf of local projects. Kearney argues that Mixtec regional identity is being forged in reaction to the attempts of both the United States and Mexico to control and take advantage of their borders. On the United States' side, the issue is one of controlling illegal immigration. On the Mexican side, it is often one of profiting from returning migrants and their remittances. In reaction to the predatory activities of both states, Mixtecs, like other Mexican migrants, constitute themselves as an increasingly self-aware community seeking to defend their major capital–their social and cultural resources. The implication for both nations is, as Kearney puts it, not ethnic assimilation but indigestion.

CHANGE IN THE AGRARIAN STRUCTURE

The final, and one of the most important, contribution is the insight provided into the agrarian structures of Latin America. Each chapter makes clear that it is inappropriate to make a clean rural/urban distinction in analyzing migration and urbanization. Few rural communities are totally dependent on agriculture for a livelihood, and, as Mitchell shows, this situation has long historical roots. Trade, craft-work, and labor migration are normal means by which families supplement agriculture. Villagers depend on the market even for the purchase of foodstuffs. The fact that village communities are highly dependent on external relations is one of the reasons why regional cultures flourish in cities. The persistence of peasant farming through diversification provides a basis for urban migrants to retain interest in their places of origin and in the land or families they left behind. In Bolivia, Peru, and Ecuador these ties remain strong, as the papers by Albó, Carrasco, and Mitchell show. The struggle over resources needed for survival at the local level becomes, in many cases, inextricably bound up with these external ties and the material and political resources they signify. It is in these struggles that regional identities are forged and acquire an urban presence.

Contacts with the city have been built up over the years as villagers came to trade, conduct official business, or seek employment as labor migrants. In recent years the move to the city has become more permanent, with settlers using the bridgeheads created by previous waves of migrants. In all the countries described in this volume, return migration from city to village or town of origin still continues. As the urban economy wanes, as Doughty points out, the flow of people and goods is reversed. As the urban economies of Latin America continue in crisis, the significance of these return flows is likely to increase. It is a question awaiting future research whether those countries with effective networks spanning city and countryside are in a better position to meet the urban crisis than those in which the agrarian structure has not provided a strong base for urban regional identities.

REFERENCES CITED

CEPAL
  1989a *Transformación ocupacional y crisis social en América Latina.* Santiago de Chile: Naciones Unidas.
  1989b "The Dynamics of Social Deterioration in Latin America and the Caribbean in the 1980s." Working Document LC/G. 1557, May 3, 1989. Santiago de Chile: Naciones Unidas.
Friedmann, John
  1989 "The Dialectic of Reason." *International Journal of Urban and Regional Research* 13:217-236.
Jelin, Elizabeth
  1987 "Introducción." In *Ciudadanía e identidad.* Elizabeth Jelin, editor, pp. 1-18, Geneva: UNRISD.
Oliveira, Orlandina de, and Bryan Roberts
  1989 "Los antecedentes de la crisis urbana: Urbanización y transformación ocupacional en América Latina, 1940-1980." In *Las ciudades en conflicto.* M. Lombardi and D. Veiga, editors, pp. 23-80. Uruguay: CIESU/Ediciones de la Banda Oriental.
Portes, A., M. Castells, and L. Benton
  1989 *The Informal Economy.* Baltimore: The Johns Hopkins University Press.
United Nations
  1987 *The Prospects of World Urbanization.* New York: United Nations.
Vila, Pablo
  1991 "Tango to Folk: Hegemony Construction and Popular Identities in Argentina." *Studies in Latin American Popular Culture* 10:107-140.

CHAPTER TWO

The Construction of Regional Identities in Urban Latin America

Teófilo Altamirano
Pontificia Universidad Católica Del Perú

&

Lane Ryo Hirabayashi
University of Colorado, Boulder

INTRODUCTION

Why do some groups of rural-urban migrants in Latin American cities sustain distinctive identities that are deeply rooted in their regional point(s) of origin? This is the key question we explore in this book. Our starting point is Roberts's finding that regional identities are characteristic of indigenous peasant migrants who retain ongoing ties with their communities of origin (Roberts 1974). From the beginning, we also want to emphasize that while such migrants often bring their native languages, their worldviews and values, and memories of their customary forms of mutual aid and social organization with them when they move, these necessarily undergo a profound transformation in the urban setting. Specifically, we seek to describe and analyze this dynamic, creative transformation that generates "regional identities" in Latin American cities. Our goal is to contribute to the clarification and understanding of this phenomenon from a fundamentally anthropological perspective.

REFLECTIONS ON THE DEFINITION OF A "REGION"

The concept of "region" can have a deceptively objective status, if only due to its material base. In this sense, a region can be defined as a territorially circumscribed, and thus readily identifiable, physical locale. According to one authority, then, a "region" is

> a homogeneous area with physical and cultural characteristics distinct from those of neighboring areas. As part of a national domain a region is sufficiently unified to have a consciousness of its customs and ideals and thus possesses a sense of identity distinct from the rest of the country (Vance 1968:377-378).

Despite such appearances, a "region" is a complex, multidimensional phenomenon, as are the forms of social relations based upon it. For our purposes here, it is worthwhile to delineate at least three dimensions of the concept of "region" that are critical in encompassing the substantive focus and data that concern us here.

Beyond its status as a culturally recognized territorial entity, a region entails, first, a "place" or "places" that at a personal experiential level become(s) a "focus of identification," and thus constituent of a regional sentiment (Johnston 1991, Tuan 1975).[1] This is basically a humanistic perspective that recognizes and privileges the individual's identification with geographical space, via the mediation, of course, of institutions such as the family and social networks of kith and kin.

A second dimension involves the region as a "medium for social interaction" (Paasi 1986). This dimension highlights the notion of the region as "locale" and as a setting for social relations. In the hinterlands, for example, many significant judicial, political, and administrative processes are played out in terms of the region, as are some economic institutions such as marketing structures. In this sense, then, following Giddens, the "locale" can be said to structure practice, but at the same time is itself structured by the strategies and actions of individuals and groups operating within its context (Paasi 1986).

Third, and very significantly, the region and regional sentiment are also the product of macrostructural institutions and dynamics. Although the region might appear to be a natural phenomenon, Bourdieu reminds us that it is an inherently arbitrary and imposed category, based on the exercise of both discursive and political power (Bourdieu 1991). In terms of the third dimension, then, regional sentiments and solidarity reflect conditions that are imposed by the state.[2] On other occasions, regionalism entails a local critique of and response to structurally based inequities, such as are generated by patterns of uneven capitalist development (Gregory 1994:508; cf. Johnston 1991:67-68).[3]

In short, we acknowledge that these three analytic dimensions–the region as a reflection of a personal sense of place; the region as locale and setting for specific kinds of social relations; and the region as imposed political and administrative unit that can generate either compliance or resistance–are all potentially part of the mix one must consider in describing and analyzing this phenomenon in the hinterlands. What implications, however, do these analytic dimensions have for understanding regional identities among rural-urban migrants in Latin American cities?

Examination of the literature indicates that region as a "personalized sense of place," which in turn provides the basis for urban social relations, has received a great deal of emphasis. We offer, below, an overview of available research that indicates the depth and strength of this phenomenon throughout the countries of Latin America;[4] we will examine the structural bases of the region in the conclusion.

In the Mexican case, for example, studies carried out by Butterworth (1962), Cederström (1989), Cornelius (1975), Kearney (1986), Lomnitz (1977), and Orellana (1973) and on Mixtec migrants, by Romer (1982) on Mixe, and by Hirabayashi (1983) on *Rincón* Zapotec indicate how the social networks of indigenous peasant migrants from distinct points of origin provide an effective social, economic, and political defense in the face of urban challenges. In Guatemala, Demarest and Paul (1981) have studied Mayan migrants to Guatemala City, with similar results.

In the Ecuadorian case, the publications of Carrasco (1988), Carrasco and Lentz (1985), Estrada (1977), Lentz (1985, 1988a, 1988b), and Pachano (1985, 1988) focus on the role that kinship and common origins play in indigenous peasant migrants' insertion into the labor force, in other agricultural, as well as in urban, settings.

The Peruvian case has received a great deal of attention due to the large volume of migration from the countryside into Lima, and because a primary outcome is the number and overall strength of regional associations. The work of Adams (1959), Altamirano (1984a, 1984b, 1988), Doughty (1970, 1972, 1976, 1978), Golte and Adams (1987), Guillet and Whiteford (1984), Isbell (1974), Jongkind (1974), Lobo (1976), Long (1973), Long and Roberts (1978, 1984), Mangin (1959, 1973), Osterling (1980), Roberts (1974, 1981), and Skeldon (1976, 1977) highlights, through the use of both ethnographic and quantitative data, the social, economic, and political significance of regional ties in Lima, and their extension back to the migrants' communities of origin.

In the Bolivian case, the studies of Albó and Preiswerk (1986), Buechler (1970), Calderón (1984), Calderón and Dandler (1984), Sandoval and Albó (1978), and Sandoval et al. (1987) illustrate the mechanisms of cultural resistance employed by Aymara in their urbanization experience in the city of La Paz. In this context, the claim to ethnic group membership on the part of the Aymara peasant migrants in the city is framed primarily in terms of their indigenous cultural and linguistic roots deriving from the point of origin.

In short, regional identities have been wrought not only in terms of migrants' sentiment that a common geographic origin encompasses and entails a common heritage and ties, but also in terms of the practical uses of relationships based on regional affiliations. From an ethnographic standpoint, then, it is worth considering the cultural bases that lie at the foundation of regional identities. We examine such bases below.

THE EXPERIENCE OF REGIONAL IDENTITY AMONG MIGRANTS IN LATIN AMERICAN CITIES

In an impressive survey of the literature, Robinson argues convincingly that, in the past and present, "place" has held a special significance and meaning in Latin American cultures (Robinson 1989).[5] Similarly, it is evident that regional identities have been salient in both the self-images and collective images of indigenous peasant migrants in Latin American cities, and that regional identities have played a key role in late modernity as a basis for migrant social relations.

Because of this, we address the question: What are the experiential dimensions, as revealed by ethnographic fieldwork, that lie at the basis of "regional identities" among indigenous peasant migrants in Latin American urban settings? On the basis of the authors previously cited, and our own field research, as well as perceptions articulated by those who are directly involved, we propose there are at least five elements that comprise the experiential matrix of regional identities in urban settings: language; religion; conceptions of time and space; arts such as music and dance; and territory. Although these elements are clearly interactive, we will outline them one at a time in order to better stress their significant characteristics and contributions.

1. *A Common Language*. The native American indian languages spoken by many urban migrants were formed over thousands of years. In spite of the fact that urbanization processes subject the manifestations of native languages to much variation, they nonetheless continue to serve as a primary means for the maintenance of tradition and culture. Especially when monolingual speakers are confronted with a language barrier in the dominant setting, the sociolinguistic ties among migrants provides a channel that serves to reinforce common origins as a basis for urban social relations. Or, alternatively, in situations where migrants are dispersed and forced to speak Spanish (or English) on a daily basis, social gatherings at which their indigenous language is the primary mode of communication become especially sought after by some, who will go hours out of their way in order to attend.

The use of native languages varies from one country to the next, and within any given sociolinguistic community. Nevertheless, language continues to be an important factor in maintaining ethnicity and identity, especially in terms of social relations outside of the workplace and outside of the formal economy. Native languages can play a significant role in work relations, too, when a business or enterprise is built on kinship ties or some other dimension of social relations deriving from the point of origin.[6]

Native languages are also reinforced in urban settings, since day-to-day family life is often transacted in such terms, especially between the female children and the senior members of the household. This occurs despite the fact that many situations in the larger urban culture and environment condition the migrants to use the language of the dominant society, which is typically Spanish. As Albó notes, because of social pressure, the use of Spanish increases in urban settings. At the same time, it is worth noting that even the content and the message of spoken Spanish can still be influenced by native indian worldviews and languages. Migrants we have spoken to also mention that, even as they are speaking Spanish, they still *think* in terms of an indigenous language.

2. *Religion*. The migrants bring with them a religious outlook and set of beliefs that are distinct from those found in the city. This is a result of a complex process known as religious syncretism—actually, a synthesis of pre-Cortesian religious elements and beliefs that have been incorporated into the Catholic religious tradition. In agreement with the concept of syncretism, migrants have the ability to reinterpret their "native" culture with forms of the "occidental" culture predominant in urban Latin American settings (Goode 1970) and create new, intermediate cultural forms (for example, Greenfield and Prust 1990). Once in the urban setting, religious values can shift more to the Christian occidental pole; nonetheless, such a process is by no means mechanical.

The best example demonstrating the continuity of regionalistic syncretic religious beliefs in the city would be the system of *cargos* (posts) that migrants, in the spirit of both religious and cultural duty, assume in order to properly honor the Catholic saints in the urban setting. These celebrations have an important function in assembling migrants from a common point of origin together, in a setting in which ties of rural kinship, friendship, and propinquity are renewed and reinforced (see Altamirano 1989, Albó and Preiswerk 1986, Guillet and Whiteford 1984, Laite and Long 1987). They are also a means of social reproduction that greatly aid single men and women to identify and meet partners, with whom they may eventually marry and start a family.

Since the end of the 1980s, the growth of Protestant churches in both provincial and urban settings throughout Latin America has created certain pressures within peasant and indigenous communities, and also within the urban zones where out-migrants reside, that tend to reinforce regionalistic sentiments. All that is entailed in regionalism or in the recomposition of cultural values found at the point of origin are seen as the equivalent of backwardness–obstacles to modernization that, for the Protestants, are to be avoided at all costs. As a response to this ideological position, migrants of Catholic faith have responded with energy, reaffirming their own cultural beliefs and principles in the face of such challenges.

3. *Conceptions of Time and Space.* The conceptions of time and space have a distinct logic among urban migrants from indigenous peasant backgrounds. Time in indigenous peasant cultures is generally cyclical and divided into flexible periods, reflecting productive (agricultural) stages. Space is constituted by conceptions of community and of territory, which in the provincial setting can be depicted in terms of a series of concentric circles. At the first, and most immediate, level there is the household. Next follow the neighborhood, the community, and then the region.

Indigenous peasants' conceptions of time and space in the urban context go through drastic modifications, yet they do not completely disappear. To begin with, time for the urban migrant is relatively unlimited in the new setting, especially in terms of his or her kinship and neighborhood ties. This, in part, helps to explain the popularized sensibility about "*tiempo Latino*" or so-called Latin time, which is characterized not so much by being late so much as by its flexibility as well as subjectivity. The concept of space continues to have the home or household as its primary focus. Next comes the local neighborhood, even though the other social actors in the latter setting may come from other regions. Migrants, especially women and children, carry out their activities in the first and second spheres: that is, in the home or in the neighborhood. Third, as we detail below, one must consider the zones of the city that are populated largely by migrants. The city itself becomes the fourth level of socio–spatial relations, replacing the community of origin. We are cognizant that conceptions of time and space vary according to class background and levels of formal education. Research carried out in Mexico City, Lima, and Quito suggests, however, that there are migrants and their children who have never been in upper– and upper–middle–class residential neighborhoods, and who have never gone to the theater or to other exclusive places of the wealthy, even though all social classes live together in the same city. Nonetheless, the four boundaries to which we have made reference continue to be maintained for migrants, ideologically, and they can take on new life and relevance when the migrant returns to his or her home village, temporarily or permanently. In short, these cognitive elements can also reinforce relative class and ethnic distinctions, as well as the regional sentiments so evident in the lives of Latin American migrants (cf. Bonfil Batalla 1987).

4. *Music and Dance.* Considered as cultural expression *par excellence*, these vary from ethnic group to ethnic group. Their content, message, and general features make ample reference to the points of origin of the migrants. This is particularly significant for the Andean and Middle American culture areas, said to be the sites of some of the most varied and rich folkloric expression on the continent. Music as well as dance, in this sense, are not merely expressions or translations of the spirit of the migrants' communities of origin but rather express everyday social and economic relations and are associated with distinct

facets of village such as individual, family, and community life. These expressions are in accordance with the fact that the music of a given region is highly valued in the urban setting (Turino 1993). Music and dance are an integral part of family events and the activities of migrant associations, both in the sense of self-affirmation, but also as counterposed to urban and occidental musical forms. In interviews we have been told that each time that a migrant listens to a *huayno*, a *ranchera*, a *mulisa*, an *unsanjuanito*, a *llamerada*, and so on, he or she can be transported back to the home setting, and thus back to memories that make up one's formative experiences including the scenery, the village, one's friends, loves, enemies, and so forth.

In summary, music and dance, as well as other complementary forms of expression such as fashion and clothes, food, drinks, and the like, make up the repertoire of regional folklore in the urban setting. They reinforce a sense of difference and uniqueness on the part of one group of migrants from others, who also manifest given characteristics and customs that link them to their own regional origins.

5. *Territory*. Considering Latin American urbanization, there has generally been a strong correlation between the social, cultural, and class composition of migrant groups and the urban areas they reside in. In this sense, there are often middle– and lower–class sections in many Latin American cities located in marginal or peripheral zones. These are known by various names in Spanish, including *barriadas, tugurios, callampas, cantegriles, vecindades, favelas, suburbios, ranchos, villas miserie*, and so on, and they are predominantly settled by migrants. Thus in the southern and eastern parts of Mexico City, in the western part of Quito, and in the southern part of Lima, the groups that live in these areas constitute the lowest level of the social hierarchy and are composed primarily of poor peasant migrants–many of whom, despite the fact that they live in the city, are functionally illiterate in Spanish, speak only an indigenous language, and are more "provincial" in cultural orientation than "urban."

Common residence in such areas allows more frequent interactions in terms of the social and cultural bases outlined above, in such a fashion that the importance of regional ties and values (including those having to do with language, religion, time and space, and the arts) may be reinforced. In the Peruvian urban setting, Aymara tend to reside in common areas in cities like Tacna, Arequipa, and Lima. Similarly, on the basis of either broad linguistic/ethnic identity, and/or a common point of origin, Quechua, Chanca, Qollas, Huancas, Waylas, and Cuzqueños live together in Lima; in Quito and Guayaquil, the Salsacas, Otavalos, and Saraguros prefer contiguous residence, as do the Bolivian Quechuas and Aymaras who reside in cities like La Paz and Cochobamba, and some groups of Mixtec, Mixe, Zapotec, as well as other migrants from southern Mexico in Mexico City. In this setting, a culture of the *vecindad* can actually develop, which is characterized by solidarity, loyalty, and reciprocity based on regional and ethnic affiliations, involving the exchange of goods and services.

In short, there has been a marked tendency for migrants with similar geographical and cultural origins, and similar urban class positions, to settle in contiguous zones of the city, at least initially.[7] This tendency generates the so-called "stains" (in Spanish, *manchas*), that constitute part of the overall morphology of the Latin American city, which are composed largely of migrants from the hinterlands. For migrants, however, these "stains," or bounded spatial areas, are sites for the production of their own forms of culture and social organization, regional or otherwise.

Finally, we note that such urban ecological divisions must be viewed in terms of class as well as cultural perspectives. In this sense, as Castells has demonstrated, to the extent that urban neighborhoods or wards are co-terminous with class strata, local community can provide a basis for workers' resistance to the state, especially insofar as issues of collective consumption become points of struggle (Castells 1980, 1983). Similarly, those who occupy the higher levels of the urban system of stratification are also set apart by common spatial denominators. As Albó emphasizes, each class lives in established ecological zones within the metropolitan urban areas of cities like La Paz. Thus, neighbors have a proprietary sense of space that they share with others like themselves.[8]

THEORETICAL PERSPECTIVES ON REGIONAL IDENTITIES IN LATIN AMERICAN URBAN SETTINGS

We have already noted that Roberts proposed that distinctive regional identities in Latin American cities–which had appeared during the early 20th century, but which were characteristic of rural-urban migrants after World War II–were typically maintained by those urban migrants from indigenous peasant backgrounds who had strong, ongoing ties with their communities of origin. Why is this the case?

Considering Latin American examples between the 1940s and the 1970s, we identify the following basic processes. Regional ties involving kinship, friendship, and *paisanazgo* (solidarity and mutual aid between migrants from the same locale) provided the basis for a pattern of chain migration to key urban centers. Chain migration is, of course, that process whereby early migrants, who usually came to the city as single men and women, and who often established themselves at great cost, facilitate the more recent migrants and their families (Goering 1989, MacDonald and MacDonald 1964, Tilly 1990).

Since the capital city in most of the Latin American countries has been the primary site of industrial development since World War II, occupational and educational opportunities abounded there, especially in comparison to any given country's secondary centers. Thus, all other factors being equal, the capital is often selected as a primary urban point of destination. In such a situation, the subsequent facilitation of new migrants led to common occupations and/or class situations, as well as initial patterns of residential concentration.

In this general context, a sense of identity that comes from belonging to a particular region is heightened when social actors who share similar cultural, economic, and ethnic backgrounds find themselves together away from home.[9] Common origins, then, are one part of the basis of a regional sense of identity in an urban setting. As the papers by Mitchell, Doughty, and Hirabayashi illustrate, to the extent that migrants maintain social and economic ties to family, kith, and kin, and/or contribute to the development of the home village or region, regional identities in Latin American cities are based on relationships spanning the points of origin and destination.

In the urban context, regional identity is also the product of a common set of experiences. This is reinforced when familiar provincial values and institutions are reconfigured in order to help individuals, families, and the members of networks and groups deal with urban adaptation. This process, however, does not occur spontaneously among migrants but is very much the product of a distinctly *urban* experience. Thus, as the papers by Albó, Carrasco (in the case of Quito), and Kearney demonstrate, when migrants find themselves in a large and unfamiliar city, and they share an ecological/social location or even specific neighborhoods, and similar occupations (if not outright labor market segregation), they may see themselves in contrast to other groups in the city, and a sense of communal interests and destiny is intensified. When migrants face challenges in the urban environment–sometimes initiated by people who are reluctant to recognize, let alone accommodate, newcomers and "others"–the sense of regional identity can become further heightened and even flower. Although respondent, in this fashion, to prejudice and discrimination, regional identity is not, it must be emphasized, simply a pale substitute for thwarted assimilation. Rather, it is a matter of an ongoing dynamic that expresses and demonstrates the capacity for cultural reorganization and recomposition on the part of the migrant population (see Figure 2.1).[10]

Four specific analytic perspectives can be identified in developing a theoretical perspective on the construction of "regional identities" as manifested in the processes of urbanization in Latin America. In essence, each perspective highlights one of four kinds of issues that migrants respond to: the need for community, services, employment, and political empowerment.

First, it has often been observed that "regional identities" provide a means of adaptation and assimilation to urban culture, especially when peasant migrants, who are often from indigenous backgrounds as well, face serious barriers due to their class and social status. This basic perspective can be found in the work of Butterworth (1962), Kemper (1977), and Lewis (1952) for the Mexican case, and the work of Doughty (1970), Mangin (1959), Osterling (1980), and Weisslitz (1973) for the Peruvian case. The central thesis of this approach is that "regional identities" help to reduce the social, cultural, and psychological marginality of new migrants in the city. This is because regional identities facilitate the reinterpretation, within the urban context, of regional and, in the cases presented below, indigenous peasant culture beyond the point of origin. In accordance with this line of thought, kinship, propinquity, solidarity, and regional identities are converted not only into a form of social organization, but also into a set of relationships that can help the new migrant navigate through the larger urban society. In this process, the "early" migrants and their families are in a seasoned state of preparedness and can facilitate the urbanization process for the new migrants who follow, whether at the individual, familial, or communal levels.

Second, pertinent to the period from the late 1970s on is the fact that "regional identities" flourish precisely in situations where urban culture, as a whole, is in crisis due to the fiscal and political problems that plague most Latin American countries. In this context, manifestations of regional inclinations, whether in terms of identity or social organization, conclusively demonstrate that migrants are far more than passive respondents to their situation. Rather, they actively utilize their socio–cultural resources in order to resolve the problems that face them, including the need to find work and to find or build housing. This becomes even more so, in terms of the crisis situation, given that the government, official political parties, the church, and private organizations have not been able to protect or provide for the migrants either economically or socially. This holds especially true for the poorer, more indigenous, sector. Altamirano (1984a, 1984b, 1988), Carrasco and Lentz (1985), Hirabayashi (1986), Long (1973), Lomnitz (1977), Roberts (1974), and Sandoval et al. (1978), among others, have advanced this perspective.

Social organization based on regional sentiments and ties can thus be utilized to generate a wide range of popular organizations: mutual aid groups or clubs made up of provincial compatriots, neighborhood associations, clubs for mothers, "popular kitchens," and so forth. Although their bases may vary, all of the above have been organized in Latin

FIGURE 2.1 MATRIX OF "REGIONAL IDENTITIES"

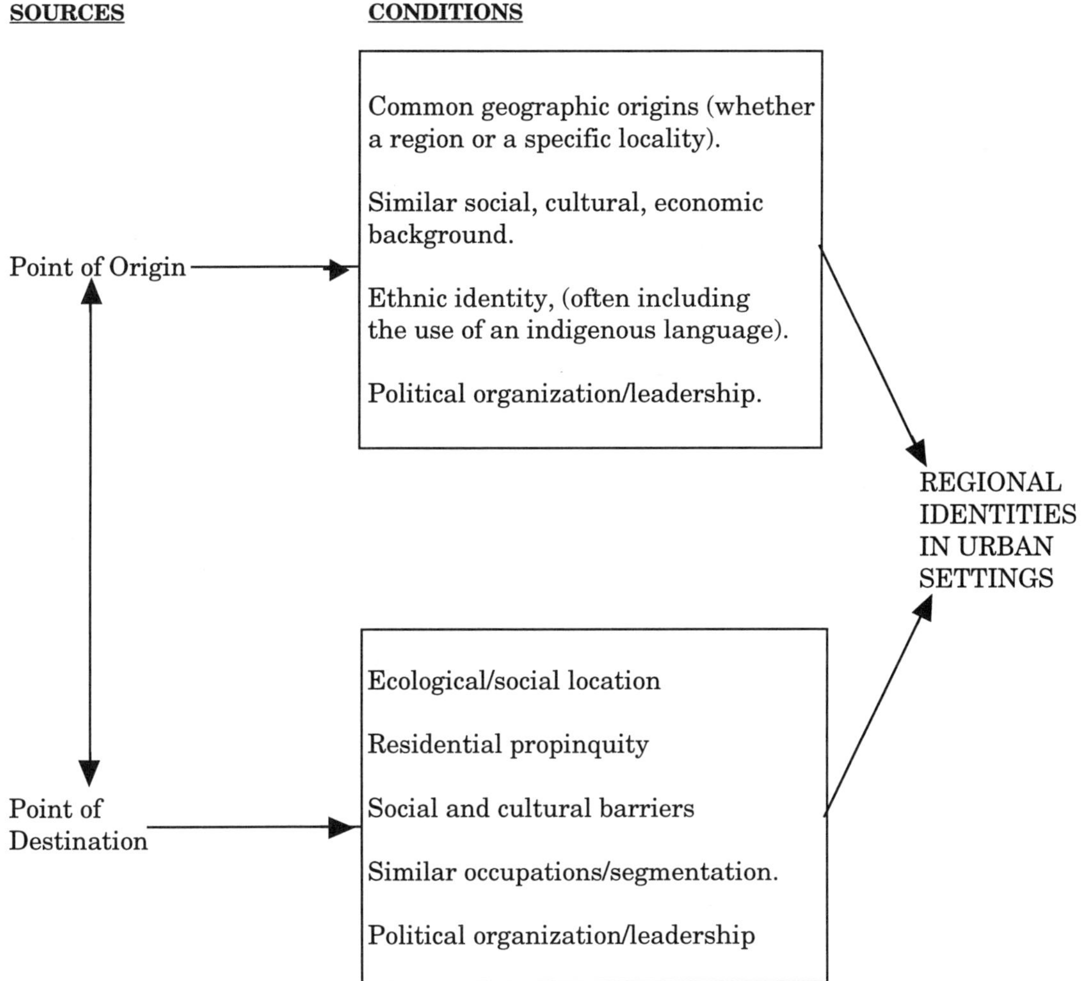

American cities in terms of common geographical, cultural, and social origins, whether these be villages, micro–regions, regions, departments, *cantones*, or states.

Third, regional identities can be seen, in part, as formed in order to gain better purchase on available economic opportunities, particularly in terms of the informal sector of the economy. In accordance with studies by Blondet (1990), Carbonetto Tortonessi et al. (1988), Grompone (1985), and Matos Mar (1984) "regional identities" entail a very pragmatic economic strategy that migrants in the low-income and even middle-class sectors of contemporary Latin American cities have utilized increasingly since the 1980s. In terms of this perspective, "regional identities" in urban settings are best analyzed vis-à-vis the informal nature of the economic and social relations of production in which migrants and their families are perforce involved (Roberts 1990), a point that we will return to in the conclusion.

Fourth, regional identities provide a vehicle for addressing issues of politics and political empowerment. At this level, we observe that regional identities are respondent to structural dynamics, involving complex sets of ties spanning the points of origin and destination. Hirabayashi has found, for example, that state development policy has generated regional sentiments and identities at micro–regional levels in the Sierra Juárez, as well as on a larger district level and beyond. The role of the state in the creation of regional and ethnic identities, however, is especially important in the case of a neighboring indigenous peasant group in Oaxaca: the Mixtec.

Driven by economic necessity and the demands of labor markets, many Latin American peasants, like the Mixtec migrants Kearney describes, increasingly venture into international settings. To the extent that they are able to reside in proximity to their compatriots, migrants form "transnational migrant communities" in various points of destination. The members of transnational communities are both linked to each other based on ties of chain migration, facilitation, mutual aid, and association, as well as because of ongoing ties to their home communities at the point of origin. The sum total of these ties, and the exchanges that characterize relationships between all parties involved, make up what Kearney terms the "articulatory migrant network" (Kearney 1986:77-92). Thus, a transnational community:

> should be understood primarily in terms of its *international* social, political, and economic components, and class relations, but not in a spatial sense and certainly not in the sense that "community" has historically been used in social science literature (our emphasis; Kearney and Nagengast 1989:2).

Kearney's research delineates the role of the state in effecting the transition from regional to ethnic identities, since the state apparatus in both Mexico and the United States has been central in creating pressures that cannot be successfully addressed by organizations based on microregional identities. As Kearney convincingly argues, such pressures have greatly contributed to the construction of pan-Mixtec identity that did not exist as such before. Thus, Kearney demonstrates that policies of the state in both domestic and in transnational settings can generate conditions at the point(s) of destination and origin that transform regional identities into broader ethnic identities. New alliances and organizations developed by out-migrants can then be used to address inequities at the point of origin, destination, or both (see Kearney 1986). In settings such as La Paz, where in-migration and patterns of resistance are deeply rooted, we can observe a situation where regional roots, while extant, and while still the basis for the social organization of recent migrants, have also evolved over a period of centuries into a pan-Aymara consciousness.[11]

In sum, the four issues that generate a context for the production of regional identities in the process of urbanization in Latin American cities can be seen as complementary. Consideration of each provides insight into a range of settings where regional identities among rural-urban migrants have been reported.

The first need, for community, is especially appropriate for understanding urbanization processes in countries that have relatively separated rural and urban structures, or where migration is a more recent phenomenon. Such a situation applies, for example, to cities like Quito, La Paz, Cuzco, Cuenca, and Cochabamba.

The second need, for basic resources, information, and services, appears to be most central in settings characterized by a number of decades of migration between the city and the hinterlands—especially when and where the urban infrastructure is weak. This is the case in Guayaquil, Monterrey, Trujillo, Arequipa, Lima, and Mexico City.

The third need, for employment, is closely related to the previous two needs, and we regard it as being quite useful, analytically speaking. This is because the period from 1980 to 1990 has been a decade of severe dislocation throughout Latin America—a crisis at once political and cultural, but especially economic. Clearly, there is a direct relationship between economic crisis, the growing importance of informal sector economic activities, and general urban conditions necessitating self-help, that influence indigenous peasant migrants to draw from regional ties in the city, whether as opposed to or in addition to other kinds of ties (Roberts 1990:42). We will return to this point again in the last chapter.

The fourth need, for political empowerment, is evident both in terms of challenges and opportunities migrants face both in the city and "back home." As Hirabayashi has specified in an earlier publication (1986), processes of politicization on the part of indigenous peasant migrants must be seen in terms of both rural and urban spheres, given that macrostructural forces and dynamics are always mediated by class and factional interests on the part of migrants and their compatriots in the city and back home. In addition, at least in terms of the case studies presented below, a range of situational variables can have an impact on the political dynamics of migrant communities, including critical mass (Fischer 1976), and the nature of state and local political structures.[12]

THE DUAL NATURE OF MIGRANT REGIONAL IDENTITIES

In conclusion, a wide range of studies of migrants in urban Latin America, including those by Bonfil Batalla (1988), Butterworth and Chance (1981), Carbonetto Tortonessi et al. (1988), Grompone (1985), Lloyd (1979), Matos Mar (1984), and Roberts (1978) emphasize the necessity of viewing the formation of regional identities not only as an expression of rural experiences, but also as an integral part of the larger process of urbanization, especially in Latin American capitals. According to these authors, regional identities have twin origins, being both provincial and urban, and these are mutually complementary dimensions. On the one hand, regional identities are "of the provinces" because the majority of those who are involved in their creation came from the countryside of a given nation. Thus, migrants' regional identities in the city are influenced by cultural patterns found at the point of origin. Regional identities, on the other hand, are also distinctly urban because they develop in response to social, cultural, and economic conditions generated in and by the urban setting. As such, regional identities form an integral part of contemporary urban life throughout Latin America. As a number of chapters below indicate, regional identities also appear to lie at the foundation of many instances of contemporary indigenous ethnic formation in Latin American urban settings.[13]

NOTES

1. We offer this formulation but note that some geographers propose that "place" and "region" are best kept analytically separate in order to differentiate subjective and structural orders.

2. Williams (1983) also provides relevant discussion of the concept of "region." In addition to emphasizing the inherently political dimensions of the "regional," Williams notes that, as opposed to the related concepts of "the province" or "the suburbs," ideology based on the former can provide the basis for a counter-discourse, critical of the excesses if not outright hegemony of the city.

3. In line with Long and Roberts's class perspective on regional identity (1984:4), we caution that there is nothing inherently progressive about regionalism, whether as an ideology, a social movement, or a theoretical orientation. The multiplicity of regionalist discourses, as expressed by those holding distinct ethnic and class positions, is the subject of a recent article by Lomnitz-Adler (1991). In his discussion of regional culture in Morelos and the Huasteca, Lomnitz-Adler presents a stimulating analysis, highlighting a "terminology and conceptual framework" for studying the politics of culture "in internally differentiated regional spaces" (1991:195).

4. Readers will note that our overview involves some generalizations about Latin American urban settings. It is important to remember that such settings are clearly more diverse than has been previously appreciated. For an outstanding example, see Doughty's article on Lima *intra*; readers can also consult articles in an anthology compiled by Lombardi and Veiga (1989).

5. Robinson notes the special importance that "place" has often had for the indigenous peoples of Latin America, especially when and where "place" involves a fit between kinship and territory (Robinson 1989:159, 161, 167). He cites, for example, the use of the Quechua term *llacta / llacctay* (which he glosses as "my soil") in communities from northern Ecuador to southern Argentina.

6. In this context, alliances between kith and kin, framed in terms of ethnic and regional identity and regulated by sentiments of loyalty and solidarity, are transformed into key resources that migrants rely upon to fulfill their aspirations. In such cases, the preference demonstrated by certain groups of migrants from the same background toward specific economic niches or occupational pursuits tangibly illustrates the linkage between ties based on regional identity and economic activity.

7. Doughty's case study *intra* is significant because the urban residential propinquity of migrants from a given rural community does not always occur; nor is it the case that regional identities in urban settings are necessarily predicated upon propinquity.

8. Sometimes, when different socioeconomic groups do come into contact, the resultant interactions can be characterized by mutual distrust and disdain. In this fashion, the very heterogeneity of the city can cause the individual members of a given subculture "to embrace [their] own social world all the more firmly, thus contributing to its further intensification" (Fischer 1976:37-38).

9. This heightening effect, which is clearly not an automatic process, indicates that regional identities are not a simple matter of cultural continuity; see Carrasco's research *intra*.

10. This figure is adapted from Altamirano 1984a.

11. Analytically speaking, regional identity may overlap considerably with ethnic identity. Our efforts here are directed toward highlighting the role of the former, especially in terms of the social and political organization of rural-urban migrants from indigenous peasant backgrounds. We also emphasize that previous research by Albó and his colleagues, as well as by Kearney and his colleagues, documents the regional bases of the pan-Aymara and pan-Mixtec ethnic identities described in their chapters *infra* (for example, Kearney 1986, 1989, Kearney and Nagengast 1989, Sandoval and Albó 1978, and Sandoval et al. 1987).

12. Two caveats are necessary at this juncture. First, regional identities should not be taken as an invitation to practice "benign neglect" toward the low-income sectors in Latin American cities because "they will take care of their own" (Henry Selby, personal communication May, 1990).

Second, as Roberts notes in his introduction, there are other key bases that urban migrants from indigenous peasant backgrounds can utilize to organize themselves in urban settings (for example, Blondet 1990). Montecino Aguirre and Willson Aedo (1983) provide an important study of Mapuche women in

Santiago, illustrating how gender provides the main organizing principle that allows these indigenous women to resist unjust conditions in their neighborhoods and work place. Generally speaking, the research literature indicates interest in a wide range of forms of urban collective identities. Class (for example, Katzman and Reyna 1979), neighborhood (for example, Taube 1986), gender (for example, Nash and Safa 1985), human rights (for example, Varese 1987), or some combination of the above elements (for example, Castells 1983; Schuurman and Naerssen 1989) have all received attention as emerging bases for social movements in Latin America. Thus, we focus on regional sentiments among indigenous peasant migrants as *one* among a number of possible dimensions of identity and organization in contemporary urban Latin America, albeit a central one.

13. For the record, we define "ethnicity" as a type of *cultural* segmentation that involves a sense of distinct geographical origins, as well as a sense of different "historical traditions, social customs, language, physical appearances, and religion" (see Thompson and Rudolph 1986:32, *passim*). The advantage of this conceptualization is that it allows the study of ethnicity alone or *in combination* with other kinds of segmentation, including class and regional, on an empirical basis.

REFERENCES CITED

Adams, Richard N.
  1959   *A Community in the Andes: Problems and Progress in Muquiyauyo.* Seattle: University of Washington Press.
Albó, Xavier, and Matías Preiswerk, editors
  1986   *Los señores del gran poder.* La Paz, Bolivia: Centro de Teología Popular.
Altamirano, Teófilo
  1984a   *Presencia andina en Lima metropolitana: Estudio sobre migrantes y clubes de provincianos.* Lima: Pontificia Universidad Católica Del Perú.
  1984b   "Regional Commitment Among Central Highlands Migrants in Lima." In *Miners, Peasants, and Entrepreneurs.* Norman Long and Bryan Roberts, editors, pp. 198-215. New York: Cambridge University Press.
  1988   *Cultura andina y pobreza urbana: Aymaras en Lima metropolitana.* Lima: Pontificia Universidad Católica Del Perú.
  1989   "La fiesta de la 'Mamacha' Candelaria de Ocobamba (Apurímac), en Lima." *Anthropológica* [Lima, Perú] 7:71-85.
Blondet, Cecilia
  1990   "Establishing an Identity: Women Settlers in a Poor Lima Neighborhood." In *Women and Social Change in Latin America.* Elizabeth Jelin, editor, pp. 12-46. London: Zed Books, and the United Nations Institute for Social Development.
Bonfil Batalla, Guillermo
  1987   "Los pueblos indios, sus culturas y las políticas culturales." In *Políticas culturales en América Latina.* Néstor García Canclini, editor, pp. 89-125. México: Grijalbo.
  1988   "La teoría del control cultural en el estudio de procesos étnicos." *Anuario Antropológico* 86:13-53.
Bourdieu, Pierre
  1991   "Identity and Representation." In *Language and Symbolic Power*, by Pierre Bourdieu. John B. Thompson, editor, pp. 220-228. Cambridge, MA: Harvard University Press.
Buechler, Hans C.
  1970   "The Ritual Dimension of Rural-Urban Networks: The Fiesta System in the Northern Highlands of Bolivia." In *Peasants in Cities.* William Mangin, editor, pp. 62-71. Boston: Houghton Mifflin.
Butterworth, Douglas
  1962   "A Study of the Urbanization Process among Mixtec Migrants in Mexico City." *América Indígena* 22:257-274.
Butterworth, Douglas, and John K. Chance
  1981   *Latin American Urbanization.* New York: Oxford University Press.
Calderón G., Fernando
  1984   *Urbanización y etnicidad: El caso de La Paz.* Cochabamba, Bolivia: Centro de Estudios de la Realidad Económica y Social.

Calderón, Fernando, and Jorge Dandler, editors
  1984 *Bolivia: La fuerza histórica del campesinado: Movimientos campesinos y etnicidad.* Cochabamba, Boliva: Centro de Estudios de la Realidad Económica y Social, and the United Nations Research Institute for Social Development.

Carbonetto Tortonessi, Daniel, Jenny Hoyle, and Mario Tueros
  1988 *Lima: Sector informal.* Lima: Centro de Estudios Para el Desarrollo y la Participación.

Carrasco, Hernán, and Carola Lentz
  1985 *Migrantes campesinos de Licto y Flores.* Quito, Ecuador: Ediciones ABYA-YALA.

Carrasco, Hernán
  1988 "Estudio de caso: Los migrantes de Puesetus en Quito." In *Caminantes y retornos.* Gilda Farrell, Simón Pachano, and Hernán Carrasco, editors, pp.109-164. Quito, Ecuador: Instituto de Estudios Ecuatorianos.

Castells, Manuel
  1980 *Multinational Capital, National States and Local Communities.* Berkeley: University of California, Institute of Urban and Regional Development, Working paper.
  1983 *The City and the Grassroots: A Cross-Cultural Theory of Urban Social Movements.* Berkeley: University of California Press.

Cederström, Thoric Nils
  1989 "Migrant Village Associations and Community Development in the Mixteca Region of Mexico." Paper presented at the annual meeting of the American Anthropological Association, Washington DC, November 15.

Cornelius, Wayne A.
  1975 *Politics and the Migrant Poor in Mexico City.* Stanford: Stanford University Press.

Demarest, William J., and Benjamin D. Paul
  1981 "Mayan Migrants in Guatemala City." *Anthropology U.C.L.A.* 11:43-73.

Doughty, Paul L.
  1970 "Behind the Back of the City: "Provincial Life in Lima, Peru." In *Peasants in Cities.* William Mangin, editor, pp. 30-46. Boston: Houghton Mifflin.
  1972 "Peruvian Migrant Identity in the Urban Milieu." In *The Anthropology of Urban Environments.* Thomas Weaver and Douglas White, editors, pp. 39-50. Boulder, CO: The Society for Applied Anthropology, Monograph 11.
  1976 "The Social Lives of Migrants: The Case of Provincial Voluntary Assocations in Lima." *Actes Du XLII Congrès International des Américanistes*, Volume 10:331-337.
  1978 "El caso de las asociaciones provinciales voluntarias de Lima: Algunos problemas metodológicos y de interpretación." In *Ensayos histórico-sociales sobre la urbanización en América Latina.* J. E. Hardoy, R. M. Morse, and R. P. Schaedel, editors, pp. 295-313. Buenos Aires: Ediciones SIAP-CLACSO.

Estrada, Julio
  1977 *Regionalismo y migración.* Guayaquil: Casa de la Cultura Ecuatoriana, Archivo Histórico del Guayas.

Fischer, Claude S.
  1976 *The Urban Experience.* New York: Harcourt Brace Jovanovich.

Goering, John M.
  1989 "Introduction and Overview." [Special issue on "The 'Explosiveness' of Chain Migration: Research and policy issues."] *International Migration Review* 23:797-812.

Golte, Jürgen, and Norma Adams
  1987 *Los caballeros de troya de los invasores: Estrategias campesinas en la conquista de la gran Lima.* Lima: Instituto de Estudios Peruanos.

Goode, Judith Granich
  1970 "Latin American Urbanism and Corporate Groups." *Anthropological Quarterly* 43:146-167.

Greenfield, Sidney M., and Russell R. Prust
  1990 "Popular Religion, Patronage, and Resource Distribution in Brazil: A Model of an Hypothesis for the Surivival [sic] of the Economically Marginal." In *Perspectives on the Informal Economy*, Monographs in Economic Anthropology, No. 8. M. Estellie Smith, editor, pp. 123-145. Lanham, MD: University Press of America.

Gregory, Derek
    1994   "Region." In *The Dictionary of Human Geography*. R. J. Johnston, Derek Gregory, and David M. Smith, editors. pp. 506-509. (Third edition). Cambridge: Blackwell.
Grompone, Romeo
    1985   *Talleristas y vendedores ambulantes de Lima*. Lima: Desco.
Guillet, David, and Scott Whiteford
    1984   "A Comparative View of the Role of the Fiesta Complex in Migrant Adaptation." *Urban Anthropology* 3:222-242.
Hirabayashi, Lane Ryo
    1983   "On the Formation of Migrant Village Associations in Mexico: Mixtec and Mountain Zapotec Cases." *Urban Anthropology* 12:29-44.
    1986   "The Migrant Village Association in Latin America: A Comparative Analysis." *Latin American Research Review* 21:7-29.
Isbell, Billie Jean
    1974   "The Influence of Migrants upon Traditional Social and Political Concepts: A Peruvian Case Study." *Latin American Urban Research* 4:237-259.
Johnston, R. J.
    1991   *A Question of Place: Exploring the Practice of Human Geography*. Oxford: Blackwell.
Jongkind, Fred
    1974   "A Reappraisal of the Role of Regional Associations of Lima, Peru." *Comparative Studies in Society and History* 16:471-482.
Katzman, Ruben, and José Luis Reyna, editors
    1979   *Fuerza de trabajo y movimientos laborales en América Latina*. Mexico City: El Colegio de México.
Kearney, Michael
    1986   "Integration of the Mixteca and the Western U.S.-Mexico Region via Migratory Wage Labor." In *Regional Impacts of U.S.-Mexico Relations*. Ina Rosenthal-Urey, editor, pp. 71-102. San Diego: Center for U.S.-Mexican Studies, U.C. San Diego.
Kearney, Michael, and Carole Nagengast
    1989   "Anthropological Perspectives on Transnational Communities in Rural California." In *Working Paper #3; Working Group on Farm Labor and Rural Poverty*, pp. 1-42. Davis: California Institute for Rural Studies.
Kemper, Robert Van
    1977   *Migration and Adaptation: Tzintzuntzan Peasants in Mexico City*. Beverly Hills: Sage.
Laite, Julian, and Norman Long
    1987   "Fiestas and Uneven Capitalist Development in Central Peru." *Bulletin of Latin American Research* 6:27-53.
Lentz, Carola
    1985   "Estrategias de reproducción y migración temporaria. Indígenas de Cajabamba/Chimborazo." *Ecuador Debate* 9:194-215.
    1988a   "Zwischen Zivilisation und Eigener Kultur." *Zeitschrift Für Soziologie* 17:34-46.
    1988b   "Los 'Pilamungas' en San Carlos." In *Población, migración y empleo en el Ecuador*. Simón Pachano, editor, pp. 167-196. Quito, Ecuador: Instituto Latinoamericano de Investigaciones Sociales.
Lewis, Oscar
    1952   "Urbanization without Breakdown: A Case Study." *The Scientific Monthly* 7:31-41.
Lloyd, Peter C.
    1979   *Slums of Hope? Shantytowns of the Third World*. New York: St. Martin's Press.
Lobo, Susan Bloom
    1976   "Urban Adaptation among Peruvian Migrants." In *New Approaches to Migration*. David Guillet and Douglas Uzzell, editors, pp. 113-130. Rice University Studies, No. 62. Houston, TX: William March Rice University.
Lombardi, Mario, and Danilo Veiga, editors
    1989   *Las ciudades en conflicto: Una perspectiva latinoamericana*. Montevideo: Centro de Informaciones y Estudios del Uruguay/Ediciones de la Banda Oriental.
Lomnitz, Larissa Adler
    1977   *Networks and Marginality*. New York: Academic Press.

Lomnitz-Adler, Claudio
　　1991　"Concepts for the Study of Regional Culture." *American Ethnologist* 18:195-214.
Long, Norman
　　1973　"The Role of Regional Associations in Peru." In *The Process of Urbanization*, 173-188. Bletch,
　　　　　Buckinghamshire: The Open University.
Long, Norman, and Bryan Roberts, editors
　　1978　*Peasant Cooperation and Capitalist Expansion in Peru*. Austin: University of Texas Press.
　　1984　*Peasants, Miners, and Entrepreneurs: Regional Development in the Central Highlands of Peru*.
　　　　　New York: Cambridge University Press.
MacDonald, John S., and Leatrice D. MacDonald
　　1964　"Chain Migration, Ethnic Neighborhood Formation and Social Networks." *Milbank Memorial
　　　　　Fund Quarterly* 42:82-97.
Mangin, William
　　1959　"The Role of Voluntary Associations in the Adaptation of the Rural Population of Peru."
　　　　　Sociologus 9:23-35.
　　1973　"Sociological, Cultural, and Political Characteristics of Some Urban Migrants in Peru." In *Urban
　　　　　Anthropology*. Aidan Southall, editor, pp. 315-350. New York: Oxford University Press.
Montecino Aguirre, Sonia, and Angélica Willson Aedo
　　1983　*Grupo de mujeres Mapuches en la ciudad: Una experiencia múltiple*. Santiago: Programa de
　　　　　Estudios y Capacitación de la Mujer Campesina e Indígena, Círculo de Estudios de la Mujer.
Matos Mar, José
　　1984　*Desborde popular y crisis del estado: El nuevo rostro del Perú en la década de 1980*. Lima, Peru:
　　　　　Instituto de Estudios Peruanos.
Nash, June, and Helen I. Safa, editors
　　1985　*Women and Social Change in Latin America: New Directions in Sex and Class*. South Hadley,
　　　　　MA: Bergin and Garvey Publishers.
Orellana S., Carlos L.
　　1973　"Mixtec Migrants in Mexico City: A Case Study of Urbanization." *Human Organization* 32:273-
　　　　　283.
Osterling, Jorge
　　1980　*De campesinos a profesionales: Migrantes de Huayopampa en Lima*. Lima: Pontificia Universidad
　　　　　Católica Del Perú.
Paasi, Anssi
　　1986　"The Institutionalization of Regions: A Theoretical Framework for Understanding the Emergence
　　　　　of Regions and the Constitution of Regional Identity." *Fennia* 164:105-146.
Pachano, Simón
　　1985　"Migración desde un pueblo serrano: Guaytacama." *Ecuador Debate* 9: 129-154.
Pachano, Simón, editor
　　1988　*Población, migración y empleo en el Ecuador*. Ecuador: ILDIS.
Roberts, Bryan R.
　　1974　"The Interrelationships of City and Provinces in Peru and Guatemala." *Latin American Urban
　　　　　Research* 4:207-235.
　　1981　"Migration and Industrializing Economies: A Comparative Perspective." In *Why People Move:
　　　　　Comparative Perspectives on the Dynamics of Internal Migration*. Jorge Balán, editor, pp. 17-42.
　　　　　Paris: UNESCO.
　　1978　*Cities of Peasants*. London: Edward Arnold.
　　1990　"The Informal Sector in Comparative Perspective." In *Perspectives on the Informal Economy*,
　　　　　Monographs in Economic Anthropology, No. 8. M. Estellie Smith, editor, pp. 23-48. Lanham,
　　　　　MD: University Press of America.
Robinson, David J.
　　1989　"The Language and Significance of Place in Latin America." In *The Power of Place: Bringing
　　　　　Together Geographic and Sociological Imaginations*. John A. Agnew and James J. Duncan,
　　　　　editors, pp. 157-184. Boston: Unwin Hyman.
Rollwagen, Jack
　　1974　"Mediation and Rural-Urban Migration in Mexico: A Proposal and a Case Study." *Latin
　　　　　American Urban Research* 4:47-63.

Romer, Marta
    1982   *Comunidad, migración y desarrollo: El caso de los Mixes de Totontepec, Oaxaca.* México: Instituto National Indigenista.

Sandoval Z., Godofredo, and Xavier Albó
    1978   *Ojje por encima de todo: Historia de un centro de residentes ex-campesinos en La Paz.* La Paz, Bolivia: Cuaderno de Investigación, Centro de Investigación y Promoción del Campesinado, No. 16.

Sandoval Z., Godofredo, Xavier Albó, and Tomas Greaves
    1987   *Chukiyawu: La cara Aymara de La Paz,* volume 4. *Nuevos lazos con el campo.* La Paz, Bolivia: Cuaderno de Investigación, Centro de Investigación y Promoción del Campesinado, No. 29.

Schuurman, Frans, and Ton Van Naerssen, editors
    1989   *Urban Social Movements in the Third World.* New York: Routledge.

Skeldon, Ronald
    1976   "Regional Associations and Population Migration in Peru: An Interpretation." *Urban Anthropology* 5:233-252.
    1977   "Regional Associations: A Note on Opposed Interpretations." *Comparative Studies in Society and History* 19:500-510.

Taube, María José de Mattos
    1986   *De migrantes a favelados: Estudio de processo migratorio.* Two volumes. Campinas, Brazil: Editora da Unicamp.

Thompson, Robert J., and Joseph R. Rudolph, Jr.
    1986   "Ethnic Politics and Public Policy: A Framework for Comparative Analysis." In *Ethnicity, Politics, and Development.* Dennis L. Thompson and Dov Ronen, editors, pp. 25-63. Boulder, CO: Lynne Rienner.

Tilly, Charles
    1990   "Transplanted Networks." In *Immigration Reconsidered: History, Sociology, and Politics.* Virginia Yans-McLaughlin, editor, pp. 79-95. New York: Oxford University Press.

Tuan, Yi-Fu
    1975   "Place: An Experiential Perspective." *Geographical Review* 65: 151-165.

Turino, Thomas
    1993   *Moving Away From Silence: Music of the Peruvian Altiplano and the Experience of Urban Migration.* Chicago: University of Chicago Press.

Vance, Rupert B.
    1968   "Regionalism." In *International Encyclopedia of the Social Sciences,* volume 13. David Sills, editor, pp. 377-382. New York: The Macmillan Co., and the Free Press.

Varese, Stefano
    1987   *Social and Cultural Conditions and Prospects of Guatemalan Refugees in Mexico.* Geneva: United Nations Instutite for Social Development, and El Colegio de México.

Weisslitz, J.
    1973   "Migración rural e integración urbana en el Perú." In *Imperialismo y urbanización en América Latina.* Manuel Castells, editor, pp. 111-137. Barcelona: Gustavo Gilli.

Williams, Raymond
    1983   *Keywords: A Vocabulary of Culture and Society.* (Revised edition). New York: Oxford University Press.

CHAPTER THREE

Pressures on Peasant Production and the Transformation of Regional and National Identities

William P. Mitchell
Monmouth University

The common construction of peasant communities as "isolated" and "self-sufficient" is incorrect and has probably never been an adequate description of Peruvian communities. Peasants are politically and economically tied to the urban world (Long and Roberts 1978, 1984; Wolf 1966). They have to deal with outside elites and officials, and often have to travel to cities to do so. They produce food and labor not only for themselves but for others (de Janvry 1981; Mallon 1983; Mitchell 1991a). Even seemingly isolated peasants supplement local production with such nonlocal resources as food, seed, medicines, clothing, and other manufactured goods. The fact that these extralocal social and economic ties are obscured by what seem to us strange language, dress, and custom does not make them any less real (Mitchell 1987).

Peasant communities, however, vary in the extent of these connections. The nature of the linkages also changes over time, shifting in response to the demands of the powerful, the economy and ecological stress. Beginning in the 1940s in Peru, for example, rapid population growth and a concomitant squeeze on the value of peasant production in national markets have transformed the country from a rural to an urban one. This metamorphosis, called by Matos Mar (1984) the "*desborde popular*," has been characterized by large scale migration, rapid urban growth, and the decline of farming. Peasants, forced off the land and into the cities, are today much more directly connected to Peru's urban world and that world to them. Even those peasants who remain in their rural communities have often abandoned farming for craft production and commerce, becoming more closely integrated into national and international markets. In the process, Lima has become an Andean city characterized by the rural regional associations and new urban identities described elsewhere in the volume.

In the first half of this century Peruvian peasants subsisted on local resources supplemented by outside cash-cropping, trade, and seasonal migration. The income from this trade and migration supplemented deficits in local production, allowing peasants to identify primarily with their home communities (Caballero 1981:163, 333-367). Taxes and rent were paid in labor (share cropping, peonage, and various labor services to local and nonlocal elites), cash, or produce. Cheap market value accorded peasant labor and agro-pastoral production (food, wool, crafts, cochineal and other raw materials) further subsidized elites and cities. Because peasant population density and consumption were low, the population was in rough equilibrium with this resource regime. Travel and communication were difficult. By necessity peasants connected more to their local region than to the nation.

Conditions changed in the early 1940s. Infant mortality declined and population began to grow very rapidly, pushing peasants against the limits of their local productive system. At the same time, various governments acted to lower urban food prices, further depressing the value of rural agricultural production. Agricultural exporters like the United States increased pressure on rural farmers by offering cheap credits for the purchase of foreign grain. A decline in the international market for cotton in the 1960s, compounded by government neglect of the cotton cooperatives in the 1970s, eliminated an important source of cyclical migratory employment that had made up for local production deficits.

To get by, peasants (especially young people without land) shifted their focus from farming to trade and petty entrepreneurship. Farming became increasingly supplemental to total household economy. Peasants migrated in greater numbers. Many remained permanently in Lima, other areas of the coast, or (until discouraged to do so by the Shining Path guerrilla war in the 1980s) the eastern tropical forests (*montaña*).

As a consequence, sierra migrants now dominate the popular culture of Lima. They have established regional clubs to facilitate their new lives and to provide resources for their home communities (Altmirano 1984a, 1984b). Lima is no longer identified as an elite creole city but as an urban cacaphony inundated with highland migrants. Ties between city and country, always present, have become stronger. Migrants have returned to their home communities playing commercial music on record players and radios, disseminating new musical styles. Sierra parents, hoping to prepare children for new commercial roles, have sent their children to school and demanded the necessary schools and teachers. Local communities that had been primarily Quechua-speaking have become increasingly bilingual and literate in Spanish. To facilitate commerce and movement, peasants have demanded and often received roads.

Most of the chapters in this volume explore such changes from an urban perspective. In this chapter, I analyze them from a rural standpoint, presenting data from the community of Quinua, a district of 6,000 people located in the sierra about an hour by truck from the city of Ayacucho. Quinua has participated fully in the Peruvian transformation (Mitchell 1991a).[1] Since 1940, internal population growth and an external squeeze on agricultural prices have encouraged Quinuenos to become even more closely tied to the national and international economy, a process intensified by the Shining Path war that began in 1980.[2] Quinuenos have migrated from the sierra and have settled in shantytowns and municipalities in and around Lima, as well as in agricultural areas along the entire central coast. In the process they and other Peruvians have transformed their country—bringing the urban world to the countryside and the rural world to the city.

LOCAL PRODUCTION

Quinua, located in the Department of Ayacucho, consists of a central town and fourteen surrounding hamlets.[3] The community covers a vertical gradient that ranges from 2,500 meters on the valley bottom to more than 4,100 meters in the high altitude grasslands. The major productive zones are the irrigated savannah (2,850-3,400 meters) and valley bottom.[4] Even though small in area, these zones contain 89.7 percent of the population (Mitchell 1991a:44).

Although most Quinuenos are farmers and grow a substantial amount of the food they eat, they are rarely able to achieve self-sufficiency. In good agricultural years, adults need one-eighth hectare apiece of good irrigated savannah land to feed themselves from their own production (Mitchell 1991a:77-86). Households usually control only a quarter to half a hectare of both irrigated and nonirrigated land, an amount insufficient to feed the average family of 4.4 people. Informants report that in most years they grow only enough food to last half the year. In poor years, of course, their situation is intolerable. Even wealthy peasants experience production deficits because they lack fields in all ecological zones or the labor to cultivate them.

Consequently, most Quinuenos have always had subsidiary occupations to earn cash to buy needed food, as well as seeds, fertilizer, coca leaves, and other goods. That they have generally worked at these occupations on a part-time basis makes them no less important to the household economy. They have also bartered services and products for food and other goods. They rarely consume their own animals and animal products but barter or sell the eggs, cheese, wool, animal fats, and animals. The poor exchange labor for food. Even wealthy peasants must barter for the food they have been unable to grow.

For as long as they can remember, Quinuenos have manufactured various goods, worked at assorted trades, and engaged in petty commerce. Artisans have produced ceramics, roof tiles, adobe bricks, cloth, ponchos, blankets, sweaters, hats, mandolins, guitars, and wooden spoons. Some Quinuenos have made bread. Every hamlet has carpenters, masons (for house construction), blacksmiths (for shoeing equids and the repair of agricultural tools), and cooks who help prepare food at fiestas. Specialists (called *perritos*) assess the value of a field to be sold; others (*tasaq*) appraise the damages caused by loose animals to agricultural fields. Less common are musicians, tailors, shoemakers, barbers, herders, mule drivers, beekeepers, curers, and witches, as well as a specialist who decorates floats and altars during fiestas.[5] Many Quinuenos engage in commerce. Alcohol, for example, has always been important and has provided income to those who sell as well as those who prepare it.

Quinuenos have earned significant income from trade outside the community. Women brought agricultural products, firewood, hats, and textiles to sell in the city of Ayacucho. Guitar makers routinely took their instruments to the Sunday fair in Huancayo (a large market city about fourteen hours to the northeast by truck) to sell or barter. Merchants (trading in such goods as home-spun cloth, cattle, coca leaves, maize, ceramics, and manufactured goods) have carried trade goods on mules throughout Peru, traveling to Huancavelica, Pampa Cangallo, and Cuzco in the sierra as well as to the coast and tropical forest.

Most Quinuenos, however, have earned the major portion of their cash needs through cyclical migration (see Collins 1983 and 1988 for a description of similar processes in the *altiplano*). In the last century Quinua sent migrants to work on the coastal guano islands. The guano boom ended in the 1870s, but some Quinua migrants were still working in guano production as late as the early 1900s.

In this century Quinuenos have worked primarily on the highway and on coastal cotton plantations. The Transportation Ministry has employed Quinuenos on highway construction and repairs in the Ayacucho region since 1924, work begun when the ministry extended the highway eastward from Quinua. Since highway work is located in the department of Ayacucho, workers can easily travel between their work and their fields. Cotton plantations are further away on the coast, but Quinuenos have been able to schedule cash-work on cotton into the rhythm of sierra farming. Cotton producers, unlike those in sugar, need cyclical labor during the sowing and harvest (Thorp and Bertram 1978:51), a periodicity that dovetails with the sierra work cycle.

Throughout the first half of the twentieth century most migration was temporary. Men set out from Quinua in search of wage work from late February through April, a period of low work demand in Quinua (after crop cultivation) but in time for the cotton harvest. This is also a time when food from Quinua's yield is running out and people need to purchase food as well as seeds and fertilizer for the next sowing.

Most migrants returned to Quinua in time for the sowing from September to December, depending on altitude and crop, although some remained away for a year or two, or even permanently. These permanent migrants, however, often maintained significant relationships with Quinua.

Most Quinua households relied (as they still do) on remittances from temporary and permanent migration (see Caballero 1981:161-163; Collins 1988; Cotlear 1988). Nonlocal and nonagricultural wages have been generally higher than local and agricultural wages (Gonzales de Olarte 1987:112). In 1967 peasants could earn (in United States dollars) $1.40 a day in the cotton harvest, and a careful person could return home with $40 to $80. Quinuenos do not consider highway work lucrative, but highway wages are nonetheless higher than those in local agriculture. In 1973 an agricultural laborer in Quinua earned $0.59 per day–but only $0.47 if the employer also provided coca leaves, cigarettes, and tools. Highway work paid nearly double–$1.10 per day, a significant difference even though highway workers had greater expenses than Quinua agricultural laborers.

Families used (and still use) migrant income and remittances not only to pay for food and materials needed for agricultural production but to buy household necessities and amenities: school supplies, clothing, candles, soap, kerosene, metal knives, forks and spoons. Many have also used the money to buy land or the trade goods for some commercial venture. In the past, many migrated to earn money to serve in the fiesta system, an institution that gave them access to farm labor and water (Mitchell 1991b). Today people still migrate to raise money for weddings and other life-passage events.

Quinuenos and other highland peasants were thus connected significantly to the nation, but–except for a minority–their primary ties were local and their absences from the community temporary. Lima remained a small coastal city with a population of about 500,000. Andean peasants worked as servants and in other occupations, but they were a clearly subordinate and unacknowledged minority. A small elite dominated the government and economy of the city; music and culture were decidedly creole (*criollo*) (Simmons 1955). Larger numbers of peasants lived on the outskirts of Lima, but they too were excluded from creole culture. Cyclical migrants often returned to their highland communities still monolingual speakers of Quechua. Even those who remained away for long periods learned little Spanish, living in Quechua enclaves on cotton plantations or in other locales organized for menial laborers.[6]

POST WORLD WAR II CHANGES

Peruvian society changed dramatically after World War II, a period when the country began to assume its modern shape (Caballero 1981:313-332; Matos Mar 1984:32-34). The number of migrants increased exponentially. Lima is now a city of more than eight million people where highland culture is a dominant force. Rural culture has similarly changed. Most young peasants are bilingual. Wage work, trade, and extralocal connections are more extensive. Pan-Andean musical forms compete with local music. In some areas Protestantism has replaced Catholicism as the dominant religion. Ecological and economic constraints on rural production, some of which have been caused by government demands on production, have been responsible for many of these changes (Caballero 1981:147-172; Collins 1988; Figueroa 1984; Mitchell 1991a; Weismantel 1988:30, 176-177).

In Quinua and elsewhere, population rapidly began to outstrip the capacity of the earlier productive regime, forcing new adjustments and new economic behavior. The growth of Quinua's population has been dramatic. In 1960 the population was increasing at an annual growth rate of 1.2 percent (Table 3.1). This itself is a high rate of increase, with a population doubling rate of 58 years. Since that time, however, population stress has increased even more. By 1980 the annual growth rate had jumped to 2.8 percent, a

---

TABLE 3.1 QUINUA BIRTH AND MORTALITY RATES, 1940-1980

Births and Deaths per Thousand Population

	1940	1960	1970	1980
Birth Rate	12.6	30.5	41.8	42.0
Mortality Rate	——	18.1	22.6	14.5
Annual Growth Rate (%)	——	1.2	1.9	2.8

SOURCE: Crude births and deaths obtained from the municipal records, District of Quinua; total population derived from the nearest national census (1940, 1961, 1972, and 1980), the data for which are found in Peru 1948, 1966, 1972, and 1983 respectively.

doubling rate of only twenty-five years.[7] Most of this growth has been caused by reduced infant mortality rather than by increased fertility. The 241 deaths of children under five years of age per one thousand births in 1955 dropped to only 100 such deaths in 1985 (Mitchell 1991a:32).

Quinuenos quickly encountered ecological limits to increasing the amount of land under cultivation to deal with larger families. Most of Quinua is unsuitable for intensive farming. High altitudes are too cold and low altitudes too dry. Only 12 percent of the terrain is farmed, and only a small proportion of that is irrigated (Table 3.2). Similar ecological conditions are widespread in Peru, severely constraining the expansion of farmland. Precise data are unavailable, but the altitudes with the most productive ecological zones (roughly, those found between 2,000 and 3,500 meters) comprise only a small portion of the total terrain in the entire Department of Ayacucho (see Degregori 1986:35).

Rapid population growth created imbalances in the population structure (Mitchell 1991b:194). Because of rapid growth, the proportion of dependent children to productive adults is high. In 1981, for example, 47 percent of Quinua's population was under fourteen years of age. When the proportion of young is this high, the adult generation has to struggle much harder than when many adults provide for few children. High male migration rates compound the problem and farmers often find it difficult to get enough labor for many necessary farm tasks, further limiting production.

Internal ecological limits to expanded farm production have been exacerbated by national and international economic policies that discriminate against peasant production. Since World War II, the Peruvian government has frequently controlled food prices and supported cheap food imports through the manipulation of foreign exchange rates.[8] These food subsidy policies favor urban wage earners at the expense of rural producers. Low food prices translate to reduced farm income; they consequently depress rural farm production and employment, pushing people into the wage economy.

TABLE 3.2 QUINUA LAND USE

	Hectares[a]	**Percent**
Natural Pasture	10,561.35	57.6
Mountains and Woods	4,345.26	23.7
Farms	2,231.44	12.2
Tree Plantations	20.88	0.1
Other	1,176.73	6.5
TOTAL	**18,335.66**	**100.1**

[a]The hectare figures are those provided in the census and are inaccurate as absolute amounts but are useful to demonstrate relationships (see Mitchell 1991a:223-224, note 11).

SOURCE: Peru 1972:466.

Throughout the 1960s and 1970s, urban food prices continued to be kept artificially low and rural-urban terms of trade became increasingly unfavorable for sierra producers (de Janvry 1981:240). Using 1961 as a baseline, the value of the principal sierra products (maize, potatoes, barley, wheat, beef, mutton, and milk) dropped 15.2 percent in 1972 compared with the price of the principle goods consumed (rice, cooking oil, fats, noodles, sugar, beer, cane alcohol, soda, textiles, school supplies, detergents, soaps, candles, kerosene, plastics, and salt) (Alvarez 1979, as cited in Caballero 1981:212). In consequence, peasants today need more sacks of potatoes to buy kerosene (and even coca leaves) than they did previously.

Because income from wages and the sale of artisan and pastoral products has not declined as rapidly as that from agricultural products (Gonzales de Olarte 1987:110), peasants have been encouraged to devote more and more labor to nonagricultural activities. Agricultural production in Peru has consequently stagnated and per capita production has declined (Thorp and Bertram 1978:315). The resulting domestic food shortages—in a vicious cycle—have further encouraged food imports (Appleby 1982; Collins 1988:20-21; de Janvry 1981; Ferroni 1980; Franklin et al. 1985; Long and Roberts 1984:60-63; Thorp and Bertram 1978; see Meillassoux 1981 for a description of similar processes elsewhere in the world).[9]

International and national policies have further affected the peasantry. After Peru began to buy United States subsidized wheat in the 1950s, commercial wheat production in the Ayacucho Valley virtually disappeared, increasing the pressures on Quinua peasants. In the 1960s the development of synthetic fabrics reduced international demand for cotton, a decline abetted by neglect of the cotton cooperatives by the Peruvian government after 1975. In consequence, these cooperatives (which had been created by the agrarian reform of the previous government of President Velasco) lacked the capital needed to buy seed, fertilizer, insecticide, and migrant labor (see de Janvry 1981:138, 212-213). In 1983, many producers on former cotton plantations told me they no longer had the money to hire migrant labor. Without capital, they had left unrepaired machinery to rust in the fields and sold their soil (once planted to cotton) to brick-makers.

The consequent decline in cotton production, combined with the decreased ability of the producers to hire workers, eliminated the most important source of temporary wage labor for Quinuenos and thereby pushed their search (and that of many other peasants) for other nonfarm work (Matos Mar 1984:28-31; Morner 1985:163-187; Reid 1985:25-27; Thorp and Bertram 1978:23-144).

Increased population, the declining profitability of agriculture, and the decrease in cyclical work opportunities have combined to create a rural crisis. Many peasants have turned to entrepreneurial activities and wage work; they continue to farm but in a more supplemental way than previously. Quinuenos have always engaged in nonfarm activities, but they have done so with increasing vigor with every new assault on their ability to feed themselves and their children. The Shining Path war of the 1980s, itself partly a manifestation of the rural crisis in Peru, exacerbated the productive difficulties of peasant farmers even more. Not only were some farms destroyed and others abandoned, but the war disrupted markets and other economic exchanges important to peasant farming.

Budget figures for a prosperous peasant family in 1973 illustrate some of the economic pressures that peasants face. Table 3.3 provides partial figures for the 1974 income of one household. The data only record monetary income obtained through cash sales and do not include the value of the food eaten or bartered. This family obtained 65.4 percent of its

TABLE 3.3 HOUSEHOLD MONETARY INCOME FOR ONE FAMILY DURING 38 DAYS IN DRY SEASON, JUNE 28, 1974 TO AUGUST 3, 1974

	Weekly Income		
	Peruvian _Soles_	US Dollar Equivalent	Percent of Total
Source of Income			
Agriculture	335.45	7.85	65.4
Animals/Animal products	78.28	1.83	15.3
Petty Commerce	89.71	2.10	17.5
Unknown	9.21	0.22	1.8
TOTAL WEEKLY INCOME	**512.66**	**12.00**	**100.0**

SOURCE: Diary of research assistant.

monetary income from agriculture, 15.3 percent from pastoral activities, and 17.5 percent from petty commerce, primarily from the wife's lively business of preparing and selling curds. These data do not include ancillary income that the couple may have factored into economic decisions. A daughter living in Lima may have been sending the family remittances of money and manufactured goods from time to time, and a son receiving an income as my research assistant may have also provided his parents with at least the expectation of his contributions.

Table 3.4 summarizes partial 1974 monetary expenses of the same family. Almost 50 percent of their expenditures were on food, despite the fact that this family owned more land than most (one hectare of good irrigated savannah land, one-half hectare of moderately good nonirrigated savannah land, and one-half hectare of poor nonirrigated land in the thorn steppe).[10] The data were gathered during the harvest, which may have influenced food purchases: the family may have been buying food for storage, a strategy that their wealth would have allowed. They bought more meat than they consumed. The family devoted 27.3 percent of its budget to agricultural production and nearly 8 percent to medicines, a relatively high percentage common in the budgets of those Peruvians who can afford them.

Although covering a period of only five-and-a-half weeks, these budget data demonstrate the pressures on peasants to raise cash. In this five-week period expenses were (in United States dollars) $31.30 greater than income (the daily agricultural wage was equivalent to $0.70). Since the data are from the harvest, when agricultural income is high but production and food expenses low, this family would have an even more difficult time balancing its budget during the rest of the year. Such budget figures prompt people to migrate and to intensify cash-producing activities.

Although owning two hectares of land and therefore prosperous, the family is not

TABLE 3.4 HOUSEHOLD MONETARY EXPENSES FOR ONE FAMILY DURING 38 DAYS IN DRY SEASON, JUNE 28, 1974 TO AUGUST 3,1974

	Weekly Expenses		
	Peruvian Soles	US Dollar Equivalent	Percent of Total
TYPE OF EXPENSE			
Consumption			
Food	362.99	8.49	47.8
Household	85.29	2.00	11.2
Personal	44.67	1.05	5.9
Medicine	59.13	1.38	7.8
SUBTOTAL	**552.08**	**12.92**	**72.7**
Production	206.96	4.84	27.3
GRAND TOTAL	**759.04**	**17.76**	**100.0**

SOURCE: Diary of research assistant.

---

unusual in its cash activities, although poorer peasants sell fewer crops. Indeed, this family had obtained its relatively favorable economic position in the community through migration. The head of household had lived on the coast for sixteen years because he and his wife could not grow enough food on the lands they had inherited, nor could they make ends meet only on the basis of Quinua income. In addition to meeting daily expenses, the couple used migrant earnings to increase their acreage and to educate their six children.

Studies suggest that monetary income (as opposed to subsistence production) represents more than 50 percent of all peasant income (de Janvry 1981:242-246; Gonzales de Olarte 1987:25-26, 85-91) and even as much as 65-80 percent (Caballero 1981:228). In a survey of the southern sierra in the late 1970s, the peasants studied obtained half of their income from monetary sources (Figueroa 1984:48-49, 129-130). Cash cropping accounted for 14 percent of total monetary income, the sale of livestock 23 percent, commerce and artisan sales 23 percent, local wages 23 percent, and migrant wages 17 percent. As in Quinua, these peasants spent most of their income on food. Their expenses were distributed as follows: production was 6.8 percent of total monetary expenditures, investment in tools and animals 4.6 percent, food 45.4 percent, nondurable goods 12.8 percent, clothing 14.4 percent, education 3.8 percent, and other expenses 12.2 percent (Figueroa 1984:49-51).[11]

LOCAL NONFARM AND CASH WORK

Quinuenos and other highland peasants have responded to ecological and economic pressures by working more in nonfarm activities. Although Quinuenos have a long-standing connection to the cash economy, many more Quinuenos today obtain significant income from cash-cropping, highway food sales, ceramic manufacture, commerce, trucking, and migration than they did in 1966 (see also Caballero 1981; Degregori 1986: 63-64; Figueroa 1984; Gonzales de Olarte 1987). In a 1987 census of twenty-five households in a rural savannah hamlet (some twenty minutes on foot from the central town of Quinua), 40 percent of the households received the majority of their income from nonagricultural work: long-distance trade (16 percent), migrant work (16 percent), white-collar work (4 percent), and store ownership (4 percent). An additional 48 percent received supplemental income from craft production (28 percent) and petty sales (20 percent). Only 12 percent of the households reported no nonagricultural work.

Changes in male employment are illustrated in Table 3.5, which summarizes data contained in municipal marriage and birth records and therefore reflects the self-

---

TABLE 3.5 MALE EMPLOYMENT–DISTRICT OF QUINUA: PERCENTAGE OF FARM AND NONFARM WORKERS, 1955-1985

<u>Percentage of Farm and Nonfarm Workers</u>

	1955	1960	1965	1970	1975	1980	1985	TOTAL
Birth Records								
Farm Work (%)	83.6	85.0	87.5	80.5	81.8	69.9	63.5	**77.7**
Nonfarm Work (%)	16.4	15.0	12.5	19.5	18.2	30.1	36.5	**22.3**
Number	146.0	160.0	216.0	231.0	203.0	249.0	260.0	**1465.0**
Marriage Records								
Farm Work (%)	75.9	62.1	79.3	76.7	69.2	——	——	**72.7**
Nonfarm Work (%)	24.1	37.9	20.7	23.3	30.8	——	——	**27.3**
Number	29.0	29.0	29.0	30.0	26.0	——	——	**143.0**

SOURCE: Municipal records, District of Quinua.

perceptions of the participants and judgments made by the municipal authorities. Both sets of records demonstrate the importance of nonagricultural work: 22.3 percent of the fathers in the birth records and 27.3 percent of the husbands in the marriage records had nonfarm occupations. The birth data show a clear trend toward the increasing importance of nonfarm work, from 16.4 percent in 1955 to 36.5 percent in 1985. This trend is also reflected in marriage data, although less clearly: nonfarm workers increased from 24.1 percent in 1955 to 30.8 percent in 1975. Since almost everyone does part-time work to raise cash, these data underestimate the number of nonfarm occupations in Quinua.[12]

Quinuenos cash-crop more today than previously, a process of intensification that began in the mid-1940s. In 1966 peasants still produced primarily for home consumption and local barter, although many also grew potatoes and (in the valley bottom) vegetables as cash crops. While still focused on household production in 1988, most farmers devote a larger portion of their crop to cash sale. In 1966 they took their crop to the city of Ayacucho or Tambo (the next major town along the highway to the northeast of Quinua), but at the present time they sell their surplus production to local highway food vendors and dealers in the Sunday market.

This increase in cash-cropping is not unique to Quinua. Peasants throughout the sierra are replacing subsistence crops, such as quinoa, broad beans, and *achita* (a chenopod, *Chenopodium pallidiculae*), for cash ones, especially maize and potatoes (Allen 1988:30; Caballero 1981:182; Cotlear 1988; Gonzales de Olarte1987:156). The declining rural-urban terms of trade have fostered this increase. Peasants have had to produce more cash crops merely to maintain their standard of living, shifting production as market conditions change.[13] In the 1950s Quinuenos reduced their wheat acreage dramatically in response to the collapsed market for the grain caused by Peru's subsidized purchase of wheat from the United States. In the 1970s some Quinua farmers began to grow lentils because of high prices. In Quinua, as in Cuzco (Gonzales de Olarte 1987:156), however, only rich peasants are able to make extensive use of cash-cropping. Poor peasants do not have enough land and capital to do so. They work primarily as day laborers in agriculture and other manual occupations.

Changes in the Sunday market reflect underlying economic trends. In 1966 the market consisted primarily of Quinuenos exchanging their surplus agricultural produce (primarily through barter), with only a few outside buyers and merchants selling manufactured goods. After the highway to Quinua was paved in 1974, however, more and more residents of Ayacucho City traveled to Quinua to make their weekly purchases and the market grew rapidly in size. By 1988 the market was considerably larger than in 1966; it contained more diverse goods, serviced more people, and lasted later into the day. Quinua is not alone in such market growth. The twenty-seven markets found in the Department of Puno in 1900, for example, had grown to 118 in the 1970s, the greatest increase taking place after 1940 (Appleby 1976a; see also Bromley 1976).

Economic activity has quickened not only in agriculture, but generally. Older Quinuenos remember that a few townspeople had small, poorly–stocked stores selling alcohol, salt, and noodles, but that they had to go to the neighboring town of Huamanguilla or to the city of Ayacucho to make major purchases. This pattern changed in 1952 when an educated peasant opened the first large, well-stocked store (*tienda*) in Quinua. By 1988 the number and quality of stores had risen significantly. There were then at least twenty-two small and poorly stocked stores that sell beer, cane alcohol, coca leaves, and a few other goods; eight larger stores that sell in addition to the above small quantities of noodles, rice, crackers, canned tuna fish, kerosene, and soda pop; and eight well-stocked ones that sell the above goods in larger quantities and that also sell some dry goods (clothing, sandals) and sundries. Nonetheless, the number of stores has declined in 1996, one consequence of the Shining Path war.

Women of the central town and countryside (known as *controlistas* or *vivanderas*) have sold food on the highway for many years. Before 1950 a few women sold maize beer, food, and forage to mule drivers and people on an occasional truck on Saturdays and Sundays. The number of food sellers expanded with increased truck traffic in the 1950s. Ten to fifteen women sold food in the plaza for half a day on Saturdays and Sundays and all day during major fiestas. By 1988 about forty women regularly sold food all day, every day of the week, in a special locale constructed in 1974. Forty more peddle food occasionally, and their children rush the trucks and cars to hawk soft drinks and candy. Travelers witness similar developments at truck and bus stops throughout the Andes.

Quinuenos have also increased commerce outside the community, trading and working in whatever they can to earn income. In the 1940s at least forty Quinuenos worked on highways throughout the Ayacucho region. Since the late 1950s their number has increased to about two hundred, about 15 percent of the district's adult male population in 1981 (those 15 years of age or older). Since men enter and exit highway work frequently, the actual percentage of households benefiting from the work is much higher.

CERAMIC MANUFACTURE

As far back as my informants can remember, most houses in Quinua have had ornamental ceramic churches or some other ceramic adornment placed on the roof during the last day of the house construction (see Arnold 1993 for a detailed description of the Quinua ceramic industry). Before 1960, ten ceramicists made these churches and other ornamental vessels on a contractual basis, but they primarily produced utilitarian pots. They bartered ceramics for food, sometimes traveling to distant communities in times of scarcity to exchange pots for maize. Shops in Quinua and Ayacucho City also sold occasional ornamental pieces. Ceramicists used the cash from these sales to purchase food, coca leaves, and manufactured goods.

In the late 1940s a few Quinua townspeople and a family of Ayacucho merchants initiated the first significant commercial trade in ceramics. They contracted with the artisans to produce churches, bulls, and crosses in return for rice, noodles, and sugar. As the ceramicists became aware of the demand for their work, they insisted on receiving cash, which provided a better return. A few ceramicists earned significant cash incomes.

At first sold only on Peruvian Independence Day, these ceramics came to be displayed regularly in shops in Quinua, Ayacucho City, and, by 1947, in Lima. A family of Ayacucho merchants exhibited the pots at Lima artisan fairs, thereby spreading awareness of the craft and demand for its production. In the early 1960s a North American owner of an artisan shop located in Miraflores, a wealthy and fashionable section of Lima, began to contract for ceramics and to suggest new forms. At the same time, a Quinua townsman set up a ceramic shop in Vitarte, an old working-class and industrial suburb of Lima. He brought six ceramicists to work in the shop and transported the paint and clay from Quinua by truck.

Many Quinuenos learned to make pots to meet the demand. In 1965, the Ministry of

Industry and Tourism established the first school in Quinua to teach ceramics. In 1966, thirty students were enrolled in the one-year curriculum, many of them recruited personally by the teachers who had gone door-to-door soliciting them. The central school began teaching the craft in 1967, and an additional artisan school teaching ceramics and other skills was established in 1974. Fewer than fifty potters practiced their trade in 1966. Today more than 500 artisans–37 percent of all men over age fourteen in 1981–produce an ever-growing variety of shapes for tourist and export consumption.

The commercialization of production and the increase in number of potters has encouraged the constant change of designs to maintain sales in a saturated market. Quinuenos produce more shapes today than in 1966, and few people make the household churches which were the start of the whole phenomenon. Similar market forces have caused declines in the monetary value of craft production in the Cuzco area (Gonzales de Olarte 1987:127).

The effect of the ceramic industry on the Quinua economy cannot be overestimated. Quinua ceramics are sold in nearly every artisan shop in Ayacucho City and Lima and are shipped to the United States, Europe, and Japan. I have seen them in the United States in museum shops, department stores, and street fairs. A household industry, it is a major source of income for producers and exporters. Townspeople participated early on as intermediary exporters. By 1988 a number of ceramicists owned their own trucks and transported their work directly to Lima, while others were involved in export to foreign countries. By 1990, fifteen households had even formed a cooperative to market their production.[14] About twenty Quinua workshops are located in Lima, employing Quinuenos and producing Quinua ceramics. One cooperative in Lima in 1996 employed two secretaries and utilized a computer and fax machine to organize its business. In addition, two brothers who live in Lima but are from a prominent town family have transmuted the Quinua ceramic tradition into lucrative industries utilizing many Quinua artisans: one producing *retablos* (a triptych form of folk art) and the other decorative plates for weddings and special occasions.

EDUCATION

Quinua parents began to educate their children in response to the changing economy (Mitchell 1994). In 1966, when I first went to Quinua, the majority of the adult population was illiterate and spoke only Quechua, but the process of creating the current literate and bilingual population (speaking Quechua at home and Spanish to outsiders) was well under way.

In 1936 (and even earlier), a girls' school and a boys' school stood in the central town and two coeducational schools in the hamlets. Each school had one teacher who taught through the second grade. Students wishing more education had to live in Ayacucho City, Huanta, or elsewhere; many did, at great expense to their families, who had to pay for their room and board. Families placed (and place) special emphasis on educating an older child, who is then expected to educate younger siblings, although many parents complain that not all older children fulfill that obligation.

School attendance accelerated in the 1940s, and in 1953 Quinuenos built a central school (*núcleo escolar*) that included all primary grades. Since then they have built many new schools. Peasants contributed free labor, and the state supplied building materials

TABLE 3.6 NUMBERS OF STUDENTS AND TEACHERS, DISTRICT OF QUINUA—1986

	Central Town		*Hamlets*		*Total*	
SCHOOLS	Students	Teachers	Students	Teachers	Students	Teachers
Nursery	57	2	63	2	**120**	**4**
Primary	623	17	925	28	**1,548**	**45**
Secondary	192	11	0	0	**192**	**11**
Technical	39	6	0	0	**39**	**6**
Ceramic	22	2	0	0	**22**	**2**
Other	31	2	219	7	**250**	**9**
TOTAL	**964**	**40**	**1,207**	**37**	**2,171**	**77**

SOURCE: Peru, Ministerio de Educación, Resumen Estadístico de Supervivencia, al junio de 1986; Ministerio de Educación, Oficina de Presupuesto y Planificación Educativa, Dirección de Estadística. The ceramic school is run by the Ministry of Industry and Tourism, rather than by the Ministry of Education.

and teachers. In 1987 ten primary schools, a secondary school, three nursery schools, and two artisan schools employed seventy-seven teachers and served 2,171 students (see Table 3.6). Not only are most young people literate, but the large number of teachers has increased the cash market in Quinua, even though most teachers commute from Ayacucho City. Many stores are located around the central school to supply the teachers and students.

The distribution of literacy by age demonstrates that the great impetus in literacy began around 1945 (see Table 3.7). In 1981 only 28 percent of rural men and 3 percent of rural women 40 years or older were literate. The figures were 89 percent and 83 percent, respectively, for their children ages ten to fourteen. The percentage of literate townspeople has always been high, but the percentage of their children who are literate is even higher. Forty-six percent of townspeople over forty were literate in 1981 compared to 90 percent of their children aged ten to fourteen.

Quinuenos began to send children to school at the same time that they began expanding market activities. Initially they only wanted to avoid being cheated by merchants, but later came to view education as improving their children's potential for employment and

TABLE 3.7 LITERACY BY AGE AND LOCATION, DISTRICT OF QUINUA— 1981

Percent Literate in Each Age Group

Ages:	5-9	10-14	15-19	20-24	25-29	30-34	35-39	40+
Central Town								
Men	56	88	100	96	90	100	88	78
Women	39	90	97	87	45	53	28	18
TOTAL %	46	90	98	91	67	76	62	46
Hamlets								
Men	39	89	94	89	85	77	71	28
Women	36	83	73	53	37	22	15	3
TOTAL %	38	87	84	69	55	46	36	14
DISTRICT TOTAL								
Men	41	90	95	91	86	81	75	32
Women	38	84	76	59	39	27	17	4
TOTAL %	39	87	86	73	58	51	40	16

Source: Peru 1983.

"upward mobility." Although most educated Quinuenos remain poor, some have become lawyers, teachers, and petty bureaucrats. In one case, a child who spoke only Quechua until he was 11 years of age went on to become a colonel in the Peruvian Air Force. Such examples have encouraged Quinuenos to use their scarce labor resources to build schools rather than to expand irrigation, even though an enlarged irrigation system would increase crop production considerably (Mitchell 1994). Quinuenos have come to view schooling as economically more important for their children than farming.

TRANSPORTATION

To deal with their population and economic pressures communities everywhere in Peru clamor for roads and schools, sometimes constructing the roads themselves to facilitate market access (Appleby 1976b). Population growth, improved transportation, and the increased commodification of the rural economy have also encouraged the development of internal markets, further stimulating demands for road construction.

Traffic to Quinua has increased dramatically since the first dirt road was built in 1924.

The growth of the city of Ayacucho, stemming from the re-opening of the University of Huamanga in 1959 and the expansion of state agencies in that city in the 1960s (Degregori 1986:46), has provided Quinuenos with a larger market for their agricultural production, stimulating the growth of traffic between Quinua and the city. The expansion of the highway to the tropical forest in the 1960s and the consequent growth of commerce led to even more traffic.

In the 1960s traffic to and from Quinua was light. Few people owned cars and few cars or trucks passed through the community. By 1988 traffic was much heavier and several Quinuenos ran their own jitney services between Quinua and the city of Ayacucho. In that year, Quinuenos owned sixteen small passenger trucks, or *colectivos*, that carried around 360 passengers each day. Some of the passengers were teachers or others who lived in Ayacucho City or along the route, but the majority were peasants traveling to market produce, make purchases, receive medical care, and resolve legal and governmental problems. Military and guerilla violence that began in 1980 has also led to increased motor transportation. Few people would walk in the countryside during the Shining Path war because of the danger.

MIGRATION

Quinuenos have also fled from their income and food pressures, joining the crowded migrant flow leaving the sierra. They have settled in Lima, other areas of the coast, various highland cities (especially Ayacucho, Huancayo, and Huanta, a provincial capital to northeast; see also Brush 1980) and in the tropical forest *montaña*. These cities and regions have grown concomitantly (Matos Mar 1984:43-47, 72-73). Some Quinua migrants have become part of a new urban class of workers, merchants, and entrepreneurs. Most of them, however, have remained poor, taking whatever odd jobs they can (*cachuelos*). To be poor in an urban area is often preferable to poverty in the highlands, where casual labor is limited and poorly paid.[15]

Many migrants now remain permanently away from Quinua. In genealogical data I collected in 1966, only 34.6 percent of one informant's kin were living outside Quinua, the town where they had been born. In 1987 more than 50 percent of people born in Quinua lived elsewhere. In one rural hamlet 61.8 percent of male children over nineteen and 55.4 percent of all children over that age had migrated, most to Lima and Ayacucho City (Table 3.8). The percentage of migrants in this generation is higher than that of their parents, of whom only 36 percent had migration experience of more than a year, a percentage close to that of my 1966 genealogical data. The Shining Path war, of course, has increased migration still more, as people have fled to Lima and other areas to escape the violence and disrupted systems of production.[16]

Despite large numbers of migrants, Quinua appears to have fewer migrants than other areas of the sierra. One survey estimated that by the late 1970s in the southern sierra 75 percent of the children had migrated permanently (Figueroa 1984:77), whereas only 55.4 percent of Quinua children over nineteen had left in 1987 (Table 3.8). The greater percentage of Quinuenos remaining at home may be the result not of reduced pressures but of substantial economic alternatives, especially ceramic manufacture, cash cropping, and commerce resulting from the highway and proximity to the city of Ayacucho.

First-generation migrants maintain active ties with Quinua. The ties are so strong that

TABLE 3.8 PLACE OF RESIDENCE OF CHILDREN BORN IN A RURAL SAVANNAH HAMLET, 1987

Percentage of Children Under and Over 19 Years of Age

PLACE OF RESIDENCE	Men			Women			Men & Women		
	0-18	19+	TOTAL	0-18	19+	TOTAL	0-18	19+	TOTAL
Ayacucho	0.0	25.5	23.0	12.5	18.9	17.8	7.1	22.8	20.8
Lima	0.0	32.7	29.5	0.0	21.6	17.8	0.0	28.3	24.5
Montaña	0.0	1.8	1.6	0.0	2.7	2.2	0.0	2.2	1.9
Other	0.0	1.8	1.6	0.0	2.7	2.2	0.0	2.2	1.9
Total Away	0.0	61.8	55.7	12.5	45.9	40.0	7.1	55.4	49.1
Still in Quinua	0.0	38.2	44.3	87.5	54.1	60.0	92.9	44.6	50.9
TOTAL N	**6**	**55**	**61**	**8**	**37**	**45**	**14**	**92**	**106**

SOURCE: Census of 25 households in a rural savannah hamlet (of which 4 had no children) made by a research assistant in 1987.

---

it would be incorrect to say that Quinua is only a highland community. Rather, it is the highland base of an extended familial and economic network. Several migrants' clubs on the coast provide emotional and social support to migrants and occasional economic and political assistance to the highland district.

People move between rural community and their migrant home frequently. Migrants return to Quinua for extended stays. Forty-four percent of migrants studied on the coast in 1983 had returned to live in Quinua for periods of a year or more; and most had remained there for more than two years.[17] Others return to Quinua permanently, sometimes after retiring from coastal employment. Return migrants are often active political officials in Quinua. The head of the Quinua community (*personero*) for more than twenty years actually lived on the coast with his family while serving in his Quinua political office. He visited Quinua periodically to arrange political matters and attend to his fields. Even though he lived on the coast, he remained a powerful figure in Quinua. Among other accomplishments, he was responsible for having registered Quinua as an official native community (*comunidad indigena*) in 1940.

Some men who migrate, especially highway workers and those living in Ayacucho City, have dual residences. They leave their wives and children in Quinua to cultivate the household fields but the men return frequently. Fewer men on the coast maintain families in Quinua, but 4.4 percent of my 1983 sample of coastal migrants had conjugal family in Quinua. Other migrants have brought their families with them to the coast.

Remittances (especially those sent by men to their wives and children to their mothers) provide significant resources for the local peasant economy. (See Connell et al. [1976:10, 68]; Manners [1965]; Philpott [1973]; and Smith [1977:51-52] for descriptions of the remittance economy in other areas of the world.) I do not have numerical data on the remittances received in Quinua, but 38.8 percent of coastal migrants interviewed in 1983 claimed to send significant remittances (money, medicine, clothing, candles, rice, and noodles) to relatives there. Assuming that this percentage means that at least 25 percent of the households in Quinua receive remittances (a not unreasonable figure that allows for exaggeration), we can see that the economic impact on the community is considerable.

Paradoxically, migrants are often unable to support themselves and their families on the basis of wage labor. While migratory laborers send cash back to the peasant community, the community also subsidizes the migrants with agricultural produce that helps them survive on their low coastal wages. Forty-two percent of Quinua migrants interviewed on the coast received at least fifty kilos of produce from Quinua annually (usually potatoes, maize, dried meat, cheese, peas, or quinoa). Most Quinuenos in Ayacucho City and 34.2 percent of those on the coast, obtained this food by actively cultivating their fields (see also Guillet 1976). They traveled to Quinua before the sowing, often using a visit to the patronal fiesta of the Virgin of Cocharcas in September as opportunity to contract for laborers or arrange for sharecropping. The migrants usually returned again in May during the harvest (see also Allen 1988:36; Collins 1988). During the Shining Path war many Quinua migrants abandoned their fields in Quinua, fearing Shining Path, the military, and the peasant militia (*ronda campesina*), but some have returned to their fomer cultivation practices with the end of most overt violence in 1996.

Others do not cultivate their fields directly but receive gifts of produce known as *encomiendas* from family and ritual kin (especially *compadres*, *comadres*, and godchildren). It is nearly impossible for people to travel without bringing gifts, no matter how small, to their relatives as well as to the relatives of kinsfolk and friends. These gifts are part of the reciprocal exchange system uniting and helping support the community. Migrants (other than school children) send medicines, clothing, other manufactured goods and cash to kin in Quinua, receiving produce in return.

Similar patterns of remittances from the home community are widespread. Roberts (1974:218, 232) suggests that such subsidies represent at least as much as the total cash crop production in the Mantaro Valley. He does not give concrete data on the amount of remittances, but since Lima receives 25 percent of its cash crop production in potatoes and certain vegetables and cereals from the Mantaro Valley, these food remittances "form an important part of Lima's household economy" (Roberts 1974:232).

A number of migrants use Quinua as a source of cheap and reliable labor. Some are labor recruiters (*enganchadores*), contracting for temporary agricultural workers. Others go to Quinua to get laborers for their own projects. In 1988 about twenty workshops were producing "Quinua" ceramics in Lima employing resident Quinua artisans. A number of other potters who lived in Lima by themselves did the same thing, using clay and paints shipped to them from the sierra community. Production in Lima places them near their primary market and reduces transportation and breakage costs. They are also better able to market their product.

The migration that has increased Quinua's access to cash has simultaneously caused local labor shortages and the abandonment of agricultural fields (Mitchell 1991b, 1994). There are too few men for many agricultural tasks. The difficulty in obtaining workers stresses household production still more, thereby encouraging additional migration (Mitchell 1991b).

CONCLUSION

Quinua's economy has changed dramatically over the last half century. Nonfarm work is much more important than it was in both 1940, when it became an officially registered native community, or 1966, when I first visited the community. The growing population has strained environmental resources and land is insufficient to feed the increasing numbers. Economic constraints have exacerbated ecological ones. The system of private tenure restricts access to idle land. The low value of agricultural goods in national markets has increased the appeal of nonfarm employment. Prices of manufactured goods have risen at a faster rate than prices of farm produce. A decline in the cotton plantations in the 1960s eliminated an important source of cyclical employment which had helped to sustain rural farming. In order to compensate for these setbacks, Quinuenos have been forced to seek alternate sources of income.

Similar processes are common throughout the highlands. In response to the inflation of the 1970s, for example, 41 percent of the peasants studied by Gonzales de Olarte in rural Cuzco worked more in wage labor than previously, 19 percent sold more cattle, 14 percent sold more artisan products, and 12 percent received more remittances from migrant relatives (1987:137).

Economic changes in Quinua have led to social and cultural ones. Almost everyone now goes to school. Women must work harder than ever in the fields to compensate for husbands who no longer work as much as they once did in agriculture. And people have dramatically changed their religious and sociopolitical organization. In the course of less than twenty years Quinuenos have abandoned much of the fiesta system and many have adopted Protestantism (Mitchell 1991a). Similar forces, of course, have also created the conditions for the growth of the Shining Path guerrilla movement (Mitchell, n.d.:a).

As peasants have entered the cash economy, household craft production has declined. People working in cash-generating activities have less time for ulilitarian crafts (Collins 1988:146). Peasants purchase what they formerly made, forcing them even more firmly into the cash economy. Today Quinuenos buy more manufactured goods of all sorts (for example, metal spoons and plates, manufactured clothing, kerosene for fuel) than they did previously.

These manufactured products have become symbols of success in the new economic order. At a fiesta, people frequently serve bottled beer as the first or second round of drinks, replacing it with cheaper maize beer and cane alcohol as the party goes on. Most Quinuenos want such consumer goods as radios and phonographs. Peasants often use records at fiestas rather than local live music, displacing the regional music of Ayacucho with that from such prestige centers as Huancayo. Some Quinuenos now have televisions. A few women dress in slacks, use rubber pants on their infants, and supplement breast milk with baby bottles.

Most people born in Quinua now leave the community. They have settled in Ayacucho City, Huanta, Huancayo, Lima, and other areas of the coast. Migrants try to preserve their connections to highland Quinua by sending and receiving remittances and traveling back and forth, but only the better off migrants in far away Lima are able to do so. The poor, who are most in need of rural agricultural remittances, usually lack capital for the gifts and travel back to Quinua needed to sustain ties of reciprocity. Many migrants nonetheless plan to return to the sierra in old age and some actually do so. Life in the sierra is cheaper, allowing them to live more comfortably on retirement income than on the coast. Life in the sierra is also cleaner and more tranquil (at least, or so they thought, before the Shining Path war). Successful migrants even return home before retirement to sponsor the patronal fiesta, maintaining through fiesta sponsorship their rights to land, labor, and water.

Such processes, common throughout the highlands, have revolutionized Peru. Cities are now the homes of rural migrants, and Lima has been transformed into a city of Andeans. The middle and upper classes have fled the once fashionable center of Lima, retreating to enclaves in San Isidro, Miraflores and La Molina. Highland migrants have not only replaced them in the central city but also surrounded Lima with shantytowns, bringing with them highland music and creating new citified lifestyles which reflect their rural backgrounds.

Life is difficult for many of these sierra migrants, who struggle arduously to make ends meet. The peasant woman, pushed by economic forces out of her home into Lima, can be found going door to door selling peeled garlic cloves. Her husband changes automobile oil in a grease pit dug into the side of a Lima street and her children, when not attending school, sell lottery tickets and chiclets. She and her family live in a shantytown with her relatives, sharing housing and child-rearing costs. They barely scrape by, enduring not only hunger but typhoid and cholera. Only a few migrants have done well, but even these well-to-do people frequently live in joint households to minimize costs. Nearly all migrants, moreover, encounter prejudices that restrict their income, limit their mobility, and subject them to police abuse.

To ameliorate their situation migrants turn to family and others from their home communities (*paisanos*). They look to *paisanos* for information, emotional support, employment, and other help. The Quinua regional associations in and around Lima are run by only a small core of people, but a great many Quinuenos attend their periodic soccer matches, barbecues (*parrilladas*), and other reunions. They come together to celebrate, get drunk, and dance. They also talk and plan. Conversation frequently turns to Quinua and its needs–for a school, a church bell, an irrigation canal. The rich acquire laborers and the poor try to get work. Everyone obtains information and social contacts. *Paisanos* provide the comfort of familiar people and familiar discourse. The ties formed and sustained at these events help migrants get by, much as ties of reciprocity and god-parenthood do in the sierra (Mitchell 1991b). The clogged Sunday streets in the areas devoted to these events (for example, the central highway) attest to their importance.

The *desborde popular* has transformed Peru, replacing regional networks and social forms with national ones. Quinua ceramics are now a part of that national culture. Many Lima households proudly display Quinua ceramics, bought by middle- and upper-class Limeños as well as by highland migrants. To the people who buy them, these crafts are symbols of a traditional order, of a self-sufficient rural peasantry that manufactures beautiful objects. But this order never existed, and contemporary ceramics are largely new, an invented tradition (Hobsbawm and Ranger 1983) engendered by economic and ecological pressures. Ceramics symbolize not tradition but the complex ties uniting rural village and city, bonds which in recent years have deepened and which have transformed Lima into a city that echoes with the sounds, culture, and regional associations of the sierra.

NOTES

Acknowledgements. Various stages of my research in Quinua have been supported by the Foreign Area Fellowship Program, the National Endowment for the Humanities, the National Science Foundation, the Freed Foundation, the Fulbright-Hayes Foundation, and the Monmouth University Grants and Sabbatical Committee. Mary Ellen York, librarian at Monmouth University, has been most helpful in locating the most obscure references. I appreciate the thoughtful comments of Monica Barnes, Jane Freed, and Barbara Jaye on the manuscript.

1. An extended discussion of my argument and the data for it can be found in my 1991 book, *Peasants on the Edge: Crop, Cult, and Crisis in the Andes* (Austin: University of Texas Press).

2. Many of these external economic pressures are related to the export economy and international capital flow (de Janvry 1981; Meillassoux 1981; Thorp and Bertram 1978), a subject beyond the scope of this essay.

3. My analysis focuses on the central town and surrounding area. In this century, most Quinuenos have been free of *hacienda* peonage, although their production had often been dominated by *hacienda* control of water (Mitchell 1994). Because *haciendas* had been affected by the same pressures on rural production that affected the peasantry, their influence and number had declined in Quinua and throughout the sierra even before the agrarian reform in the 1970s.

4. See Mitchell (1991a:35-46 and n.d.:b) for a complete description of Quinua's ecological zones.

5. We find evidence of Indian tailors, shoemakers, and church musicians in Peru at least as early as the sixteenth century. These occupations exempted indians from the forced labor of the *mita* (Monica Barnes, personal communication, March 1992).

6. I do not wish to dismiss the complexity of Andean coastal culture, which contains many European, Asian, Middle Eastern, and African subgroups. I wish only to emphasize the marginal nature of Andean peasants.

7. Population growth, of course, is not a completely independent variable (see de Janvry 1981:142-143; Meillassoux 1981:130, 159). People make decisions about the size of their families in ecological and economic contexts that encourage certain decisions over others.

8. Peasant subsidies of the urban sector also characterized colonial Peru. The mid-eighteenth century Bourbon "reform" known as the *encomienda de ventas* (forced purchase) required rural producers to exchange their products (wool, hides, potatoes, maize, et cetera) at unfavorable rates for commercial products (mules, cloth, hardware, candles, et cetera) (Monica Barnes, personal communication, March 1992).

9. The impact on peasant communities of the economic changes initiated by President Alberto Fujimori during the early 1990s is not yet clear.

10. Collins (1988:119) has found that families purchased 7 to 12 percent of the food they consumed in 1980 in one Aymara community in the *altiplano*. Ferroni (1980:60) has calculated that purchased foods represented 35 percent of the monetary value of all foods (both home produced and purchased) in rural Puno, 45 percent in the rural southern sierra, 69 percent in the rural central sierra, and 69 percent in rural Junin.

11. The small amount spent on production in this study, as compared to the information from Quinua, results from aggregating alcohol, coca leaves, and cigarettes as consumption rather than production expenses.

12. The data probably underestimate nonfarm employment still more because I counted the men classified as *obreros* in the municipal records as farm laborers. At least some of them work primarily in manual labor rather than in agriculture.

13. Although the general trend in the Andes has been to increased cash sale, periodic crises have sometimes led to increased barter (Appleby 1982; Collins 1988:14; Orlove 1986:94-95). Such fluctuations occur in Quinua, but these are restricted to particular crops rather than to the overall pattern. In Quinua the deterioration in rural/urban terms of trade has tended to encourage greater cash-cropping to earn the cash needed for such important expenses as education. At the same time, the growth of the nearby city of Ayacucho and the increased food sales to travelers have created new markets for Quinua produce.

14. This information on the ceramic cooperative is from the *Pueblo to People* (Houston, Texas) Spring 1990 catalog. The fact that Quinua ceramics are advertised in this catalog is, of course, yet another indication of the importance of ceramic production in the local economy and the transnational nature of that production.

15. Poverty is difficult everywhere, but people lacking land in rural highland areas usually leave their homes to find work elsewhere. Some poor are able to remain in rural areas by using significant social ties to obtain work and resources, but the availability of such aid is limited.

16. With the end of the Shining Path war in the mid-1990s people have begun to return to their highland communities, including Quinua.

17. The data on coastal migrants is from a study that commenced in 1983 in which 107 migrants from Quinua were interviewed. These data are only partially analyzed, and the figures reported may change when the study is completed.

REFERENCES CITED

Allen, Catherine J.
  1988   *The Hold Life Has: Coca and Cultural Identity in an Andean Community.* Washington, DC: Smithsonian Institution Press.
Altamirano, Teófilo
  1984a   *Presencia andina en Lima metropolitana.* Lima: Fondo Editorial, Pontificia Universidad Católica del Perú.
  1984b   "Regional Commitment among Central Andean Migrants in Lima." In *Miners, Peasants, and Entrepreneurs: Regional Development in the Central Highlands of Peru.* Norman Long and Bryan Roberts, editors, pp. 198-216. Cambridge: Cambridge University Press.
Alvarez, Elena
  1979   Politica agraria y estacamiento de la agricultura, 1969-1977. Ponencia presentada al Primer Seminario sobre Agricultura y Alimentación en el Perú. Chaclacayo: Pontificia Universidad Católica del Perú.
Appleby, Gordon
  1976a   "The Role of Urban Food Needs in Regional Development, Puno, Peru." In *Regional Analysis,* volume 1, *Economic Systems.* Carol A. Smith, editor, pp. 147-181. New York: Academic Press.
  1976b   "Export Monoculture and Regional Social Structure in Puno, Peru." In *Regional Analysis,* volume 2, *Social Systems.* Carol A. Smith, editor, pp. 291-307. New York: Academic Press.
  1982   "Price Policy and Peasant Production in Peru: Regional Disintegration During Inflation." *Culture and Agriculture* 15:1-6.
Arnold, Dean E.
  1993   *Ecology and Ceramic Production in an Andean Community.* Cambridge: Cambridge University Press.
Bromley, Raymond J.
  1976   "Contemporary Market Periodicity in Highland Ecuador." In *Regional Analysis,* volume 1, *Economic Systems.* Carol A. Smith, editor, pp. 91-122. New York: Academic Press.
Brush, Stephen B.
  1980   Peru's Invisible Migrants: A Case Study of Inter-Andean Migration." In *Land and Power in Latin America: Agrarian Economies and Social Processes in the Andes.* Benjamin S. Orlove and Glynn Custred, editors, pp. 211-228. New York and London: Holmes and Meier Publishers, Inc.
Caballero, José María
  1981   *Economía agraria de la sierra peruana; antes de la reforma agraria de 1969.* Lima: Instituto de Estudios Peruanos.
Collins, Jane
  1983   "Seasonal Migration as a Cultural Response to Energy Scarcity at High Altitude." *Current Anthropology* 24:103-104.
  1988   *Unseasonal Migrations:The Effects of Rural Labor Scarcity in Peru.* Princeton: Princeton University Press.
Connell, John, et al.
  1976   *Migration from Rural Areas:The Evidence from Village Studies.* Delhi: Oxford University Press.
Cotlear, Daniel
  1988   "La economía campesina en las regiones modernas y tradicionales de la sierra." *Allpanchis* 31:217-244.
Degregori, Carlos Ivan
  1986   *Ayacucho, raíces de una crisis.* Ayacucho:Instituto de Estudios Regionales José María Arguedas.

de Janvry, Alain
1981   *The Agrarian Question and Reformism in Latin America.* Baltimore: The Johns Hopkins University Press.
Ferroni, Marco A.
1980   *The Urban Bias of Peruvian Food Policy:Consequences and Alternatives.* Ph.D. dissertation, Cornell University.
Figueroa, Adolfo
1984   *Capitalist Development and the Peasant Economy in Peru.* Cambridge Latin American Studies, volume 47. Cambridge: Cambridge University Press.
Franklin, David et al.
1985   *Consumption Effects of Agricultural Polices:Peru; Trade Policy, Agricultural Prices and Consumption:An Economy Wide Perspective.* Report Prepared for USAID/PERU. Raleigh, NC: Sigma One Corporation.
Gonzales de Olarte, Efraín
1987   *Inflación y campesinado:Comunidades y microrregiones frente a la crisis.* Lima: Instituto de Estudios Peruanos.
Guillet, David
1976   "Migration, Agrarian Reform, and Structural Change in Rural Peru." *Human Organization* 35:295-302.
Hobsbawm, Eric, and Terence Ranger, editors
1983   *The Invention of Tradition.* Cambridge: Cambridge University Press.
Long, Norman, and Bryan R. Roberts, editors
1978   *Peasant Cooperation and Capitalist Expansion in Central Peru.* Austin: University of Texas Press.
1984   *Miners, Peasants, and Entrepreneurs:Regional Development in the Central Highlands of Peru.* Cambridge: Cambridge University Press.
Mallon, Florencia E.
1983   *The Defense of Community in Peru's Central Highlands; Peasant Struggle and Capitalist Transition,1860-1940.* Princeton: Princeton University Press.
Manners, Robert A.
1965   "Remittances and the Unit of Analysis in Anthropological Research." *Southwestern Journal of Anthropology* 21:179-195.
Matos Mar, José
1984   *Desborde popular y crisis del estado.* Perú Problema 21. Lima: Instituto de Estudios Peruanos.
Meillassoux, Claude
1981   *Maidens, Meal and Money:Capitalism and the Domestic Community.* New York: Cambridge University Press.
Mitchell, William P.
1987   "The Myth of the Isolated Native Community." In *Global Interdependence in the Curriculum:Case Studies for the Social Sciences.* Judy Himes, editor, pp. 35-49. Princeton: Woodrow Wilson National Fellowship Foundation.
1991a   *Peasants on the Edge: Crop, Cult and Crisis in the Andes.* Austin: University of Texas Press.
1991b   "Some Are More Equal Than Others: Labor Supply, Reciprocity, and Redistribution in the Andes." In *Research in Economic Anthropology,* volume 13. Barry L. Issac, editor, pp. 191-219. Greenwich, CT: JAI Press.
1994   "Dam the Water: The Ecology and Political Economy of Irrigation in the Ayacucho Valley, Peru." In *Irrigation at High Altitudes: The Social Organization of Water Control Systems in the Andes.* William P. Mitchell and David Guillet, editors. Washington, DC: American Anthropological Association, Publication Series of the Society for Latin American Anthropology, volume 12.
n.d.:a   "Detour onto The Shining Path: Constructing a Field of Andean Violence." In *Deadly Developments: Anthropological Analyses of the Contemporary World.* Stephen P. Reyna and R. E. Downs, editors. Philadelphia, PA: Gordon and Breach Publishers, Inc.
n.d.:b   "Multizone Agriculture In An Andean Village: The Ecological Basis Of Peasant Farming." To be published in *The Prehistory of the Ayacucho Basin, Peru, Volume 1,* Richard S. MacNeish, ed. Ann Arbor: University of Michigan Press. In Press.

Morner, Magnus
  1985   *The Andean Past: Land, Societies, and Conflicts.* New York: Columbia University Press.
Orlove, Benjamin
  1986   "Barter and Cash Sale on Lake Titicaca: A Test of Competing Approaches." *Current Anthropology* 27:85-106.
Peru
  1948   *Censo nacional de población de 1940*, volume 6. Lima: Ministerio de Hacienda y Comercio, Dirección Nacional de Estadística.
  1966   *Sexto censo nacional de población: Primer censo nacional de vivienda, 2 de julio de 1961, tomo I, volumen de centros poblados.* Lima: Dirección Nacional de Estadística y Censos.
  1972   *Segundo censo nacional agropecuario, 4 al 24 de setiembre, 1972, Departamento de Ayacucho.* Lima: Instituto Nacional de Estadística.
  1983   *Censos nacionales; VIII de población, III de vivienda, 12 de julio de 1981; Resultados Definitivos, Departamento de Ayacucho.* 3 Volumes. Lima: Instituto Nacional de Estadística.
Philpott, Stuart
  1973   *Indian Migration: The Montserrat Case.* New York: Humanities Press.
Reid, Michael
  1985   *Peru: Paths to Poverty.* London: Latin American Bureau.
Roberts, Robert R.
  1974   "Interrelationships of City and Provinces in Peru and Guatemala." In *Latin American Urban Research*, volume 4. W. Cornelius and F. Trueblood, editors, pp. 207-235. Beverly Hills and London: Sage Publications.
Simmons, Ozzie G.
  1955   "The Criollo Outlook in the Mestizo Culture of Coastal Peru." *American Anthropologist* 57:107-117.
Smith, Waldemar
  1977   *The Fiesta System and Economic Change.* New York: Columbia University Press.
Thorp, Rosemary, and Geoffrcy Bertram
  1978   *Peru: 1890-1977: Growth and Policy in an Open Economy.* New York: Columbia University Press.
Weismantel, Mary J.
  1988   *Food, Gender, and Poverty in the Ecuadorian Andes.* Philadelphia: University of Pennsylvania Press.
Wolf, Eric R.
  1966   *Peasants.* Englewood Cliffs, NJ: Prentice-Hall.

CHAPTER FOUR

The Politicization of Regional Identities among Mountain Zapotec Migrants in Mexico City

Lane Ryo Hirabayashi
University of Colorado, Boulder

INTRODUCTION

Since the 1950s–but especially during the 1970s–some scholars asserted that there was little substantive difference, culturally, between Mexico's indigenous peoples and the rest of the country's *mestizo* population. At one level, this occurred as anthropologists studying specific indigenous/peasant communities, in rural and urban settings, argued that being "indian" in Mexico was more a matter of class dynamics than of cultural heritage (for example, Arizpe 1975:148-153, Friedlander 1975:xv). At another level, this occurred as historians systematically revealed the fundamentally colonial, and thus occidental, nature of contemporary Mexican society (for example, Borah 1976).

In similar fashion, regarding the Zapotec of Oaxaca, one anthropologist suggested:

> By the end of the Spanish Colonial period, the Zapotec had been reduced to a peasantry, or, more properly, to communities of peasants. Little that was distinctively Zapotec remained of their culture and society; instead, the rural indian peasant culture of central and southern Oaxaca was a conglomeration of things pre-Spanish and things Spanish.... Although the Spanish designation *zapotecos* may have entered their vocabulary, Zapotec ethnicity, on a larger level, was of little consequence, as there were (and are) few, if any, social forms that gave it unity (Whitecotton 1977:219).[1]

This view, however, has not been borne out by recent events. During the 1980s there have been significant signs of a reemergence of Zapotec ethnicity in both the isthmus and in the sierra.

The resurgence of "regional assemblies" in the Sierra Juárez during the 1980s is one indication of the salience of a regional problematic in the highlands of Oaxaca, Mexico. For example, the *Asamblea de Autoridades Zapotecas de la Sierra*, a coalition made up primarily of Mountain Zapotec from villages speaking the *Cajonos* dialect, is an important advocate of local customs as well as the right of Zapotec, Mixe, and Chinantec villages to organize for the purpose of self-determination. Through its newsletters and publications, the assembly repeatedly stresses the importance of communal practices such as popular governance, community service, mutual aid, as well as the production of local agricultural specialties and crafts, as key to the integrity of each sierran community.[2]

The above values, deeply rooted in the postconquest organization of individual Mountain Zapotec villages as *la república de indios* (Nader 1989), provide an excellent example of what might be called "regional identities" in the rural setting. Regional identities, in this sense, are not simply an analytic concept but a phenomena that Mountain Zapotec villagers, themselves, recognize, employ, and organize around.[3]

As among rural-urban migrants of similar backgrounds, regional identities are of great importance in the initial adaptation of Zapotec out-migrants, especially in urban settings where their numbers are significant. Ethnographic and literary analysis indicates that regional identities evolved among Mountain Zapotec migrants in Mexico City in the following fashion. Ties involving kinship, friendship and *paisanazgo* provided the foundation for a pattern of chain migration to Mexico City. Since Mexico City has been the primary site of industrial development since World War II (Muñoz at al. 1982), occupational and educational opportunities abounded there between 1960 and 1980, especially in comparison with those available in Mexico's secondary urban centers. Thus, the capital was selected as the main urban point of destination. The subsequent facilitation of new migrants led to common occupations and class situations, as well as initial patterns of residential concentration (Hirabayashi 1993).

Concrete manifestations of regional identities in Mexico City include: (1) shared lifestyle, customs, food preferences, religious beliefs and practices, and—in all but one case described below—language; (2) exchange based on reciprocity, and the practice of mutual aid; (3) facilitation in terms of jobs and housing; (4) visiting, parties, and the celebration of rites of passage among *paisanos*; (5) pursuit of hobbies such as sports and music; (6) networks based on common work place; and (7) formal migrant village or regional associations. Such manifestations should not be seen as an *extension* of rural values and institutions to the city; rather, they constitute a unique synthesis of social elements, many of which may be based on rural experience, but which are creatively tailored to new purposes in the urban setting.

In this chapter, I focus on the *politicization* of regional identities among Mountain Zapotec migrants in Mexico City between 1960 and 1980. By *"politicization"* I mean a situation in which regional identities become a medium for debate, formal organization, and action among migrants. This emphasis controverts both assimilationist and oppression oriented interpretations of indigenous peasant culture and community. It is also methodologically inspired: focus on the politicization of regional identities helps to reveal how and why its dynamics are respondent to ongoing linkages between the points of origin and destination.

ETHNOGRAPHIC PROBLEM

The bulk of ethnographic material I present focuses on a group of *Rincón* Zapotec migrants, originally from a village I have chosen to call "Lahoya" (a pseudonym), living in Mexico City.[4] In order to better analyze the Lahoyan case, I will contrast it with a recently published account of migrants from the town of Villa Alta, the *cabecera*, or administrative seat, of the district.

Both groups of migrants arrived in significant numbers in Mexico City between 1960 and 1980. Most were able to adjust relatively quickly, in part, because they arrived in a process of chain migration. Migrants from both Villa Alta and from Lahoya facilitated compatriots and provided mutual aid in order to help each other adapt to and compete in the new urban setting. The politicization of regional identities occurred as both groups of migrants formed village associations. In fact, if one examined these two groups of migrants *only* in the urban setting, their broad patterns of adaptation might appear to be quite similar.

The apparent similarities between these two cases are ultimately unsettling, however because of the background and characteristics of the two distinct points of origin. Lahoya, for example, is an agricultural village whose residents speak the *Nexitzo* dialect of the Zapotec language. For a variety of reasons discussed below, however, the social organization of the Lahoyan villages does not revolve around a strong tradition of mutual aid practices, nor are there a range of extrafamilial groups that create cross-linking ties among the citizenry. Why, then, would Lahoyan migrants in Mexico City engage in a variety of mutual aid practices, including the formation of village associations, in a fashion similar to more communally oriented Mountain Zapotec migrants? And why, despite their best efforts to aid each other in the city and to facilitate development in the home village, did the two Lahoyan migrant associations formed in Mexico City end up fighting one another?

The case of the migrants from Villa Alta, on the other hand, is as surprising since it is generally regarded as a Spanish-influenced *mestizo* town, whose administrative and commercial functions set it apart from the surrounding Zapotec villages (De La Fuente 1965). Given that migrant associations in Mexico are usually formed by those from indigenous peasant backgrounds, why would Villalteco urban migrants form migrant village associations in Oaxaca and Mexico City, like migrants from neighboring villages that are composed primarily of Zapotec-speaking peasants?

In order to answer these questions, I will present data pertaining to adaptations in the points of origin and destination of the Villalteco and Lahoyan migrants, since both have had an impact in the creation and dynamics of regional identities, especially the migrants' village associations. In addition, I propose that analysis must be based on a broad historical perspective that emphasizes the complex linkages that tie the Sierra Zapoteca to the larger Mexican society. *Specifically, the intensification of regional identities among Mountain Zapotec migrants in Mexico City occurred during a period from the late 1960s through the 1970s, when the state's postrevolutionary program for "development" and "national integration" began to impact the Sierra Zapoteca quite significantly.* In short I hope to demonstrate that this perspective provides a coherent framework within which the politicization of regional identities among Mountain Zapotec in Mexico City is effectively studied and interpreted.

I will first outline the case of migrants from Villa Alta, drawing extensively from a recent publication by anthropologist Philip C. Parnell (1988). Subsequently, I present a second case study, based on original research, that focuses on migrants from Lahoya in Mexico City.

VILLA ALTA: THE DISTRICT SEAT

Villa Alta is a postconquest Spanish settlement, originally established as the administrative center for the district as a whole. Villa Alta also served as a regional marketing center (Chance 1989). As a result of such origins, Spanish is the primary language spoken, and residents have traditionally been regarded as "Spanish" (De La Fuente 1965). This has undergone some change over the course of the twentieth century, since there has been a marked pattern of out-migration on the part of residents to Oaxaca and to Mexico City, as well as some in-migration on the part of Zapotec from surrounding villages. Today, Villaltecos are more properly seen as being *mestizo*.

Parnell's account (1988) indicates that Villa Alta's function as administrative center, and seat of local representatives of the state and national systems, has served to channel power and wealth into the town from the villages in the surrounding hinterlands. Administrative power within the district exists in combination with mercantile interests such as credit financing and the brokerage of cash crops.

Interestingly enough, according to Parnell, despite these characteristics, and despite its status as the district seat, civil *cargos*, *tequio* duties, and vestiges of the *mayordomía* religious institution–practices that might otherwise be ascribed to an indigenous peasant tradition–are still extant and practiced in Villa Alta.[5] These communal traditions exist simultaneously with political bossism and provide the two key ways that "Villalteco males achieve prestige and power" (Parnell 1988:39).

Since the 1950s, the political and social dynamics of Villa Alta have been dominated by a division between competing factions of *caciques* and their followers. On one side, there are the *Caleros*, whose programs revolve around two key principles: to minimize the importance of village development projects (and accompanying and associated burdens such as quotas, *tequios*, and the growth of the town's governmental bureaucracy), and to maximize the input of local representatives and supporters of the Catholic Church, in regard to village life and governance.

Opposed to the *Caleros* are the "Progressives," affiliated with the political boss (or *mero cacique*) of Villa Alta, David Mendiolea. A local businessman who actually resides a good deal of the time in Oaxaca City, Mendiolea and his followers have championed the use of government development programs in order to further the progress of Villa Alta. Specifically, their contributions involve bringing electricity and potable water to the village, repairing the Catholic church, constructing a new municipal building and offices, building secondary as well as "technical" schools, and bringing a rough road into the town from the neighboring community of Yalalag (Parnell 1988:44).

Eventually, the *Caleros*, who generally opposed such projects, ostensibly because they create onerous burdens that have to be assumed by citizens of Villa Alta, could not remain idle in the face of the challenge that new public works represented to their status. According to Parnell, the *Caleros*'s particular contribution in this regard consisted of constructing a new road, since the old road was not totally functional:

The new one-lane dirt road, federally funded and maintained, ran through the district of Zacatepec;

unlike the older road it passed through few of the Villa Alta district villages that opposed the seat and its residents (Parnell 1988:48).

Cognizant that internal divisions could weaken social solidarity within the community as a whole, the citizens of Villa Alta are careful not to let factionalism get out of hand. This is done, in part, by emphasizing the principal ethic which guides Villa Alta's relations to the outside world–namely, to maximize the overall strength and self-determination of Villa Alta vis-à-vis all external threats. This general rule, it might be added, holds whether the threat is exogenous, say, in the form of Protestant evangelists or agencies of the state, as opposed to endogenous, such as the various regional assemblies of the sierra (Parnell 1988:71).

By 1984, when Parnell left the field, "the political groups of the divided district seat were locked as more or less equal opponents in dispute over principles of governance and the nature of village boundaries" (1988:50).

VILLALTECO OUT-MIGRANTS

Although Parnell's account focused mainly on the town and immediate region of origin, there are some data regarding the urban Villaltecos, that are briefly outlined here. Generally, Parnell found that "urban Villaltecos in Oaxaca City and in Mexico City are organized politically around opposed village political groups, the Caleros and Progressives" (Parnell 1988:11).

The urban *Calero* supporters are reported to be an older, more financially secure, and more tightly organized group, in contrast to the younger urban supporters of the Progressives. According to Parnell, this group includes a number of influential professionals and bureaucrats in Mexico and Oaxaca City. The Calero group was particularly active in Oaxaca City, setting up an organization called the Villalteco Cultural Association, to support the Calero faction back in the town. The level of security and sophistication of the Caleros in Oaxaca City is partly reflected in the fact that

> The Villalteco Cultural Association...published a book that chronicled the Caleros' role in the construction of the new road. It included copies of their correspondence with state and federal officials (Parnell 1988:48).

This, to my knowledge, is the first time a migrant association from the region has initiated and carried out a project along these lines.

As teachers, and operators and office workers in the national telegraph and postal service, many of the urban Progressives are clustered in the same types of occupations that their parents pursued. As organized groups in Oaxaca and in Mexico City, they are opposed to the urban *Caleros*.

Although younger and less economically secure, urban Progressives in Mexico and Oaxaca City support Mendiolea's group's development projects morally and financially. Because their zeal extended to both general fundraising as well as individual donations, Mendiolea expressed his firm faith in the out-migrants as "responsible villagers" (Parnell 1988:56).

Urban progressives also facilitate the political connections and petitions usually needed in order to win governmental financial backing. For this reason, the urban migrants constitute an important base of support for Mendiolea and his supporters.

Parnell notes, however, that as federal and state agencies provided monies for the further development of Villa Alta:

> The seat's isolation in the district increased. Regional assemblies and Protestant churches brought organization and new alliances among outlying villagers who opposed both the state and the district seat (Parnell 1988:49).

Thus, the political dynamics of the region have had a direct impact upon the motivations for creating support groups among urban residents and the solicitation of their moral and monetary support for the causes of the district seat.

Beyond this, urban residents (as Parnell puts it) are active in terms of forming "committees for annual village fiestas, in addition to the contributions they make to family members still residing in the seat" (1988:11). Commitments of the former kind are described by Parnell in terms of the participation of a Mexico City committee's involvement in the *mayordomía* involving the *Santo Entierro*.

> One week before the fiesta, representatives of the village's Mexico City committee arrive in Villa Alta. Each year an image of the Santo Intierro [sic] is taken from Villa Alta to go from house to house in Oaxaca City or Mexico City. Village urbanites pay their city's village committee for the privilege of hosting the image in their homes (1988:27-28).

Funds, gathered in this fashion, are then used by the committee to support the organization of the Santo Entierro fiesta in subsequent years.

In this fashion, whether adherents of the *Caleros* or the Progressives, and whether or not they have been able to achieve occupational and financial security as individuals or as families, Parnell observed that the out-migrants from Villa Alta in Oaxaca and Mexico City "continue to participate in the politics, conflicts, disputes, and economy of their native village" (1988:5).

THE AGRICULTURAL VILLAGE OF LAHOYA[6]

Lahoya was a preconquest Zapotec settlement (Chance 1989). The limited data available indicate that during the nineteenth century Lahoya was a somewhat poor, subsistence-oriented agricultural village with a fluctuating, yet gradually growing, population. Between the 1940s and the middle of the 1950s, sugar cane (which could be processed into *panela*, or unrefined brown sugar) became a major cash crop in Lahoya. Despite the strenuous nature of its production, *panela* was in great demand and thus a very profitable pursuit before the mid-1950s. Unfortunately, the boom did not last. The fertile, extensive fields of the Valley of Oaxaca were more easily modernized and more central to routes of trade and transportation. Competition undercut Lahoya's market for *panela*, and by the late 1950s the village entered a long period of economic stagnation.

Today, the municipality of Lahoya is made up of the village of Lahoya and a small *rancho* that is attached to the village. As in other *Rincón* Zapotec villages, male citizens owe service to the municipal government. Civic service is given in two principal ways. First, every man must serve his share of posts in the municipal government. Second, every able-bodied man must provide his fair share of labor in the village *tequios*.

During the twentieth century, the main agricultural technique of the Lahoyans was similar to "slash and burn." The practice is not to return to the same fields the following year in order to allow the soil to fallow. In contrast to the style of agriculture in Ralu'a, Lahoyan women and older children of both genders actively participate in agricultural tasks along with the men, and sons continue to work with their fathers after adulthood and even marriage.

According to a national census taken by the Mexican government in 1970 (D.G.E. 1973), the land base of Lahoya was held in approximately one hundred and seventy parcels, almost two-thirds of which were under five hectares in size. However, the other third of the land, held in units greater than five hectares, actually represented one-half of all arable land. Although basically everyone in the village farms, interviews suggested that stratification developed after World War II as the wealthier families obtained some of the best lands in the immediate vicinity of the village. Apart from formal institutions and offices of the municipal government, Lahoya since the 1950s has been run by a small group of families who can influence village affairs but cannot totally control them. Their hold over the village appears to be based on prestige (especially their higher educational levels), and on their superior land holdings. An important aspect of their power also lies in their connections with the outside world, for the heads of the important families have become brokers in the larger legal-political system linking Lahoya to Villa Alta, the district seat.

In 1950, when the population of the *municipio* peaked at 1,177 persons, 85 percent of the households were made up of nuclear families–either married couples, or couples and their children.[7] About 15 percent of the population was attached to a nuclear family-based household. Demonstrating the importance of the household as a basic unit of both production and consumption in a self-provisioning economy, less than one percent of the populace lived alone.

Lahoyan families go out to work in their fields for weeks at a time. They live there for the better part of the year, dispersed in their lean-tos. Many families return to the village only for periods of rest or when they need to fulfill civic duties, religious observances, and so forth. Beyond the immediate family, then, the social organization of Lahoya is largely formal in nature, and revolves around activities in two interrelated areas of village life: civic and religious service. Beyond their spiritual significance, the religious festivals integral to the *mayordomía* system have been the main village-level cultural and economic events in which families and individuals participate collectively.[8] Otherwise, Lahoyans appear to lack the many intravillage associations and institutions of reciprocal exchange characteristic of neighboring Mountain Zapotec villages.

The relative impoverishment of Lahoya becomes clear when examining traditional occupations: in fact, there appear to be few besides farming; nor are there crafts outside of making "home brew." Development projects have been initiated in Lahoya through a combination of different sources of leadership and money: out-migrants, state and federal agencies and officials, and the local elite. A potable water system was installed in 1965, and electricity became available in 1968. Even by 1980 there was no store in Lahoya, although there were several houses where soft drinks and liquor could be obtained. Lahoya hosts no agencies or governmental commissions. A few men have managed to leave the village in order to become primary school teachers. Lahoya has access to postal and telegraphic service only via the services of a neighboring town, which is also the regional marking center. Through *tequio* and government grants, a road was completed between that center and Lahoya in the early 1970s, but it is not passable during the rainy season, even by truck. There is no landing strip in Lahoya, so the main means of transportation in and out of the village is still by foot.

Because of its isolation and stagnation, Lahoya appears to be a traditional mountain Zapotec village.[9] Zapotec remains the primary language, and vestiges of the traditional (albeit postconquest) religious *cargo* system are still in existence. Even by the 1980s few Lahoyans in the village went beyond primary school. In short, Lahoya is one of the poorest and most conservative villages of the sector. In no small part because of the dearth of economic alternatives or opportunities, over the past 40 years the population has gradually declined to about 50 percent of its 1950 size, largely due to the high rates of out-migration.

LAHOYANS IN MEXICO CITY[10]

Facilitation and mutual aid were practiced extensively among the Lahoyan migrants in Oaxaca City, which was the first primary urban point of destination after World War II. There were, by contrast, very few early migrants from Lahoya in Mexico City in the early 1950s. Facilitation there was almost impossible due to few numbers of migrants, and because most of them were not in a financial position to help others. In both cities, women tended to be employed in domestic services, while men worked as servants, in the service sector, or sold wage labor in unskilled manual jobs in the informal sector of the urban economy.

By the late 1950s, though, the number of Lahoyan migrants in Mexico City had grown substantially. It had become evident to Lahoyans in Oaxaca City, as well as in the village, that the capital offered the widest range of occupational and educational opportunities. At this point, the possibility of receiving help from relatives or friends influenced many people to make the move. The selectivity of types of migrants broadened. Facilitation was generalized but limited in its duration since few families could promise indefinite lodgings or meals, even for close relatives.

As industrial development "took off" in Mexico City and the migrants obtained new experience and skills, the patterns of occupation and mobility changed. Despite continuing patterns of domestic work for women and wage labor for men, by the middle of the 1970s many men held "tenured" jobs (that is, jobs protected by formal contract) that paid steady minimum wages. At the same time, however, analysis of occupational histories in my possession indicate that Lahoyans' work experiences were still characterized by stigmatization, frequent horizontal mobility, shifts in and out of formal sector occupations and sometimes, periods of unemployment.[11]

In the 1970s, young unmarried women continued to migrate to Mexico City specifically to work as maids. Women were attracted initially to Mexico City by the high wages and comparatively favorable working conditions. By the 1980s this pattern seemed to be slackening but had not stopped entirely.

Data on Lahoyan households in the 1970s were limited but indicated that most arrangements were either nuclear or involved nuclear families extended by the inclusion of close relatives being facilitated until they were able to move out on their own. Many of the Lahoyan migrants own land and houses in the capital and have settled in neighborhoods in relative proximity to compatriots from the village. Three of these areas are on the periphery of Mexico City, and two of the areas involve land invasions: Lahoyan migrants squatted and claimed land by participating in larger (that is, non-Lahoyan) squatter's movements. Because of residential clustering, patterns of interaction and reciprocity between Lahoyans can have a strong day-to-day basis, especially when they are reinforced by kinship or work relationships.

The formal dimension of the social organization of the Lahoyan migrants in Mexico City, which revolved around two migrant village associations, has evolved through distinct stages and so must be seen from a historical point of view.

Initially, migrant social organization was a matter of informal social networks. As noted, these networks were based on ties of kinship and neighborhood, mutual interests, a common workplace, or a common occupation. Parties and activities were the main events bringing Lahoyan migrants together. Young women who had come to Mexico City to work as maids, for example, gathered every weekend for a party and invited their friends. Two other networks began to cluster at the homes of two early migrants, both of whom had prestige among their compatriots because they had completed professional careers.

One of the latter networks was centered around parties at the house of Miguel Bautista Ambrocio, who was born in Lahoya but who grew up in Mexico City. This man (whom the Lahoyans called *Profesor*) had been orphaned at an early age. Brought to the capital as a child, he was eventually able to complete his education at an institute that trained elementary school teachers. Over the years he had also established many political connections throughout the official bureaucracies in Mexico and Oaxaca.

During the course of many gatherings at his house in the late 1950s, Bautista came up with several ideas, all of which revolved around projects to improve the basic infrastructure of the village. It should be pointed out that such projects had the potential for being funded by the Mexican government, especially since the national policy of that time was to extend basic services into the rural hinterlands. Finding that there was great enthusiasm among his compatriots regarding these ideas, Bautista eventually decided to organize a formal village association in Mexico City, named The Lahoyan Development Association, to carry out these projects. The leader of the second main network of migrants, which was also a formal village association by then, agreed to work with Bautista for the common benefit of Lahoya. The two leaders thus decided to put their groups together and take turns being the president of a single unified migrant association.

Bautista took the first turn and quickly took control of the organization, largely because of his ability to draw from his many personal contacts and friends in the middle echelons of the federal government. Through these contacts he was able to petition for and obtain funding and the technical assistance to initiate a series of local development projects, including a telegraph service and electrification. Work toward the construction of a passable road, without doubt the most important of the projects conceptualized and initiated by Bautista, also began in 1959. Although definite achievements were realized during this period, overt factionalism within the unified Lahoyan migrant village association also began to occur as early as 1959. Although the nature of the division is not fully clear, it appears that Bautista was unwilling to yield the leadership position once his term of office was technically over. Since he was the sole person with government contacts, and since payments for projects were issued in his name, it was almost impossible for any opponent or rival leader to challenge or to unseat him.[12]

Feeling that the initial promise to share the leadership of the united migrant village association had been broken, the leader of another group of Lahoyan migrants became angry and withdrew, taking all of his people with him. This split, which occurred around 1960, was definitive and final. The two leaders and their respective followers were subsequently at odds for many years. In addition, because the members of elite families in Lahoya had their own contacts at the local and state levels of government, they had been able to launch their own program to undermine Bautista and his group. With the joining of, and then the split between, the two groups in 1960, the rival leader in Mexico City, who was opposed to Bautista, threw his support to the leading families back in Lahoya. Thus, the division of the migrant community in Mexico City was soon replicated by corresponding divisions in Oaxaca City and in Lahoya itself. In the following decade, animosity and conflict between Bautista's association, the rival migrant association in Mexico City, groups affiliated with both sides in Oaxaca City, and factions within Lahoya itself became quite intense.

By 1968, three-fourths of the new road had been completed, and the fourth that remained had already been mapped out by the engineer. The plan for the last fourth of the road called for a completely new route into Lahoya, avoiding the traditional paths that had been utilized for decades.

Interestingly enough, the Lahoyans became concerned at this point that intracommunity factionalism was impeding efforts to obtain further government support for development projects. On September 28, 1968, a number of community leaders got together to pledge cooperation and to commit the moral and financial resources of the village as a whole toward the progress and benefit of the pueblo. Nonetheless, because conflicts continued to arise, it became clear that intracommunity divisions were not going to subside very quickly or easily. In the heat of many struggles–struggles that resulted in old friendships being torn asunder, and even the issuance of death threats designed to silence principal actors–some migrants in Mexico City began to drop out of the Lahoyan community in the hope of avoiding further struggles and controversies.

In 1970 Bautista was killed under mysterious circumstances. No one was ever charged in regard to his death. Soon afterward, the leadership of the rival association, in alliance with elite families in Lahoya, began to feel that they had an opportunity to get everyone together again under their newly asserted guidance and leadership. This vision, however, turned out to be quite difficult to realize. Federal aid was never again obtained at the same levels for Lahoyan development projects, including the completion of the road.

With one-quarter of the new road still to go, Bautista's opponents decided to complete the final fourth of the road by widening an old path that had traditionally linked Lahoya to the regional marketing center. Unfortunately, this path was located on a section of the sierra that had a very steep incline. Thus, when the job was finished between 1970 and 1971, the road was quite poor. It was difficult, for example, for a loaded truck to transverse the road during the dry season, and the road was basically impassable during the rainy season. In short, after years of great sacrifice and labor, there was little to show for all the efforts that had been made.

By the middle of the 1970s in Mexico City, these events had exacted their toll. There were only a few ad hoc organizations extant among the Lahoyan migrants in the capital, which still focused primarily on development issues in the home village, although their efforts had bogged down due to continued infighting.

ETHNOGRAPHIC ANALYSIS

Informal uses of regional identities among Mountain Zapotec migrants appear to be adaptive and efficacious. This may be because they are inherently voluntary. Thus, while informal ties based on and carried out in terms of regional identities can be and sometimes are subject to abuse, they can also be terminated easily, which acts to protect the provisioner of support. In addition, in terms of the two groups considered here, it can be said that each of the migrant communities has made use of informal aspects of regional identities in order to enhance their primary interactions and the "quality of life" in the capital.

From an instrumental and material perspective and in terms of occupational placement, facilitation appears to be effective, albeit within limits. Migrants' initial jobs and their subsequent occupational trajectories, that is, tend to reflect the levels of education and opportunity available in the point of origin. This is most clearly illustrated in terms of the Villalteco migrants, whose occupational clustering in professions related to either teaching or the national telegraph reflects specializations long practiced in the town itself. In this manner, training in and experience with either of these two professions have been utilized by many Villaltecos in pursuit of geographical and upward mobility.

Again, what is striking about the strength and the range of urban facilitation and mutual aid practices described above is that, especially in the case of the Lahoyans, such an emphasis is not apparent in the rural setting. In my view this indicates that mutual aid among indigenous peasant migrants is not always a matter of the direct *transfer* of a rural communal orientation but rather reflects the fact that the city presents an overwhelming set of challenges in the beginning. Social solidarity is intensified in such a setting because rural migrants prefer to face such challenges in alliance with each other rather than individually.[13]

Finally, it must be said that informal dimensions of regional identities, based on customs and institutions learned in the rural point of origin, are sometimes creatively recast in the new urban setting in new and original ways. This is certainly the case with the mechanisms for the resolution of serious domestic conflicts among Zapotec migrants from the town of Ralúa in Mexico City, as I illustrate in a recent study (Hirabayashi, 1994).

In this fashion, social relations entailed in chain migration among the Mountain Zapotec initially reinforced regional identification and solidarity. With the exception of networks based on common workplace, however, most informal aspects of regional identities have manifested little potential, to date, for politicization.

Moving to the primary issue at hand, both cases described above involve formalized expressions of regional identities in Mexico City. For the Villaltecos and Lahoyans in the capital, this has taken the form of migrant village associations, designed to support development projects in the point of origin. What is striking is that this process appears to be inseparably linked to a dynamic involving the regional policies pursued by the Mexican state, on one hand, and local political structures, on the other.[14] How did this linkage evolve?

Since the Mexican Revolution, regional development in Mexico, vis-à-vis Mexico's indigenous peoples, has been based on an "integrationist" approach spearheaded by the Mexican government (Adams 1967:476-477; King 1967:530-531). Based on the assumption that the modernization and economic integration of the hinterlands with the larger nation would be the best way to ensure the entrance of Mexico's indians into the larger society and polity, many economic and sociocultural programs directed toward "culture change" (read: assimilation) were implemented by the Mexican government following the revolution (Ewald 1967). The concrete manifestations of this policy in the Sierra Juárez have had a long and complex history (for example, Berg 1974). Beyond the impact of the national educational system (see Varese 1983),[15] the most tangible local form taken by the government's development policy was the Papaloapan Basin project, initiated in the 1950s (Poleman 1964). Because the Sierra Zapoteca was in the extreme southern periphery of the project, the overall impact of the project appears to have been much more benign than in the neighboring Mazatec region (for example, Barabas and Bartolomé 1986:67-68; Boege 1988). For example, under the direct auspices, or influence, of the Papaloapan Commission, rural villages in the *Rincón* were eventually provided with a wider range of infrastructure and services, including roads, schools, health care, water, electricity, communications, and so forth (Nader 1964:214).

What is ironic–at least in terms of Mexican public policy aims–is that government-supported programs of regional development were supposed to promote a national sense of identity in the rural hinterlands. The fact, however, that "every Zapotec village has a sharp sense of itself, such that its members always feel superior to people from other villages" (De La Fuente 1965:31; my translation) was further exacerbated as each community competed to win the benefits of governmental programs operating at the national and state levels. In the urban setting, the corollary of this process took place as the migrants supported (or, in the Lahoyan case, initiated) such efforts and presented petitions to governmental officials requesting resources to enable development in their communities of origin.

Keeping this in mind, the resultant point is as follows: the Mexican government's philosophy and approach to regional development, at least as it was manifested in the Sierra Zapoteca between 1950 and the mid-1980s, appears to have intensified locally framed conceptualizations of identity. Furthermore, because out-migration from the Sierra Juárez also "took off" simultaneously as new opportunities for state funded projects became available, rural development policies also set the stage for the fluorescence of Zapotec village and regional associations throughout the decade of the 1970s.[16] How migrant associations were manifested, and whether or not their pursuits proved salubrious for the migrants or the village in question, appears to have a great deal to do with local power structures (cf. De La Peña 1986).

Since its establishment, Villa Alta has traditionally been surrounded by less powerful indigenous peasant villages (De La Fuente 1965:51). Presently, the town is confronted politically with new kinds of alliances and levels of resistance, including those represented by both regional assemblies, on one hand, and Protestant converts, on the other. The major forms of political linkage Villaltecos have sought, in order to address these challenges, have been either (1) ties to the state and the nation, established by individual *caciques* and political brokers; or (2) the Villalteco out-migrants (Parnell 1988). In the latter case, as we have seen, each of the two primary village *caciques* and their followers have cultivated support groups among out-migrants in Oaxaca and in Mexico City in order to bolster their power. One *cacique* in particular, David Mendiolea, began to broker development projects, funded by the state, in order to create improvements and generate more political support for his group. What is quite notable is the extent to which the formal urban associations of Villaltecos in Oaxaca and in Mexico City are predominantly extensions of the key rural factions. Migrant factionalism in the urban setting is thus basically a reflection of extant factions in the town. Moreover, politicization and much of the direction and thrust of the urban associations appear to revolve around village leadership and village dynamics. In any case, factionalism seems to be kept under control in rural and urban settings through the use of *la voz pública* (popular opinion) and, failing that, informal and formal dispute management techniques, all of which are based on the postulate that Villaltecos should retain control over their own affairs.

By contrast, the Lahoyan migrants' village associations were initiated and controlled by out-migrants, although their ultimate fate was heavily impacted by political dynamics back in Lahoya. Formal associations had their base in informal networks that Lahoyan migrants drew from in order to mitigate the occupational disadvantages of being raised in a Zapotec-speaking, primarily agricultural setting. In addition, through their associations, migrants were able to collectively respond to the fact that the village of Lahoya was sorely in need of services and infrastructure in order to revitalize its stagnant economy. While extant among the migrants, factionalism was ultimately intensified when the elite families of Lahoya fought tooth and nail to prevent Miguel Bautista and his followers from completing their version of the road, among other projects. Subsequent events highlight the fact that formal migrant associations can often produce division and factionalism among both the migrants and their communities of origin when and if development projects threaten intrenched political interests back home. For this same reason, the formation of associations, and their overall impact upon the Lahoyan migrants, not to mention the village itself, serves as an example that regional cultures need not have a positive dynamic or outcome.

CONCLUSION

As I have indicated, regional identities among first-generation Zapotec immigrants in Mexico City remains fairly strong at both the informal and formal levels. It should also be noted that the cases described here do not capture all extant variations. In another article (Hirabayashi 1983), for example, I have outlined how and why, among the migrants from the regional marketing center of Ralúa in Mexico City, manifestations of regional identities took on a pan-regional thrust during the 1970s, both in the city and vis-à-vis the point of origin. In any case, I believe that regional identities, as these are manifested in Mexico City, can often (but not always) be seen as a creative and dynamic aspect of contemporary Zapotec culture.

In this same sense, it appears likely that, contrary to theoretical projections of the 1970s, regional identities among Zapotec in either provincial or urban settings are not solely the product of either cultural continuity or class oppression, but must be viewed in terms of the political configurations that frame specific communities within the larger Mexican society. Such a view greatly helps us to understand why "regional origins" are sources of new forms of cultural and social organization among Zapotecs and *mestizos* from the sierra–that is, whether they are from communities like Lahoya or Villa Alta, and whether they are residents in the provinces or in the city.

Over time, it is possible that the maintenance of community and of regional identities in urban settings among migrants from the Sierra Zapoteca will become much more tenuous. The general process whereby regional identities undergo attrition is not a given, though. Regional identities in the urban setting, in this sense, are influenced by developments and processes in the highlands of Oaxaca. For example, in the 1980s, regional assemblies such as the *Asamblea de Autoridades Zapotecas de la Sierra*, the *Unión de Pueblos del Rincón*, and *Organización para la Defensa de los Recursos Naturales de la Sierra Juárez*, began to organize on a larger pan-Zapotec, pan-regional, and even pan-sierran basis. Each organization can be seen as a response to political and economic threats to the self-preservation and self-determination of Sierra Zapotecan communities that were caused by the direct or indirect activities of the Mexican State (cf. Stavenhagen 1988; 1989). Similarly, other processes taking place in the sierra, ranging from land and boundary disputes to religious movements, unite and divide the residents of the area in new and sometimes unexpected ways.

Thus, if the long-term future of regional identities among Zapotec in urban settings like Mexico City is not yet clear, what is clear is that we are not talking about a lineal or a cumulative process of assimilation. Within the broad context of a "regional identities" perspective, Zapotec ethnicity as a whole, it seems to me, is emergent. It is respondent to a broad dialectic that conjoins the "rural" and "urban" dimensions of the larger Mexican society, and thus is most effectively studied in terms of a holistic view of regional dynamics and the kinds of extant linkages that tie the center and the periphery together (cf. Gledhill 1988; Kearney 1989; Nugent 1989). What transpires in the years to come, in this regard, certainly deserves continuing attention.

NOTES

1. A recently published study of the Sierra Zapoteca by Chance (1989) corroborates historians' general observation that much of what appears to be "indigenous" culture and social organization, actually has strong colonial roots (for example, Borah 1954, 1976). Nonetheless, what is at issue is precisely what was selected, and how it was reinterpreted and articulated with indigenous cultural elements, according to local world view (Kearney 1972; Nader 1989).

2. The various observations and analyses offered by Martínez Luna (1984), Mejía Piñeros and Sarmiento Silva (1987:95-96), Basañez E. (1987:71-72; 85-91), and Parnell (1988:82-85), concerning the different regional assemblies, indicate that they have similar orientations in terms of the values outlined above. All three organizations described by these authors fulfill the criteria for a "regional social movement" as specified by Slater (1989:206).

3. Nader's comments about the historical roots of *la república india* clarify why it is that the Mountain Zapotec identify so strongly with their natal village, and also why out-migrants are so oriented toward village-level associations (Nader 1989). In addition, Wolf notes that "the atomism of local communities in Oaxaca has increased, if anything...since the passage of the law of 1938 granting communities greater administrative autonomy from their regional centers" (1967:306).

4. Throughout this chapter the term "Mountain Zapotec" will be used to differentiate the Zapotec communities of the sierra, as a whole, from the Zapotec of the Rincón, specifically. There are some twelve communities in the core area of the Rincón (see maps in Nader 1964).

5. Civil *cargos* are offices in the local government that male citizens are required to assume. *Tequio* involves labor for civic projects and works that every male citizen is required to give to the community. *Mayordomía* involves religious duties and services. All of these institutions are central in the organization of the community; all are carried out, without remuneration, as part of the service that citizens owe to the larger community.

6. Funding for this research was generously provided by the Department of Anthropology, University of California, Berkeley, the Center for Latin American Studies, University of California, Berkeley, and the Inter-American Foundation. I would also like to acknowledge the helpful comments of Henry Selby and other scholars during a formal presentation of this paper at the "Regional Cultures in Latin American Cities workshop," May 12, 1990, at the Institute for Latin American Studies, the University of Texas, Austin. I alone am responsible for the data and interpretations advanced here.

7. The 1950 census was selected for discussion here, simply because it provides the most detailed statistics on household composition (D.G.E. 1954).

8. Lahoya's church houses a large collection of saints, many of which are said to be antiques. Lahoyans believe that the saints can act as intermediaries between man and God; thus, one can pray to a saint for a

cure from sickness, on behalf of one's children, or for any special wish. During the *mayordomía*, when the saints are honored, they are taken from the church, paraded around the village, and may be placed for a period of time in individual homes. Although these traditions appear to be in decline, my own data, along with subsequent reports on religion in the sierra offered by Marroquín (1987; 1989), indicate that Protestant evangelists have made little headway in this particular village.

9. Even by the 1970s, slightly over one-fourth of the Lahoyan population was monolingual Zapotec in 1970 (D.G.E. 1954, 1963, 1973), and a full third of the Lahoyans could neither read nor write. In fact, the primary school in Lahoya includes only the first three grades out of a six-year primary school education. A comparison between the neghboring marketing center and Lahoya in 1960 provides a clear picture of the differential impact of development on the region. In 1960 the marketing center had 163 persons in occupations outside of agriculture; Lahoya had only six. Although an improvement in this area is suggested by the national census figures for 1970, interviews with migrants who had recently visited the village indicated that little had changed substantively.

10. The population of Lahoyan migrants in Mexico City was on the order of three hundred adults in 1978. Several circumstances impeded an accurate estimate of the total population of, as well as the selection of a large sample from, this group. First of all, since there has traditionally been either friction or mutual disregard between Lahoya and the regional marketing center of the area, Ralúa, the fact that I had worked with the Ralúan migrants (for example, Hirabayashi 1983) made some of the people from Lahoya suspicious of my motives. Second, Lahoyans and Lahoyan migrants in Mexico City have themselves been divided into factions, thus producing a general climate of suspicion and confict. As a result of this sitation, data collection took the following form. Initially I made contact with the leaders of all factions, and gave long open-ended interviews on the reasons for Lahoyan migration and the present situation of Lahoyans in the capital. Then I selected a small number of key informants, whom I interviewed over a period of six months. The information gathered in this manner was checked and expanded by interviews with thirty-five nonrandomly selected migrants from three key neighborhoods where there was a pattern of Lahoyan residential clustering. These comments provide an idea of the limitations of the sample: (1) interviews were nonrandom; (2) access to people and information was often quite limited; and (3) I probably spoke with migrants who were more "attached" to Lahoya, both in terms of other Lahoyans in Mexico City and back in the village. Finally, for obvious reasons, names and some details have been adjusted in order to protect the identities of individuals.

11. Since the educational attainment of the Lahoyan migrants was (understandably) low, they were the first to suffer from the standard policy of many Mexican companies in the 1970s: to fire unskilled and semi-skilled workers before they could obtain tenure or before their "compensatory" fees became too high.

12. Representatives from each of the two factions had their own interpretations of this basic situation. His detractors claimed that Bautista was clearly corrupt because he arranged to have government monies for road construction signed over in his name. This arrangement was clearly outside of "proper channels," that is, the municipal authorities back in Lahoya. Bautista's supporters, on the other hand, claimed that he was an upright citizen. Moreover, his move in regard to receiving government monies directly was both a logical and an intelligent strategy because in this fashion he circumvented the village power structure.

13. I also hypothesize that migrants from an indigenous peasant background tend to phrase mutual aid practices in terms of an egalitarian, communal worldview, while *mestizo* migrants are more likely to phrase mutual aid and facilitation in terms of vertical "patron-client" relationships (see Rollwagen 1974).

14. I would like to acknowledge the influence of Susan Buck Sutton, whose research (1978) on the relationship between the government's regional development projects and migrant associations in Greece attuned me to this process among the Zapotec.

15. Varese's research (1983) on the impact of official Mexican educational policy in Oaxaca provides an important, if tragic, study of the resultant damage to Zapotecan culture and self-image. It is notable that his subsequent work was aimed at redressing this situation (Varese 1985), and that this same theme was pursued by Bonfil Batalla (1987).

16. A cursory review of the ethnographic literature suggests that similar processes characterized the formation of migrant associations among other groups from the highlands of Oaxaca in Mexico City, including Mixtec migrants from Tilantongo (Butterworth 1975) and Mixe migrants from Totontepec (Romer 1982).

REFERENCES CITED

Adams, Richard N.
  1967   "Nationalization." In *Handbook of Middle American Indians,* Volume 6. Manning Nash, editor, pp. 469-89. Austin: University of Texas Press.
Arizpe S., Lourdes
  1975   *Indígenas en la ciudad de México: El caso de las "Marías."* Mexico City: Secretaría de Educación Pública, Sep/Setentas.
Barabas, Alicia M., and Miguel A. Bartolomé, editors
  1986   *Etnicidad y pluralismo cultural: La dinámica étnica en Oaxaca.* Mexico City: Instituto Nacional de Antropología e Historia; Colleción Regiones de Mexico.
Basañez E., Miguel, editor
   1987 *La composición de poder: Oaxaca, 1968-1984.* Mexico City: Instituto Nacional de Administración Pública.
Berg, Richard Lewis Jr.
  1974   *El Impacto de la economía moderna sobre la economía tradicional de Zoogocho, Oaxaca y su área circundante.* Mexico City: Instituto Nacional Indigenista.
Boege, Eckart
  1988   *Los Mazatecos ante la nación: Contradicciones de la identidad étnica en México actual.* Mexico City: Siglo Veintiuno Editores.
Bonfil Batalla, Guillermo
  1987   "Los pueblos indios; sus culturas y las políticas culturales." In *Políticas culturales in América Latina.* Néstor García Canclini, editor, pp. 89-125. Mexico City: Grijalbo.
Borah, Woodrow
  1954   "Race and Class in Mexico." *Pacific Historical Review* 23:331-42.
  1976   "Legacies of the Past: Colonial." In *Contemporary Mexico.* James W. Wilkie, M. C. Meyer, and E. Monzon de Wilkie, editors, pp. 29-37. Berkeley: University of California Press and the Colegio de México.
Butterworth, Douglas
  1975   *Tilantongo: Comunidad Mixteca en transición.* Mexico City: Instituto Nacional Indigenista.
Chance, John K.
  1989   *Conquest of the Sierra: Spaniards and Indians in Colonial Oaxaca.* Norman: University of Oaklahoma Press.
De La Fuente, Julio
  1965   *Relaciones interétnicas.* Mexico City: Instituto Nacional Indigenista.
De La Peña, Guillermo
  1986   "Poder local, poder regional: Perspectivas socio-antropológicas." In *Poder Local, poder regional.* Jorge N. Padua and Alain Venneph, editors, pp. 27-56. Mexico City: El Colegio de México/CEMCA.
Dirección General de Estadística
  1954   *Sétimo censo de la población–1950.* Estado de Oaxaca. Mexico.
  1963   *Octavo censo de la población–1960.* Estado de Oaxaca. Mexico.
  1973   *Noveno censo de la población–1970.* Estado de Oaxaca. Mexico.
Ewald, Robert H.
  1967   "Directed Change." In *Handbook of Middle American Indians,* Volume 6. Manning Nash, editor, pp. 490-511. Austin: University of Texas Press.
Friedlander, Judith
  1975   *Being Indian in Hueyapan: A Study of Forced Identity in Contemporary Mexico.* New York: St. Martin's Press.
Gledhill, John
  1988   "Agrarian Social Movements and Forms of Consciousness." *Bulletin of Latin American Research* 7:257-276.
Hirabayashi, Lane Ryo
  1983   "On the Formation of Migrant Village Associations in Mexico: Mixtec and Mountain Zapotec Cases." *Urban Anthropology* 12:29-44.

1986   "The Migrant Village Association in Latin America: A Comparative Analysis." *Latin American Research Review* 21:7-29.

1993   *Cultural Capital: Mountain Zapotec Migrant Associations in Mexico City.* Tucson, AZ: University of Arizona Press.

1994   "Mountain Zapotec Migrants and Forms of Capital." *PoLAR [Political and Legal Anthropology Review]* 17(2):105-116.

Kearney, Michael
1972   *The Winds of Ixtepeji: World View and Society in a Zapotec Town.* New York: *Holt, Rinehart and Winston.*

1989   "Mixtec Political Consciousness: From Passive to Active Resistance." In *Rural Revolt in Mexico and U.S. Intervention.* Daniel Nugent, editor, pp. 113-124. San Diego: Center for U.S.-Mexican Studies, U.C. San Diego.

King, Arden R.
1967   "Urbanization and Industrialization." In *Handbook of Middle American Indians,* Volume 6. Manning Nash, editor, pp. 469-489. Austin: University of Texas Press.

Marroquín Z., Enrique
1987   "Presencia protestante en las comunidades indígenas de Oaxaca." In *De sectas a sectas, Una aproximación al estudio de un fenómeno apasionante,* pp. 35-46. Oaxaca: Claves Latinoamericanas; Universidad Autónoma "Benito Juárez" de Oaxaca, Instituto de Investigaciones Sociológicas, México.

1989   "El campo religioso en las comunidades indígenas de Oaxaca." *Cristianismo y Sociedad* 27:59-71.

Martínez Luna, Jaime
1984   "Resistencia comunitaria y cultura popular: El caso de la 'Organización en Defensa de los Recursos Naturales y el Desarrollo Social de la Sierra Juárez, A.C.'" In *Culturas Populares y Política Cultural.* Guillermo Bonfil Batalla, editor, pp. 65-78. Mexico, City: Museo de Culturas Populares/Secretaría de Educación Pública.

Mejía Piñeros, María Consuelo, and Sergio Sarmiento Silva
1987   *La lucha indígena: Un reto de la ortodoxia.* Mexico City: Siglo Veintiuno Editores.

Muñoz, Humberto, Orlandina de Oliveira, and Claudio Stern
1982   *Mexico City: Industrialization, Migration and the Labour Force, 1930-1970.* (Reports and Papers in the Social Sciences 46. Selected Studies on the Dynamics, Patterns and Consequences of Migration, I). Paris: UNESCO.

Nader, Laura
1964   *Talea and Juquila: A Comparison of Zapotec Social Organization.* Berkeley: University of California Press.

1989   "The Crown, the Colonists, and the Course of Zapotec Village Law." In *History and Power in the Study of Law: New Directions in Legal Anthropology.* June Starr and Jane F. Collier, editors, pp. 320-344. Stanford: Stanford University Press.

Nugent, Daniel
1989   "'Are We Not [Civilized] Men?': The Formation and Devolution of Community in Northern Mexico." *Journal of Historical Sociology* 2:206-239.

Parnell, Philip C.
1988   *Escalating Disputes: Social Participation and Change in the Oaxacan Highlands.* Tucson: The University of Arizona Press.

Poleman, Thomas
1964   *The Papaloapan Project.* Stanford: Stanford University Press.

Rollwagen, Jack
1974   "Mediation and Rural-Urban Migration in Mexico: A Proposal and a Case Study." *Latin American Urban Research* 4:47-63.

Romer, Marta
1982   *Comunidad, migración y desarrollo: El caso de los Mixes de Totontepec, Oaxaca.* Mexico City: Instituto National Indigenista.

Slater, David
1989   *Territory and State Power in Latin America: The Peruvian Case.* New York: St. Martin's Press.

Stavenhagen, Rodolfo
  1988   *Derecho indígena y derechos humanos en América Latina.* Mexico City: Instituto Interamericano de Derechos Humanos, El Colegio de México.
  1989   "Comunidad étnicas en estados modernos." *América Indígena* 49:11-34.
Sutton, Susan Buck
  1978   *Migrant Regional Associations: An Athenian Example and its Implications.* Ph.D. dissertation, University of North Carolina.
Varese, Stefano
  1983   *Indígenas y educación en México.* Mexico City: Centro de Estudios Educativos.
  1985   "Cultural Development in Ethnic Groups: Anthropological Explorations in Education." *International Social Science Journal* 37:201-216.
Whitecotton, Joseph W.
  1977   *The Zapotecs: Princes, Priests & Peasants.* Norman: University of Oklahoma Press.
Wolf, Eric R.
  1967   "Levels of Communal Relations." In *Handbook of Middle American Indians,* Volume 6. Manning Nash, editor, pp. 299-316. Austin: University of Texas Press.

CHAPTER FIVE

Life Goes On:
Revisiting Lima's Migrant Associations

Paul L. Doughty
University of Florida

A PREFACE FROM THE PAST

"Fellow countrymen," said the president, "the sons of Chalhuanca, like those of Caráz, those of Jauja, those from Huamancucho already have their Cultural Sports Centers. There are hundreds of Andean provincial organizations in Lima. These centers look after the interests of their own provinces; they defend their communities from abuses by the landowners, authorities and priests. And they are raising the cultural level of their members by organizing public lectures, even receptions, libraries and even by publishing magazines. These centers also keep the memory of our own part of the country alive; they have their typical orchestras, and hold their festivals in their hometown ways. There are now more than 2,000 of us Lucaninos in Lima, and we're all asleep. Meanwhile the big landholders and petty politicians keep on exploiting the comuneros, just as their ancestors did 200 years ago. . . . We who have had our eyes opened and our consciousness freed should not let them get away with skinning our brothers alive. I put the organization of a Lucanas Union Center to a vote!"
José María Argüedas, *Yawar Fiesta* 1941[1985]:70).

DEMOGRAPHY AND SOCIAL ORGANIZATION OF PERUVIAN MIGRATION

Demographic data only hint at the nature or possibilities of social organization, social action, and cultural content. If we view the growth of the Peruvian population from 1940 to the present, for example, we see that there has been a massive change in both the prehistoric and historic pattern of distribution and settlement as highlanders moved to coastal cities seeking urban employment, facilities, and access to participation in national policy and power decisions and economy.[1] The majority of Peru's people live along the urbanized desert coast instead of in the Andean valleys.

Peruvian migration did not conform in all ways with the patterns of similar phenomena elsewhere, particularly in the European and North American nations, where, since the onset of industrialization, peasants, craftsmen, and others moved into urban environments. In many areas, such as the United States, it was the female population that predominated in the movement off farms and into cities; in other instances it was the men who were first called to new arenas of employment. Often it was observed in the stressful urban settings that migrants were hard put to maintain viable social groups in the face of economic and social strains on the traditional relationships and norms that governed behavior and formed the basis of neighborhood and community structures.

The generalizations that emerged from this literature guided many of the first attempts to discover just how the migratory process in Latin America operated and what its characteristics were. Thus, for example, Oscar Lewis sought to highlight some of the differences he saw in Mexico that apparently distinguished the new urban life there from United States experience. The title of Lewis's (1959) article, "Urbanization without Breakdown," expresses the concern well, addressing what was, perhaps, a negative ethnocentric generalization often made about erstwhile "universal" aspects of urbanization. In contrast to the sociological literature that appeared to emphasize social disintegration, urban anthropological research tended to focus upon structure, organization, interactive social process, solidarity, and group identity–those cultural practices that shaped, nourished, and reinforced group patterns. The individual in the anthropological perspective was to be seen, always, as a role player in an ongoing social context, not to be isolated from the sociocultural matrix from which one drew the status, obligations, and expectations that formed the basis of daily life.

It was not surprising that the experts on small rural communities and tight-knit tribal nations should carry their theoretical packages with them to the city like so many *encomiendas*[2] in the back of a *mixto*, winding down the flanks of the Andes to Lima. Anthropological inquiries into urban life thus carried with them the strong rural accent, developed in the context of the community study tradition, long debated as a method and theoretical issue, but one that continues to dominate the literature. This is for good reason, of course: people throughout the world continue to live in definable forms of community, with a wide range of variation in form, content, and purpose. That culture, kin, and community should be discovered as organizing principles in urban life is surprising only in that these factors often fail to appear as variables in research, and especially in that which attempts to focus on the proverbial "big picture" and "macrolevel" analyses.

Like the migrants themselves, the students of towns and rural villages literally followed "their" people into the cities. In my own case, the interest began when my wife and I were living in Huaylas, Ancash (Peru), studying the impact of electrification on that Andean district, "nailed in the heart of the Andes." Typically for the time, I had not even considered the migrants as part of our study population as such. They no longer lived in Huaylas. On our periodic trips to Lima, however, our neighbors would always ask us to take boxes of food and gifts "in trust" to their relatives in the capital. In delivering these *encomiendas* I learned of a substantial Huaylas "colony" in Lima comprised of *paisanos* who were not only in close touch with their homelands but who welcomed both the gifts and messengers with a ready friendship. We were, after all, now part of the community and came recommended and trusted. Village hospitality patterns had not disappeared in the city, and we unexpectedly discovered that we automatically and unknowingly had acquired a very large web of relationships in Lima. Not only were we well known among the Huaylinos in Lima, but, as in the village, we were expected to be part of their Lima community.

This relationship has never abated. In later years, when we lived in Lima, they played an important role in our social life. To meet our needs we would be referred unhesitatingly to Huaylinos who were tailors, shoe repairmen, nurses, pharmacists, doctors, carpenters, lawyers, maids, diplomats, market vendors, and other useful specialists.

LEARNING ABOUT LIMA

All of this was an exciting social revelation of major import: it was not possible to study Peruvian life without an urban component, and it was incorrect to visualize any Peruvian as being "outside" of or in fact "marginal" to the national socioeconomic and political system. This was important not only for anthropologists who worked in the hinterlands but also for other social scientists who concentrated most of their efforts in capital city and "upper level" national affairs. In the decade of the 1960s, just as Lima was flooded with migrants, so Peruvians were visited by increasing numbers of researchers of all types from several countries, criss-crossing each others' paths and creating their own visions of the urbanization process and its meaning.[3] To paraphrase more recent popular jargon, Lima was being "penetrated" by peasants, and that was followed by the "expansion of social scientism."

Generalizations about urban growth in Peru have tended to overlook the fact that Lima's "new look" was already developing in the last century and that population growth was part of a long trajectory. The removal of the "new" city walls built in 1685 was accomplished under the aegis of erstwhile "Yankee Pizzaro" Henry Meiggs to make room for growth in 1872 (Dobyns and Doughty 1976:185-207). Pierola's second term as president in 1895 marked the onset of modernization of urban Lima, catching up with social changes which were forced by the fatal War of the Pacific and being introduced by English and other European immigrants who were taking control of Peru's economy. Symbolic of this were the athletic clubs that sprang up to encompass novel interests in tennis and *fútbol* among the elites and quickly were popularized as organizational forms throughout Lima and ultimately to the provincial hinterlands as regionalist publications of the time make clear.

Of course, since its founding Lima had been an attraction not only for colonial administrators but for those persons who managed to slip through viceregal regulations that greatly limited the free movement of individuals. Early censuses of Lima even in the seventeenth century found hundreds of *provincianos* ensconced in urban neighborhoods dominated by them. By the beginning of this century, that pattern was fully developed. In 1920, 32 percent of the residents in Lima came from elsewhere in the republic. The local census conducted in Lima and Callao in 1931 revealed a population pyramid that, like a man of prosperous middle age, was not only adding a smooth coat of new tissue all over the body but developing a pronounced bulge in the midsection; in this case, the 20-29 year age cohort representing the most mobile sector of the population.

MAP 5.1   PERUVIAN CITIES AND DEPARTMENTS

SIX PATTERNS OF URBANIZATION IN LIMA

Lima's dramatic growth in the twentieth century has been a "national" event, uniting Peruvians in ways heretofore unachieved. The collection of data in Table 5.1 reviews the demography of provincial migration to metropolitan Lima, which includes Callao as well as the Province of Lima, with its many districts (see Map 5.1). When scholars and politicians turned their attention to Peru's urban conditions the population of greater Lima seemed to be "exploding," as many authors chose to phrase it. Triggered by the emergence of the anchovy fishing industry in the early part of the 1950 decade, no one predicted that the quiet, nonindustrial coastal towns were to be engulfed by a provincial population long regarded by urban creoles as ignorant, uncultured, and brutish. The first migration pattern is that, in broad context, the regional origins of migrants to Lima have lasted over a century. The highland and coastal provinces of the department of Lima itself have led all others in migration to the capital city. Besides this, however, the departmental migration pattern has been surprisingly constant since the beginning of the century, with six of the eight leading departments figuring among the top six contributors to Lima's growth throughout the period. Half of those departments are adjacent to Lima, but the others are not.

Given the fact that Cajamarca, Puno and Piura are among Peru's most populous departments, it seems somewhat surprising that they have not been a more prominent part of the movement towards Lima until one sees that their migrants have been filling the urban niches closer to or within their borders, as is the case with Piura. Puno, on the other hand, has supplied large numbers of Amazonian colonists in addition to being the major contributor to the growth of the cities of Juliaca and Arequipa, while the north coastal cities of Trujillo and Chiclayo have drawn most from Cajamarca hinterland (see Table 5.2).

A second major feature of this demographic review is that before 1920 no less than 32 percent of the people resident in Lima were born outside the capital. The surprising fact is that the 1981 census registered the smallest percentage of birthright *provincianos* living in Lima since the beginning of this century. For the moment, at least, the migrants of yesteryear are producing a "baby-boom" of new *Limeños–masamoreros*[4] who have tipped the numerical balance between migrant and native. In percentage terms, the migrant flow has slowed substantially from its high point registered between 1940 and 1961 (see Table 5.1).

The third historic feature of this migratory stream is the sociocultural diversity represented by the departments: Ancash and Ayacucho being strongly rural in nature and part of what was lamentably referred to by some writers by that infelicitous (not to mention derogatory) name, the *"mancha india"*;[5] Arequipa and Ica being urbanized *"criollo"* populations; and the highland parts of Lima department and Junín, classically thought of as *cholo*, whose migrants came primarily from recognized indian=cum=peasant communities such as Acolla, Mito, Muquiyauyo, Chongos, and dozens of others. The highlander migrants were characteristically bilingual and bicultural *mestizos* or self-identified *cholos*. Indians–that is, monolingual Quechua and Aymara speakers wearing regional clothing, unschooled farmers, and impoverished rural villagers–were not the main current of the migrant stream contrary to some journalistic opinion. Those indians who did come to Lima throughout this time found themselves under enormous stress and altered their cultural identities by rapidly learning Spanish and changing their clothes as they denied their

TABLE 5.1 THE GROWTH OF THE GREATER LIMA POPULATION AND ITS PROVINCIAL ORIGINS, 1920-1981

Greater Lima (Thousands)	1920	1931	1940	1961	1972	1981
Metropolitan Lima	255.0	410.0	643.0	1,641.0	3,294.0	4,836.0
Callao	51.0	68.0	81.0	205.0	321.0	454.0
Lima	204.0	342.0	562.0	1,436.0	2,973.0	4,382.0
TOTAL % GROWTH	»33.5	60.7	56.8	159.6	129.3	46.8
Ancash	11.0	18.2	44.5	105.0	155.0	231.0
Lima (outside Metro Lima)	nd	26.8	nd	83.5	146.9	§212.7
Junín	11.5	18.7	32.1	68.0	110.0	158.0
Ayacucho	5.0	9.0	19.8	77.0	131.0	**157.0
La Libertad	5.5	11.0	24.7	64.0	96.0	118.0
Cajamarca	2.8	5.7	10.8	40.0	81.0	**113.0
Arequipa	9.0	17.2	23.3	62.0	96.0	100.0
Apeurímac	1.0	2.2	4.3	40.0	81.0	**99.0
Ica	9.9	18.0	26.3	51.0	75.0	98.0
Piura	4.3	6.0	9.2	38.0	84.0	**91.0
Cuzco	1.8	3.0	5.4	26.0	63.0	80.0
Huánuco	2.0	3.9	7.4	25.0	53.0	**72.0
Lambayeque	3.2	5.5	10.2	35.0	59.0	72.0
Huancavelica	2.0	2.9	7.2	28.0	49.0	**68.0
Puno	1.0	2.0	2.3	14.0	40.0	**51.0
Pasco	*	*	*	16.0	30.0	43.0
Loreto	-1.0	1.5	3.3	15.0	33.0	35.0
San Martín	-1.0	-1.0	1.0	7.0	18.0	27.0
Amazonas	-1.0	-1.0	-1.0	6.0	17.0	**21.0
Ucayalí	*	*	*	*	*	**11.0
Tacna	3.7	4.3	3.7	5.0	7.0	8.0
Tumbes	-1.0	1.0	1.4	2.0	7.0	8.0
Moquegua	1.5	1.9	2.2	3.0	2.0	7.0
Madre de Dios	-1.0	-1.0	1.0	1.0	1.0	**2.0
Tarapaca	3.8	2.6	*	*	*	*
TOTALS	84.0	164.4	241.1	811.5	1,434.9	1,882.7
% MIGRANTS IN LIMA	32.0	40.0	37.0	52.6	43.0	34.9

¶ From Peru Censo de Lima y Callao 1931; Censos Nacional de Población de 1940; VI Censos Nacional de   Población 1961; Censos Nacionales VII de Población, 1972; Censos Nacionales VIII de Población, 1981.

+ Departments by order of the numbers of migrants censused in Lima in 1981.

* Departments not in existence at time of census.

§ Estimated.

» Growth from 1905/8 census of Lima-Callao when the metropolitan area held 191,243 inhabitants, to 1920.

** Departments with rural populations exceeding 52% of their total.

TABLE 5.2 PERUVIAN CITIES AND THEIR GROWTH, 1961-1990

City*	Major City Population Growth*				% Growth	Department	% of National Urban Population
	1961	1972	1981	1990	1961-90		
Lima/Callao	1,64.0	3,294.0	4,836.0	6,414.0	290	Lima	58
Arequipa	158.0	304.0	447.0	634.0	301	Arequipa	6
Trujillo	103.0	241.0	355.0	531.0	415	La Libertad	5
Chiclayo	95.0	189.0	280.0	426.0	348	Lambayeque	4
Piura	72.0	126.0	186.0	324.0	350	Piura	3
Chimbote	59.0	159.0	216.0	296.0	401	Ancash	3
Cuzco	79.0	120.0	182.0	275.0	248	Cuzco	2
Iquitos	57.0	111.0	185.0	269.0	359	Loreto	2
Huancayo	64.0	115.0	165.0	207.0	152	Junin	2
Ica	49.0	73.0	111.0	152.0	210	Ica	1
Tacna	27.0	55.0	92.0	150.0	473	Tacna	1
Pucallpa	26.0	57.0	92.0	129.0	396	Ucayali	1
Juliaca	20.0	38.0	77.0	121.0	505	Puno	1
Sullana	34.0	60.0	80.0	113.0	229	Piura	1
Ayacucho	23.0	34.0	68.0	101.0	339	Ayacucho	-1
Cajamarca	22.0	37.0	60.0	92.0	318	Cajamarca	-1
Puno	24.0	41.0	66.0	90.0	275	Puno	-1
Talara	27.0	29.0	57.0	89.0	229	Piura	-1
Huacho	22.0	36.0	42.0	87.0	278	Lima	-1
Huanuco	24.0	41.0	53.0	86.0	258	Huanuco	-1
Tarapoto	13.0	21.0	37.0	77.0	492	San Martin	-1
Pasco	21.0	47.0	72.0	76.0	211	C. de Pasco	-1
Huaraz	20.0	29.0	45.0	65.0	225	Ancash	-1
Tumbes	20.0	32.0	48.0	64.0	220	Tumbes	-1
Chincha	20.0	28.0	40.0	51.0	155	Ica	-1
Barranca	15.0	28.0	31.0	40.0	166	Lima	-1
Tarma	15.0	28.0	38.0	40.0	166	Junin	-1
TOTALS	**2,772.0**	**5,414.0**	**8,014.0**	**11,985.0**	**332**		
PRIMACY RATE¶ 41.8				**46.1**			

* From Peru VI Censo Nacional de Población, 1961; Censos Nacionales VII de Población, 1972: Censos Nacionales VIII de Población, 1981; Proyecciones Especiales de Población, (1984).

+ It is a challenge to discover the populations for Peruvian cities because "cities" are not reported as such in the Census as analytical categories, but only as urban populations of districts or provinces. Because several districts may comprise a city, one must know which ones are included as these are not indicated in Census materials. The only place in the 1981 census which this information is to be found for example is in the "Preliminary Results" volume (Perú, Resultados Provisionales, 1981.)

¶ The primacy rate represents the total population of leading secondary cities divided by that of the metropolitan capital. Here, the populations of the eight largest cities are compared to that of Lima.

cultural origins (Myers 1973). Those who could not make such a change, like the migrants' elderly parents, remained essentially "out of sight" at home or took up the most marginal urban existence. Those who could not effect any of these strategies returned home or moved to more congenial settings elsewhere.

A fourth and continuing quality of the migratory process is the stratagem of almost always following in the footsteps of relatives and *paisanos* to the chosen destination (Dobyns and Vazquez 1963). People do not as a rule simply strike out on their own, without references and potential support already in focus but as part of a family enterprise. Persons who do undertake a solitary adventure, characteristically have great difficulties, as Patch's classic example of the "villager who met disaster" illustrated (Patch 1967). This is confirmed by Altamirano, who notes:

> The migrant who has no relatives, or has only a small number in the city, increases his risks of unemployment and loneliness; consequently increases his marginality with respect to other social groups, including those that come from the same place of origin (1988:35).

Although there are some who do accept the risk of entering upon a "Columbian" adventure, the vast majority of migrants to the great Andean metropolis invariably direct themselves to a known social "beachhead" from which to start and survive in the new life. They are not "castaways" on a deserted island.

Seen from the *Limeño* viewpoint, migration is an overwhelming fact of life that has engulfed not only their space but their social traditions as well.[6] While by and large ignoring the influx of provincials, especially highlanders (*serranos*), into Lima prior to the early 1960s, the sharp rise in their presence in that decade provoked many changes and problems. The growth of squatter settlements (discussed below) was only the most obvious aspect of this. Andean music was now frequently heard on the radio, provincial *mixtos* were a common sight in Lima streets. Highland folk arts and crafts, which were denigrated and not a part of creole urban home decor or style, suddenly became popular mid-decade with the development of a permanent craft market in a plaza of La Victoria district in central Lima.[7] Indeed, the importance of highland migrants was strongly emphasized in the political campaigns of 1962 and 1963, when Fernando Belaunde Terry conducted a vigorous effort to gain provincial votes and was especially effective in attracting the support of migrant colonies in Lima (see below). For the first time in Peruvian history a truly nationwide campaign was waged because Belaunde's strategy forced even APRA's aging Victor Raul Haya de la Torre onto horseback over mountain trails.[8]

A fifth trait of the Peruvian migrant is that this person is decidedly prone to joining social and political institutions such as migrant associations, sports clubs, or settlement and neighborhood mutual assistance groups of various sorts. The ubiquitous nature of these voluntary groups is not only one of the most striking features of modern Lima, it is also one that may not be readily visible, identified, or, as it turns out, understood. Given the fact that migrants originate in rather diverse departments, it is interesting to raise the question of whose idea it was to organize a provincial association. Which departmental society was the first to organize a group calling itself by some such name as "The Mutual Aid Society of the United Sons of Incaland"? The Departmental Club of Arequipa appears to be the oldest of its genre, being organized in 1871, but there may have been others more senior.[9] Lima became famous for its squatter settlements whose special attribute, besides their ubiquity, was and remains, as we shall see, their high degree of organization, a fact that came quickly to the attention of social scientists, planners, and journalists.[10]

The motivations, mechanisms, and causes that induced and guided Peru's millions to migrate are varied and complex. Collectively, these form a sixth pattern in this vast social configuration because they conform to the conditions created by the overarching norm of the Peruvian state: the political, cultural, economic, social, infrastructural, and operational primacy of the capital city. The immediate reasons given by most center around the search for more lucrative and steady employment, the quest for schooling and vocational training, and the need to accompany other family members to gain access to health services and, in general, to go somewhere where there is *movimiento*. There are also many "push" factors as well that come into play: the loss of or lack of farmland; disaster; poverty conditions; lack of employment options; and a host of personal reasons.

Seen in a more system-oriented perspective, however, the conditions that stimulate migration should be collectively placed in the context of the state structure and the policies that operate therein. This milieu is governed by the colonial, if not Incaic, principal that the capital is the "navel of the universe." The Spaniards moved that center from Cuzco to Lima, resulting in the indisputable consequence that the major social, economic, and political fact of Peruvian life is that Lima is a primate city (Browning 1967; Deitz 1976; Doughty 1976, 1979b). With almost 30 percent of the national population consuming approximately 75 percent of the country's resources, Lima's institutional forces control the political, economic, and bureaucratic life of the nation absolutely. That migrants are predominately attracted to Lima over other places is thus no surprise. But it also means that the nation's social policy is skewed sharply in favor of the residents of the capital. Lima has the best jobs, the best education and public facilities, uses most of the electricity, and, of course, is the undisputed power center of the nation. It is not surprising that Lima is both hated and loved by *provincianos* who are engaged in unequal struggle for access to the nation's wealth and power.

Peru's urban growth, however, is not limited to Lima, despite the norm of primacy. Lima's dominance over its hinterland, which ranked that city among the most preeminent in the world in that category (Doughty 1979b) has declined slowly since 1961. Even so, it remains vastly more significant than the secondary urban areas (Table 5.2), despite the spectacular growth of Chimbote, Trujillo, Tacna, Juliaca, Tarapoto, Piura, Pucallpa, or Chiclayo, which in percentages greatly exceeded that of Lima. In fact, Lima's percentage increase from 1961 to 1981 was less than the national urban average. All of this change was entirely at the expense of small town and rural populations whose absolute numbers have remained virtually the same even as the rural percentage dropped from 53 percent in 1961 to 35 percent in 1981.[11] By 1990, of Peru's twenty-five departments, only nine in the highlands and Amazon basin retain a majority of rural residents (Table 5.1). With migration–prone Ayacuchanos, Cajamarquinos, and Apurimeños among these, the generalization that the migration process primarily moves people from city to city rather than country to city now seems suspect. What has been happening for some time is that people have flocked to Lima from both small towns and highland cities, as well as from the *estancias* and *aldeas*, a fact to which the abundant numbers of migrant regional associations uncontrovertably attest.[12]

EDDIES OF MISCONCEPTION

Tracing migrant pathways through space and time lends itself to diagrammatic portrayals of Peru's migration, but the imagery and patterns are open to question.

Skeldon, for example, imagines an evolutionary sequence from 1910 to the present in which

> the earliest movements tend to be circular with migrants returning to their communities after short absences. These periods away from their communities tend to become prolonged as the volume of the population movement increases and migration evolves to what can be termed semi-permanent. Permanent migration, the later phase in the evolutionary sequence varies...to a stage during which people are brought up to migrate and all contacts and interest are towards the urban environment (1977:507).

His view of the Peruvian migration process is a kind of "folk-urban" continuum, with people close to Lima being the first ones attracted to the city, and ones farther away coming later as the earlier people lose their interest in hometowns.

Contrary to this neat theory, we see from the census records (Table 5.3) that persons from both "near" (Lima department, Ancash, Junín, Ica) and "far" (Arequipa, Ayacucho, La Libertad) migrated to Lima from the beginning of the century.[13] That they tended to remain permanently in Lima is testified to by their unslacking interest in migration and the constant growth of the city before the turn of this century. To be sure, people have always moved back and forth between metropolis and homeland, but the ability to take up permanent residence in Lima reflects the employment and income status of the migrants as well as their sociocultural adjustment.

While step migration occurs in some cases (Ghersi and Dobyns 1963), this was not the universal pattern visualized by Skeldon (1977:507-508). The path followed by most migrants was a direct one to the capital, without intermediate stopovers to serve as a practice stage for living in metropolitan Lima. There are of course, several forms of migration: permanent residential moves to new places; seasonal; cyclical or short time moves for purposes of work, education or health; retirement; and "experimental" moves to try out a new situation before making commitments. People are engaged in every type of migratory action, and the categories are not exclusive.

As noted, people migrate to places where they know people, and this includes provincial cities as well as the capital. The major facet of this migrationary fact is that no matter what form it may take, the vast majority of such movements are undertaken in the context of

---

TABLE 5.3 DEPARTMENTS WITH THE MOST MIGRANTS IN LIMA, 1920-1981

Rank	1920	1931	1940	1961	1972	1981
1	Lima	Lima	Ancash	——	——	——
2	Junín	——	Lima	——	——	——
3	Ancash	Ancash	Junín	Ayacucho	——	——
4	Ica	Ica	——	Junín	——	Ayachucho
5	Arequipa	Arequipa	——	La Libertad	Cajamarca	La Libertad
6	Ayacucho	La Libertad	——	Arequipa	La Libertad	Cajamarca

Note: Derived from Table 5.1; excludes the nonmetropolitan areas of the Department of Lima.

some family group strategy, not by individuals acting alone. The form of migration—seasonal, return, and cyclical—is inevitably tied to and governed by some family interest.

Beyond the extended family, Peruvians are surely the Latin American champions at self-organization. One of the singular features of Peruvian migration is the demonstrated capacity of people to constitute themselves into formal groups in their new city of residence, despite severe difficulties in logistics and communication. The primary form of migrant organization is clearly the type dedicated to obtaining land and housing. Lima as the primary target for migrants has offered a wide variety of residential options: inner city "alleys with one spigot";[14] decrepit residences built at the end of the colonial period; rental apartments of every description and suburban housing developments. Most of all, however, Lima was internationally famous for its boundless squatter settlements, which rose in spectacular fashion over unoccupied urban lots and the peripheral sands beyond the reach of ancient irrigation ditches and modern plumbing. The provincial immigrants to Lima are and have been widely scattered throughout the entire range of residential opportunities. Quite rightly, social scientists have found this an irresistible research attraction, as hundreds of publications demonstrate.[15] One of the outstanding aspects of the squatter settlement movement developed in Lima (and other coastal cities) was its high degree of organization and ability to gain strong allegiances among participants. First called *barriadas*,[16] settlements were unfailingly raised over the objections of authorities, followed by the maturing of a political organization in each settlement, which ultimately led to official recognition and the creation of many new municipalities throughout the province of Lima.[17]

Earlier migrants to the metropolis, however, had already been pioneers in the matter of organization. Before the turn of the century, provincial clubs had been formed by migrants to maintain a friendly social and cultural context for their own benefit as well as that of their home communities. These associations identify themselves with the four levels of Peruvian political structure: departments, provinces, districts, and district subdivisions called annexes, *barrios*, communities, or other titles. In fact, virtually any settlement with a name might have migrants who organize themselves into a club of some sort. The number of clubs rapidly increased in a manner most likely commensurate with the expansion of migration as such. Because these organizations were independent of the "*barriada* movement," since the migrants from a particular place tended to be scattered throughout Lima and were not necessarily concentrated in the same residential area, their mutual occurrence is unrelated.

The clubs, which are invariably named after the hometown or region, are engaged in a calendrical round of activities, including dances and parties; sports (*fútbol, tiro al sapo*);[18] dinners and commemorative events such as Mother's Day; the celebration of the patronal fiestas of the hometown; lectures and educational events; exhibitions and presentations of regional folk music and dance;[19] the publication of newsletters and monographs about the homeland (usually referred to in reverent fashion as one's *terruño*, that is, native soil, or *patria chica*, "little fatherland") and political activities to promote and lobby for government policy and projects to benefit the place of origin. On virtually every festive occasion sponsored by a club the members are also in the process of raising money for a specific project, either in Lima to benefit members, or for the *terruño*. As a phenomenon confined to *provincianos*, the existence of the clubs provoked little interest or recognition among *Limeños*, who have generally maintained patronizing attitudes towards provincial pretensions to "culture."

The regional clubs were "discovered" as a research topic by William Mangin (1959) and subsequently caught my interest and that of others.[20] The conclusions we drew from our studies were that the clubs provided many migrants with a significant venue for social life and psychocultural validation in an often stressful and insecure environment; that they were important in giving people a sense of social solidarity among their peers in Lima as well as retaining their sense of belonging to the homeland and its values; that recreational and other personal needs could be met in the club context (such as meeting members of the opposite sex); and that they could provide for a sphere of action in which members could address needs they felt as a group either in Lima or in the homeland.

The literature on the topic, however, is not particularly abundant, and the subject of voluntary associations in general is rather thin with regard to the Third World arenas of urban change. Nevertheless, some questions have been raised with respect to the early work on regional clubs by Jongkind (1971, 1974a, 1974b, 1986), who has insisted that what Mangin and I reported did not mean what we thought it did, and that my data in particular were suspect on several counts. His principal objections were that the clubs did not serve the purposes I suggested; that they were an urban as opposed to rural phenomenon; that my estimates for their numbers and membership counts were exaggerated; and that my methodology was wanting.[21] Jumping into the fray, Skeldon (1976) attempted to resolve our dispute by suggesting some alternative interpretations, using data compiled several years after mine. He followed many of the same procedures I did with similar results, although he fails to make these comparative connections. Interestingly enough, Skeldon discovered that regional clubs divided their activities in the same patterns of interest and relationship that I found earlier. His percentages are even "better" than mine, although he doesn't make note of this.

As I pointed out, Jongkind's material suffers from many inadequacies including its representativeness, sample size, and slavish dependence upon suspect survey data (Doughty 1972, 1978, 1979a). His most recent foray into this domain simply rehashes his earlier assertions, ignoring the refutations by both Skeldon and myself. Since these are somewhat scattered they should be summarized here so that we may move forward. First, Jongkind asserts that the Lima-based regional associations do little to assist their home communities. Comparing the data of the three studies in Table 5.4, we find that our data are not that different in pattern. What differs is what each of us considers important, and I fear that this will not be resolved. Jongkind denigrates the efforts of the migrants to assist

---

TABLE 5.4 WHOM DO REGIONAL CLUBS RAISE MONEY FOR?

Purpose of events	Doughty 1966-7 N=443	Jongkind 1969-70 N=46	Skeldon 1974 N=98
Percent of clubs supporting hometown projects	39	35	46
Percent of clubs supporting only club affairs	61	65	54

their fellows at home because he thinks the value of their contributions is insignificant; I choose to see it the other way (Doughty 1972, 1978:305-307), placing them in the context of the characteristic impoverishment of rural areas. This is not Jongkind's perspective. For me, the fact that almost 40 percent of the clubs (amounting to over 55 percent of their activities) chose to donate their hard-earned capital to village projects is an amazing feat of altruism that in percentage terms, at least, compares very well with what analogous university "alumni" associations give to their "alma maters" in the United States (see, for example, Ursinus College [1990] or University of Florida Foundation [1990]).

Migrant regional organizations abound. It is difficult to know just how many there are because relatively few of them are duly registered in legal fashion.[22] The problem in ascertaining the approximate numbers rests in the fact that there is no prescribed registry and the vast majority of clubs do not have permanent locales in which they meet. Most utilize private homes or rented and borrowed facilities; many do not publicly advertise their meetings, and others only do so in limited fashion. This led me to utilize the assistance of Lima's *Radio Agricultura*, a station that caters entirely to provincial migrant interests, to help me collect information.[23] Perhaps the most common type of club at the lowest end of the hierarchy, those representing subdistrict sectors of the migrants from a district, are the sports clubs that play furious soccer tournaments on weekends and holidays. Using *Radio Agricultura*, a list was compiled of seventy-three empty lots, factory areas and equipped playing fields regularly used by regional clubs.

All have names no matter what their condition. On a given Sunday, the favorite time for such events, as many as twenty different teams would play "round robin" tournaments on a field starting at seven in the morning. Thus, on a holiday weekend, as many as 1,000 migrant sports clubs could well be playing! I concluded that a reasonable minimum estimate would be about 5,000 migrant clubs for metropolitan Lima, because in the relatively complete materials available for Ancash, Junín, Ayacucho and Apurimac there were an average of five clubs per district. Present data now suggest that this number, if anything, has increased, and that more provinces and districts are involved.

Yet, the number of clubs in metropolitan Lima and their respective memberships is disputed by Jongkind, who alleges that there are both far fewer clubs as well as members.[24] As I pointed out elsewhere, he misunderstands what is meant by different classes or levels of participation and "membership," as well as the reasons for the widespread popularity of the clubs. Since that time, however, Altamirano (1984a) has recalculated this estimate and concludes that there are at least 6, 000 such associations. Since there are now 1,680 districts in Peru there could be as many as 8,400 regional migration associations in Lima, and a figure between six and seven thousand is not an unreasonable estimate. With respect to actual club members, Altamirano also produces very convincing data on membership that support my original material, Jongkind's unsupported assertions notwithstanding.

Finally, the critique made by Jongkind misconstrues the meaning of "provincial" by confusing it with "rural" and thus introduces yet another eddy of misconception with respect to whether these institutions are "urban" or "rural" (Doughty 1978). This has lead to a series of contemplations, alas, about "residual ruralism" and the "ruralization" of the city. Let there be no doubt that these organizations are urban–they are, after all, found in cities! But more than that, the type of formal institution that the associations represent is an organizational form found throughout Peru. The organizational traits that typify migrant structures are highly standardized from the metropolitan setting to the village and *comunidad*, where sports clubs, brotherhoods, and civic committees show the same features and principles of operation, style, and membership patterns (Doughty 1968:175-188; Tulles 1970:85-184). It is quite likely that this uniformity of organizational style has achieved a countrywide diffusion through a strong assist from migrant networks. If so, it is a quite different and much larger process than Jongkind's strawman theory suggests (Doughty 1978:301-302, 1979b). As Altamirano (1984a, 1984b) has shown in a convincing fashion, migrant behavior within the context of the clubs reflects many customs that are clearly based in rural highland culture,such as strong community-centered values and reciprocity.

THE PERUVIAN MIGRATION SYSTEM

Explaining the needs, interests, and operations–the raison d'être–of migrant voluntary associations (alas, can the word *function* still be used?) has to be viewed in the perspective of a national socio-cultural system. As a special part of the migration process that is the undercurrent that courses through every vein of Peru's body politic, the regional club phenomenon is also part of a response to the chain of national dilemmas that national policy has failed to resolve.

The state system of governance, economy, and social relations has been often described by Julio Cotler as one of "internal colonialism" in which the dominant elites extract resources and wealth from the hinterlands while returning very little in the form of "value-added" goods and services; when they do so, it is at a high price. Such an arrangement is exploitative in principle in the same ways that classic colonial administrations governed their provinces from the "Age of Discovery" into this century. The Peruvian model derives directly from its colonial ancestor and in many ways has simply replicated and conserved a colonial spirit and style. Traditional Peruvian capitalism has always operated on this model, which is driven more by monopolistic codes and assumptions than by marketplace demands. Exclusiveness is thus favored in such a system whose strength derives from a concentration of power in the bodies of central government and the elites who manage it. An intimate part of this archaic edifice is the notion of centralization focused upon the city of Lima, which has blossomed into one of this century's singular primate cities (Doughty 1979b) ,with all the attributes that implies. The effects of primacy are repeatedly seen in the skewing of national wealth distribution (Doughty 1976; Wilson and Wise 1986:96-101) and the continuation of this pattern in terms of the conditions affecting each individual (Glewwe 1988), despite numerous overt attempts to reach out to provincial needs as was the case with the first Belaunde administration, the Velasco reform period, and with USAID programs.[25]

Simply put, to live in Lima, despite its obvious poverty, is to be better off in virtually every material index of social condition than people in other areas, especially the highlands (Glewwe 1988). Response to the fundamental injustice of the system of internal colonialism and primacy in Peru is neither surprising nor novel. Whenever the opportunity presents itself, geographic mobility and migration throughout history have been preeminent options to entrapment in such exploitative systems. It is no accident that persons concerned with thwarting change and maintaining a status quo seek to discourage freedom of movement as the South African and Soviet cases amply demonstrated. Indeed, the Andean peonage system operated under such controls until recently.[26]

In this context, the ability to move one's residence has a great deal to do with gaining dignity and respect as well as gaining access to those other rationed commodities such as wealth and power, values in which all would enjoy an equitable share. In the traditional repressive Peruvian state, migration takes on a far larger meaning because it has to do with the acquisition of and access to a greater sharing of what McDougal et al. (1980) have described as fundamental life values.[27] In terms of a much overworked but underemployed concept, human rights, the Peruvian migrants are seeking redress from unacceptable conditions. It is not by chance that the people of Lima have traditionally described the provincial–especially highland–poor as living in conditions that were *infrahumanas*.

Therefore, when one hears the personal histories of migrants and their individual, family, and community responses to and strategies for coping with poverty and repression, the role of Lima in the complex of available alternatives is a critical variable, as Altamirano (1988), Isbell (1978), and Matos Mar (1986) have shown. People remain an active part of their extended kin and communal networks as well as develop new relationships with neighbors in the new environment. This universe is a social whole necessary to their existence, not an either/or proposition. Although every case will be different, the overall effect of this migratory experience is to weave a new cloth in which the patterns of regionalism serve as the weft and the metropolitan society as the warp that runs the length of the fabric, uniting all the parts. The cultural plaid of Lima results in the kind of heterogeneity that Schaedel (1979) sees in the course of metropolitan evolvement.

The people who have migrated to Lima often hold a strong sense of duty and obligation to the familial homeland. Indeed, Peruvians generally describe themselves as being from a particular place, a kind of ascribed status that does not change through life. A person is thus known by his or her village or place of birth: one is referred to as an Arequipeno, Huaylino, Puneño, Vicosino, or Chalaco. Place and social identity are strongly intertwined. One may speculate that this regionalist orientation has very deep roots in the Andes, where fertile valleys and high mountain niches have created special ecological environments known for their unique qualities and products. In the pre-Columbian era there were dozens of languages spoken here, and the archeological record hints at the ethnic diversity of the region that was modified by Inca conquest and decimated by postconquest disease and policy. Nevertheless, the colonial period created a greater isolation than the Inca regime because it served the colonial administrators as a device of conquest and control, and the conquered as a means of protection in some instances.

Entering the post-Pacific war period (1885), Peru was a strongly regionalized state with the centers of creole power ensconced in Lima, Arequipa, and Trujillo. It is not surprising that the early immigrants to Lima carried strong regional allegiances as well as desires for greater personal and familial opportunity. The first regional clubs were probably formed by local elites who found themselves seeking recognition in the capital. Thus, Arequipa, a place of political power and prestige, historically known as the "cradle of revolutionaries," was the first department to have a formal club in Lima, as noted earlier. The publications of these organizations, on the one hand, reek with pretension and undisguised longing for cultural respectability in metropolitan society; on the other hand, they protest the indignities of their homelands and the exploitation they perceive there. The atmosphere here may seem contradictory.

The highland migrants arriving in Lima in the first decades of the century entered a hostile cultural sphere. They responded by leading demands for an indianist policy that would surmount the abuses as they envisioned them encouraged by Gonzalez Prada (1960[1894]), Valcarcel (1914, 1927), and later Mariategui (1928). The regionalist publications were aggressive protectors of the dignity and rights of highlanders, exalting the beauty of the land, the need for progress, and their role as leaders and communicators. Their titles tell the tale: *Acomayo: Por la Cultura y el Progreso de la Provincia* ; *El Indio:Vocero Crítico, Independiente y Informativo. Consagrado a la Defensa de los Supremos Intereses del Departamento de Junín.*

A similar 1930 publication of the provincial club Juventud Huaylina (Huaylas Youth) held fifty pages devoted to photographs of the homeland; political caricatures; a long editorial about the development potential of Huaylas; a section on Huaylas folklore and history; an article about feminism in Huaylas; poems; sports activities; the club activity calendar; a long article on the indian rebellion in the Callejón de Huaylas of Atusparia in 1885; a world news round-up; and a list of club officers. Although these contents are typical of their time, there is much that carries over from this date to the present. Although the sample of the genre is small it nonetheless reveals a great consistency in content (Table 5.5). Similarly, a review of regionalist works recorded in the *Anuario Bibliográfico* published by the Biblioteca Nacional del Perú indicates that of 102 items published by regional associations, 40 percent were edited by district-level clubs, 25 percent by provincial-level groups, and the rest by departmental and multiclub organizations.

The quotation from José María Argüedas' book with which we began this discussion outlines the concerns of migrants very well and provides reasons for their act of organizing: to defend the interests of their district; protect against abuses of the powerful; to "raise" the cultural levels through education; to publish news and information; to promote folklore and music; to "remember the homeland"; and, as conscientious persons, to accept the responsibility to halt the humiliation of their families and communities. We now turn to

---

**TABLE 5.5 TOPICAL CONTENT OF PROVINCIAL ASSOCIATION
PUBLICATIONS**

Content or Topic	Percent of Publications	Content or Topic	Percent of Publications
Ethnography	93	Regional Art & Photographs	50
Migrant Club Activity	75	Regional Personalities	41
Regional History	73	Hometown Problems	41
Opinion & Editorial	66	Andean Language	32
Folklore and Tales	66	Regional Advertisements	30
Poetry	57	Regional Music	25
Hometown Events	52	Short Stories by Local Authors	23
		Women's Issues	18

Note: The departmental origins of the clubs publishing these works corresponded roughly in pattern with the numbers of migrants from each area (Table 5.1): Ancash, 19%; non-metro Lima, 17%; Junín, 12%; La Libertad, 6% [n = 44].

---

a century-long example of regional club activity.

THE HUAYLAS MIGRANT COLONY: 1895-1990

To illustrate dimensions to these generalizations, the institutional history of one district's migrants provides a useful case study, albeit in a somewhat abbreviated form.[28] The people of the Huaylas district come from the Callejón de Huaylas in the highland center of the department of Ancash, the foremost contributor of migrants to metropolitan Lima through this century. Consequently, their experiences can be presented as representative to some degree. The first record of any Huaylas migrant organization occurs in faint records from 1884 discovered in the Huaylas Municipal office. These reported that several Huaylinos who had been attending the university in Lima until the Chilean invasion had returned to their homes with a plan to open a private secondary school in the district. A municipal primary school had been in operation since 1874. The Instituto El Progreso did indeed open that year, followed by at least three other schools. In 1895 the Huaylas colony in Lima sent a set of instruments to the district to start a municipal band. The early publications of the Huaylas colony were strongly oriented to intellectual interests, with poetry, commentary, and some local history, often the work of university students. They also carried commercial advertisements placed by Huaylas-connected businesses in Lima and a few from Huaylas itself or Caráz, the neighboring provincial capital.

The people doing these things were members of the district's upper class from a town of about 1,300 persons in a district whose total population was about 5,000. It was an area without serfdom, whose people engaged in small-to-medium farming on ancient terraced *chacras* that, as they climbed the sides of the Cordillera Negra, passed from corn and alfalfa production to wheat, rye, and potatoes. The town and rural hamlets were a close knit but competitive society, with the several *barrios* vying with the others over local issues. All Huaylinos spoke Quechua, and about two-thirds spoke some Spanish as well. The district had a regional reputation for its "progressive" character.

The interplay between the district and Lima has been active now for over 115 years. The population of the district has remained at the same level, indicating that the equivalent of the entire natural increment of between 150 to 200 persons a year regularly migrated. Over the past 90 years an estimated 16,000 persons have left the district, a great majority to Lima; some went to adjacent districts and to Caráz the nearby provincial capital; since 1955, some migrated to Chimbote, the steel and fishing center on the coast. Throughout this time there have probably been as many Huaylinos in Lima as in the district at any given time, and, predictably, there have been several regional associations organized by them. In 1920 the principal club in Lima was called the Círculo Huaylino which sponsored a soccer team, published a magazine, and conducted a variety of activities, not the least of which was the celebration of the patronal fiestas of the district. In 1931 the Asociación Distrital Huaylina (ADH) was founded and has lasted to the present, with several of its original members still in attendance at reunions.

During the 30 years I have known the club, its paying membership has fluctuated between forty and sixty-five persons, with a larger circle of about 300 followers who regularly turned out for festive events of various types.[29] The association has continuously maintained its cycle of activities and interests, divided about evenly between serving the local social interests of its following and hometown affairs. Events include regular biweekly meetings of the fifteen elected officers of the club; celebration of the Feast of Saint Elizabeth, Patroness of the Harvests of Huaylas; the Feast of the Virgin of the Assumption, Patroness of Huaylas; Peruvian Independence Day; Mother's Day; Christmas; New Year's; the anniversary of the club's founding; and special meetings to discuss projects and problems as they arise. Invariably, the festive events include a fund-raising drive either to promote some need in Lima such as refurbishing the club headquarters or, more commonly, to support a project in the district itself.

Over the many years of its existence, the ADH has raised funds for many development, construction, and repair efforts in Huaylas. These have included funds and materials for road building over many years; school construction, repair, and equipment; paving the sidewalks of the town plaza; the municipal electrical system; construction of the district library to house the collection donated by a Huaylino living in New York; repairing the church tower and altars; donating litters for the processions of Saint Elizabeth and the Virgin of the Assumption; irrigation projects; repairing of the municipal market; and for many other other municipal needs.

In addition to these types of activities, club members have steadfastly lobbied for Huaylas interests in government agencies, Parliament, and private institutions. In 1963 for example, a committee from ADH went to president-elect Belaunde's house (with me as "window dressing") to present him with a plan for his proposed *Cooperación Popular* local development programs. The Huaylinos sought to establish an operations center at the Huallanca district hydroelectric plant,[30] a proposal that was accepted and resulted in numerous material benefits for Huaylas. On the other hand, Huaylinos were sharply divided on the issue of recognizing the *Comunidad Indígena* in the late 1930s. Groups both supporting and opposing the establishment of the communal organization actively lobbied Lima authorities until the legalization of the *comunidad* was given in 1940.

A period of intense club activity occurred after the enormous earthquake in 1970, when the town of Huaylas was destroyed and 90 percent of rural homes were damaged or lost. The "colony" sprang into action, collecting clothing, food, and money that they sent as emergency aid to the district even as the dust was still settling. Three days after the disaster, with communications to the region completely disrupted and all roads blocked, a caravan of over thirty Huaylinos walked over the Cordillera Negra to deliver the first assistance the district received. ADH became a clearinghouse for all the other clubs, with an emergency committee organized to lobby, seek aid and materials, and help victims and their families. From that time forward the association has labored in various ways to help meet the massive reconstruction needs. The largest project they undertook was the reconstruction of the district "mother church," which had been bulldozed away. With no funding available from government sources, the ADH began collecting funds and eventually secured a $20,000 donation from the German Bishops' Fund to begin the rebuilding process in 1979. In this postquake period, the association raised an additional $10,000 to assist the homeland, a very appreciable amount in inflation-ridden Peru. The reconstruction has taken over 12 years but nears completion: it is a massive building intended to memorialize the victims as well as aggrandize the district.[31]

The club also maintains contact with other regional institutions with varying degrees of intensity, depending upon issues that may involve some collaborative effort–or rivalry. The other groups from Huaylas are always invited to ADH events, and these acts are reciprocated. Over the years there have been numerous other Huaylas clubs organized to represent particular interests and sectors of the population. Because the ADH largely embodies people of varied socioeconomic backgrounds from the town of Huaylas, the other organizations specifically claim their following from other parts of Huaylas, including six of the barrios and a subarea with political desires to found a separate district (which was created in 1990 as one of President García's last acts). There are also two religious groups: the Comité Pro-Piedad and the Brotherhood of Saint Elizabeth; at least two musical groups, Lira Huaylina, and the Conjunto Santo Toribio; and no less than three soccer clubs. These interest groups have ties to one or more of the clubs but run their own affairs. As of 1990, there were fifteen Huaylas organizations in Lima, with an estimated involvement of about 310 activists and a wider following of 1,200.

At the present time, the ADH enjoys the use of its own locale in the center of old Lima in a spacious but decaying postcolonial building. It was the bequest of one of the club founders, a successful engineer. For him, social mobility had become possible through a stratagem (and in his case it was just that) of migration from his small-town background in Huaylas to Lima for higher education; constant activity and alliance-building in the provincial networks in Lima; and, through these connections, becoming a candidate and winning a seat in Parliament as deputy for the Province of Huaylas in 1945. His role in provincial clubs expanded as he systematically cultivated club support throughout the very extensive Ancash club network. In the next decade, as a former deputy, his active club affiliations perpetuated his role as a powerful force in regional politics, leading to his election as president of the Ancash Departmental Club, an institution comprised of the Ancash elite in Lima. It was a career of over 50 years intimately tied to club activities at the district, provincial, and departmental levels.

The political interests of the club have been essentially nonpartisan, however, and candidates for national offices from Huaylas tend to be encouraged irrespective of party affiliation because it is in the interest of the district to do so. To gain influence with the Lima power structure is an all important consideration. During the earthquake aftermath between 1970 and 1980, Huaylinos were frustrated by the fact that while they had always enjoyed effective political connections under the military regimes of Generals Velasco and Morales, they were cut off because, as the club president put it, *"no tenemos militares huaylinos, carajo!"* ("we have no Huaylas military men, damn it!").

The lobbying system, of course, works on the basis of kin, community and club connections, and these are carefully plotted out in an effort to influence policy and material decisions. The connections of club members are explored, examined for their manipulative potential, and commensurate strategies are meticulously arranged to achieve the goals set. The persons targeted for persuasion are interviewed, entertained, invited to club functions, and in some cases, taken to Huaylas to see the great fiesta of Saint Elizabeth or other local events. It helps in these endeavors if there is an appropriately prominent Huaylino available to host such guests, and support persons are recruited to play their role even if they have not been active in club affairs. The details of these political affairs are as complicated as anyone might imagine, sometimes with important wider consequences linked to major policy issues.[32]

The Huaylas case finds the club performing continuously over a sixty year period without abatement, much longer in fact if the operations of predecessor organizations are taken into account, since they involved many of the same persons. In terms of activities, the members engaged in all of the tasks outlined by Arguedas' fictional club president and perhaps some others as well: that they are dedicated to the defense of their district and its people there can be no doubt; that they see a duty in helping out at home, even after a half century of absence, is clear; that they engage in the rituals of renewal and reconfirmation of loyalty is undisputed. Although the club and its members are "urban" by any definition, there can also be no doubt that they unabashedly identify themselves as *provincianos* and highlanders with some pride. This has led to the association's playing an important role in hometown affairs throughout its long history and being a good example of an independent, voluntary, self-help organization confronting many great difficulties with patience, thoughtful strategy, and considerable sacrifice. Far from being unusual, it is part of a long tradition shared over the breadth of Peru's Andean communities.

SIENDO MUY AVANZADA LA HORA, SE CERRO LA SESSION

Association minutes inevitably close with the ritualistic phrase "being such a late hour, the session was concluded." By way of conclusion here it is important to note that the topic of voluntary associations, of which migrant clubs are but one example, is far from exhausted. Indeed, there are many questions of an ethnographic, theoretical, and applied nature that remain. Hirabayashi's query (1986) about why some people do not organize seems particularly germane to the Lima situation, precisely because such large numbers of people do belong to clubs at some point in their migrant life. The dynamics of these voluntary associations would make an interesting comparison to those from other areas in the Third World as well as in industrial societies. They are, of course, specialized types of voluntary organizations, and these should thus be viewed in this larger context that is so central to urban life. Urban societies distinguish themselves from rural, kin-based communities, small towns, and tribal societies in the fact that they are replete with organizations that are independent of kin criteria as a necessary component of membership. This is one of the features that helps to provide the "freedom" for socioeconomic mobility that is one of the major driving motivations for all migration. One of the aspects for the study of any migration and urbanization process, then, should include research on the development of voluntary associations, ones whose conditions for belonging are not based on ascription but rather on achievement. This is a theme that seems to be touched upon only briefly in Latin America.

In the case of Peru, however, the interest in migrant clubs derived, as I pointed out, not from an interest in urban society per se but rather from the curiosity about the fate of provincial villagers usually studied by anthropologists. What was discovered was that Peru's unique regional migrant associations constituted a very special cultural adaptation, an institutional bridge between a deprived and exploited hinterland and a privileged and powerful primate capital. The clubs thus functioned as mechanisms by which people could "live in two worlds." On the one hand, membership and definition of interests are derived on the basis of ascription (on the place of birth and thus kin-community orientation); but, on the other hand, the formal organizational style and procedure grow out of and respond to urban institutional, bureaucratic, political, and economic mandates. They are a kind of hybrid organization that continues to reflect the longstanding nature of Peru as a nation of mixed sociocultural ancestry.

The critiques of the regional club research are not substantiated by further investigation, time, or case experience. Not only has the trend of club development continued unabated, but there is every indication that it has grown, even in the face of the last desperate decade of Peruvian life. This is as we might well have predicted judging from the fact that when seen in response to high stress (Huaylas in the earthquake) and deep need (Altamirano and Isbell's cases) the regional clubs have reacted, often in impressive fashion.

There are, however, important questions with respect to regional associations as they have customarily operated in light of two major national issues that are altering or will alter the way the nation functions and is structured. The impact of ongoing "low intensity warfare" waged by the Sendero Luminoso, other such groups, and the military in the provinces as well as in Lima has been devastating in some areas. The ability of people to conduct their normal affairs is dramatically altered, as the report to the Peruvian Senate graphically outlined (DESCO 1989). Although clubs are certain to remain faithful to their mandates, how they will fare now is another matter.

A second source of impact on migrant club affairs rests in the proposal to "decentralize" the structure and operations of the national government, in effect, to restructure the government completely and the way it does its business, as outlined with respect to elections, representation, and bureaucratic organization (Chico Colugna 1989). Should this attempt succeed in altering the primate, colonial structure of Peru, it would predictably have a large impact on regional associations with respect to the strategies they follow and perhaps, even influence the trends of migration to emphasize the growth of provincial cities even more.

Based on the fact that clubs made frequent and often important gifts to their home communities, was there any way in which that force for constructive self-help might be enhanced and supported with greater resources? Having discovered that clubs often reflected long-standing factions extant in the communities of origin, the mechanisms that might be employed in maximizing interclub efforts were illusive. My recommendation (Doughty 1964) to some Peruvian agencies as well as international organizations that they might be able to undertake some effective small scale projects through club initiatives never met with any bureaucratic interest to work with such self-directed and independent organizations with their own strong agendas. In the meantime, the clubs proceed with their own programs of activities and hometown help, retaining control, self-respect, and the sense of achievement and solidarity when they succeed. To gain a share of these values could be called success.

NOTES

1. There is of course much discussion about the motives for migration in Peru. These have been amply discussed by numerous researchers. See for example: Alers and Applebaum (1967), Beyer (1967), Browning (1967), Deitz (1976), Dobyns and Vazquez (1963), Doughty (1963, 1976, 1979), and Roberts (1974, 1975, 1978) among many others. The summary by Alers and Applebaum noted above is particularly useful as a review of the the early literature and summary of the numerous propositions and hypotheses which have been examined regarding both motive and pattern.

2. In modern Andean usage, *encomienda* refers to some item entrusted to someone for delivery to a third party. Commonly, provincial residents ship goods from village to city and back in this manner, often loaded onto a *mixto*, a type of large commercial vehicle, half truck, half bus, that plies provincial roadways.

3. The vast literature of the post-1960 period more than equals everything that went before, and it is not my intention here to review it. Martínez (1980:18) records the sharp increase in urban research between 1955 and 1975 when over 485 works were published on the subject in Peru. One might begin to review this material starting with Butterworth and Chance (1981), Dobyns and Vazquez (1963), Doughty (1983), Mangin (1959, 1965), Martínez (1980), Matos Mar (1961), Osterling and Martínez (1983),and Wallace (1984) among numerous other works such as the Sage series on *Latin American Urban Research* issued annually for several

years after 1971.

4. A birthright Lima resident may be colloquially referred to in a humorous vein as one who loves to eat *masamora,* a pudding made from purple corn and associated with Lima's creole cuisine.

5. The "indian blemish" region included all or parts of Ancash, Ayacucho, Huancavelica, Apurimac, Cuzco, and Puno (Cotler 1976, Lowenthal 1975:23) in theory "disarticulated" from effective national relations and thus dominated by Lima's "colonial" authority.

6. There are several excellent commentaries on this issue. Patch (1967) and Schaedel (1979) offer perceptive analyses of the sometimes subtle, but always complex, process by which the *criollos* cope with the highland migrants.

7. Under the Velasco regime this market was moved to its present location and developed as a very extensive commercial strip along Avenida de la Marina between Pueblo Libre and Magdelana districts in Lima.

8. Belaunde's pursuit of provincial support initially resulted in the participating in the government of such prominent champions of highland interests as José María Argüedas, who was head of the newly reformed Casa de la Cultura. While Belaunde can be credited with bringing this development to fruition, the political events of the Odria era witnessed perhaps the first manifestation of highland provincial political force. Military dictator Manuel Odria (1948-56), himself a Tarmeño from the Junín department, greatly favored that region's development, and his wife, María Delgado, became famous for distributing sewing machines and other appliances to the women in squatter settlements.

9. Other departmental clubs were founded later such as La Libertad (Trujillo) in 1895; but Club Ancash was not founded until 1949.

10. See Dietz (1969), Lloyd (1980), Lobo (1982), Mangin (1963, 1967), and Turner (1965), for various descriptions and analyses of squatter organization and effectiveness.

11. In 1961 the rural population of Peru numbered 5.2 million; by 1981 it had increased by 13 percent to a total of 5.9 million persons. In contrast, urban Peru had 4.6 million in 1961 but mushroomed to 11.1 million in 1981, an increase of 140 percent (Peru 1981).

12. The classifications of "urban" and "rural" in the Peruvian census materials are quite arbitrary and depend largely upon political rank. All district, provincial, and departmental capitals are considered "urban" by definition, no matter what their size or other characteristics. On the other hand, there are coastal *haciendas* counted as rural, that have larger urbanized populations in terms of settlement pattern than the capital of their district. In my research on the subject from 1963 to 1967, however, I found there were probably well over 1,500 clubs representing rural villages and hamlets. There were even more purporting to represent districts whose populations were essentially rural, although not classified as such.

13. The question as to what constitutes "near" and "far" in the era before wheeled transportation was dominant is interesting and perhaps difficult to determine from today's perspective. Junín was connected by railroad to Lima in the later decades of the nineteenth century, but everyone else was quite equally isolated until the construction of vehicular roads begun during the second Leguia regime in the 1920s. Along the coast, people traveled via packet ship, first having to descend the Andes on horseback. Thus, from the "adjacent" department of Ancash, migrants needed up to two weeks to reach Lima until the coming of motorized transportation in the 1930s.

14. This is an archetypical inner-city slum environment populated by the creole descendents of African slaves and highland migrants, memorialized in Victoria and Nicodemes Santa Cruz' popular *vals criollo,* "Callejón de un solo caño," (El Virrey Industrias, Lima, No VY-A-1198).

15. Voluminous literature on this subject arises in the 1950s. Various aspects of the topic are found in Collier (1976), Deitz (1969, 1976), Lloyd (1980), Lobo (1982), Mangin (1963, 1967), and Matos Mar (1961, 1986) among many others.

16. The name *barriada* carried the negative connotations of being a messy slum and an undesirable place in general. *Limeño* middle class fears about such places and the people who lived there, gave rise to considerable discriminatory attitudes, some going so far as to describe the *barriadas* that surrounded Lima as analogous to the "scummy ring around the bathtub" (Henry Deitz, personal communication). Squatter respectability arrived in 1970 when the Velasco government officially renamed the settlements *pueblos jovenes* or "young towns," a title that has since remained.

17. In 1920 the provinces of Lima and Callao were comprised of 18 and 3 districts, respectively. In 1981, there were 40 districts in Lima and 6 in Callao, all primarily the result of migration and squatter movements.

18. A popular "Sunday afternoon" drinking game, the "toad throw" features competitors who pitch small brass disks at a brass toad mounted on a special stand to see who can score the most by tossing the disc into the toad's open mouth. A former Peace Corps volunteer began producing replica games in the United States

and for a while these elegant versions of the Andean barroom game could be purchased at Nieman Marcus stores!

19. See John Cohen's film on *Mountain Music of Peru,* for examples of this activity.

20. See other descriptive details about club activities in Altamirano (1984a, 1984b, 1988:66-72), Doughty (1969, 1970, 1972), Long (1973), Long and Roberts (1984), and Osterling (1980:157-184). The Lima organizations are compared to similar groups elsewhere by Hamilton (1979), Hirabayashi (1986), and Sassen-Koob (1979). Kerri's (1976) useful comparative article, however, does not deal with any Latin American cases. Jongkind (1974a, 1974b, 1986) and Skeldon (1976, 1977) review and critique this literature.

21. The "intellectual" history of these erstwhile disagreements may be enlightening. Having previously addressed all of his complaints in previous work to which he has never responded, one feels caught up as on an old phonograph record that goes round and round repeating itself. The background to this quarrel began in 1969 when I was introduced to Jongkind, then undertaking his doctoral research in Lima on the subject of regional clubs. We talked over a pleasant supper at his apartment. Having recently arrived in Peru, he was quite unfamiliar with both Lima and, of course, the highlands, which he was not to visit. In the course of our conversations I gave him the names of several of my informants, addresses of key locales such as the Asociación de Clubes Departamentales, Jardín Villa Campa dance hall, and Radio Agricultura, among others, in addition to suggesting that he try to work with the "upper class" departmental clubs as much as he could because I felt they had not been adequately studied. The next I heard of his work was indirectly from friends in Lima who were excited by his attacks on my previous work. (*"Los gringos están peleando."*) My first response to him was in 1972, followed by one in 1978, and another in 1979 wherein I addressed all his critiques. Jongkind's most recent effort (1986) ignores all of this, however, citing only my 1970 chapter in Mangin's book.

22. I attempted to use the registry at the Prefecture of Lima, which theoretically tracked all voluntary organizations, but found that source very inadequate since I had records on many more clubs than it did. The same was true in the Social Security office, which was so wanting and dated that I did not pursue it. Skeldon (1976), however, summarizes this data for the 293 groups registered there from 1936 to 1972.

23. See Doughty (1972) for a sample of this station's broadcasting style and content. The station saved all the advertisements they carried on the air for almost a year (between 1966 and 1967), and I was able to use these to gather the club names, dates and places of their activities, names of club officers, and the nature of what they were doing. This was fine except for the fact that many clubs did not use this station. Thus I had to supplement this source of information in a variety of other ways to build an inventory of the club universe from which to develop a sample for further study. Skeldon, Jongkind, and Altamirano have subsequently used this technique as well; Altamirano has greatly expanded on it, with more complete results.

24. That guess, however, is based on his small, skewed sample of 46 associations and their members; my estimate came from a registry of over 1,500 clubs from which I used a sample of 443 associations to develop detailed information including interviews with eighty-six presidents and hundreds of members, in addition to archives, extensive observations and published data.

25. Despite the rhetoric of public policy, these efforts–if that is what they were–failed to significantly change patterns of distribution. The USAID policy, for example, was supposed to work mostly with the rural poor through its programs, yet in the period of its greatest expansion in 1983, the largest project in its portfolio, the PL480 Food for Peace program, was placing half of its resources in Lima (Doughty et al. 1984).

26. The impact of this freedom of movement is seen in the case of Vicos after 1952, a classic Andean manor where serfdom was abolished after 350 years (Alers et al. 1965).

27. As outlined by McDougal et al. (1980), they include the values of power, wealth, skill, enlightenment, respect, rectitude, affection, and well-being. In their theory, individuals and societies seek what they consider equitable shares of these qualities; social and cultural systems arrange for their distribution.

28. My research in Huaylas began in 1960 and has continued to the present, although my most recent trip there was in 1995. I have worked in the district on many trips in thirteen different years, and in Lima for a longer time, where I have been in contact with the Huaylas provincial associations. In 1963-64 I was "Secretary of Culture" of the Asociación Distrital Huaylina and have attended dozens of meetings and events of the group, most recently in August 1991.

29. Club supporters are generally thought of as being "militants" (*militantes*) who accept offices and responsibility for association activities; "members" (*socios*) who regularly attend club affairs and form a pool of possible candidates for future roles as militants; and "sympathizers" (*simpatizantes*) who attend regular festive events or special activities but otherwise are not involved and do not pay dues. Most persons fall in this category. By their general affiliation with the club, I consider all of these as part of the "membership" although, technically, only those who pay dues are. This is where Jongkind and I disagree: he only counts

those who are paid up, whereas I opt for a less rigid definition. The paying membership, of course, changes through time: some persons remain active for many years, others for only a few, and many drop out completely for a while, only to renew interest later on.

30. Huallanca is a district which was formerly part of Huaylas and is heavily populated by Huaylinos who work at the power plant. The mayors of Huallanca have often been Huaylinos, and the two districts are closely allied in interest. The construction of the power plant and its subsequent political, economic, and social effects are analyzed elsewhere (Doughty 1987).

31. There were many such projects supported and funded in other Ancash districts by their regional clubs at this time. The Huaylas club activities were typical and not exceptional.

32. When I accompanied a Huaylas delegation to visit president-elect Belaunde at his home in 1963, there were many other provincial associations in line with us. One of them was a fifteen-member delegation from a provincial club from San Pedro de Cajas, Junín. They approached the president-elect with a magnificent gift of an alpaca tapestry depicting one of his campaign posters. As Belaunde held the gift, the club members announced that they were there to assist the new president in his goal of achieving land reform, and requested that in his inaugural address, Belaunde put forth the policy of supporting the recuperation of land usurped from the *Comunidades Indígenas*–"land which has been ours from time immemorial." Belaunde dissembled and would not commit himself. The San Pedro group included several prominent persons whose influence was considerable. Three days after Belaunde's waffling, and a day after his inauguration, the *comuneros* of San Pedro invaded their usurped lands and set in motion the massive land nationwide invasions that followed.

REFERENCES CITED

Alers, José Oscar, and Richard Applebaum
1968   "La migración en El Perú: Un inventario de proposiciones, estudios de caso." *Población y Desarrollo* [Lima] 1:1-43.
Alers, José Oscar, M. C. Vazquez, A. R. Holmberg and H. F. Dobyns
1965   "Human Freedom and Geographic Mobility." *Current Anthropology* 6:336.
Altamirano, Teófilo
1984a   *Presencia andina en Lima metropolitana: Un estudio sobre migrantes y clubes de provincianos.* Lima, Perú: Pontíficia Universidad Católica del Perú.
1984b   "Regional Commitment Among Migrants in Lima." In *Miners, Peasants, and Entrepreneurs.* Norman Long and Bryan Roberts, editors, pp. 198-216. New York: Cambridge University Press.
1988   *Cultura andina y pobreza urbana: Aymaras en Lima metropolitana.* Lima, Perú: Pontíficia Universidad Católica del Perú.
Argüedas, José María
1941[1985] *Yawar fiesta.* Frances Horning Barraclough, translator. Austin: University of Texas Press.
Beyer, Glenn H., editor
1967   *The Urban Explosion in Latin America.* Ithaca, NY: Cornell University Press.
Browning, Harley L.
1967   "Urbanization and Modernization in Latin America: The Demographic Perspective. In *The Urban Explosion in Latin America.* Glenn H. Beyer, editor, pp. 71-92. Ithaca, NY: Cornell University Press.
Butterworth, Douglass, and John K. Chance
1981   *Latin American Urbanization.* New York: Oxford University Press.
Chico Colunga, Franco
1989   *Elecciones: Compendio concordado de legislación, jurisprudencia y doctrina.* Instituto de Desarrollo de la Información Legal. Trujillo: Línea Editores, SA.
Collier, David
1976   *Squatters and Oligarchs: Authoritarian Rule and Policy Change in Peru.* Baltimore: John Hopkins University Press.
Cotler, Julio
1976   "The Mechanics of Internal Domination and Social Change in Peru." In *Peruvian Nationalism: A Corporatist Revolution.* David Chaplin, editor, pp. 35-74. New Brunswick: Transaction Books.

Deitz, Henry
    1969   "Urban Squatter Settlement in Peru: A Case Study and Analysis." *Journal of Inter-American Studies* 11:353-370.
    1976   "Metropolitan Lima: Urban Problem Solving under Military Rule." *Latin American Urban Research* 6:205-226.

DESCO y la Comisión Andina de Juristas
    1989   *Violencia y pacificación. Comisión especial del senado sobre las causas de la violencia y alternativas de pacificación en el Perú.* Lima, Perú: Senado de la República del Perú.

Dobyns, Henry F., and Paul L. Doughty
    1976   *Peru: A Cultural History.* New York: Oxford University Press.

Dobyns, Henry F., and Mario C. Vazquez, editors
    1963   *Migración y integración en el Perú.* Lima, Peru: Editorial Estudios Andinos.

Doughty, Paul L.
    1963   "Huaylas: Un Distrito en la Perspectiva Nacional." In *Migración y integración en el Perú.* H. F. Dobyns and M. C. Vazquez, editors, pp. 111-127. Lima, Perú: Editorial Estudios Andinos.
    1964   "La Migración Provinciana, Regionalismo y el Desarrollo Local." *Economía y Agricultura* (Lima) 1:203-211.
    1968   *Huaylas, An Andean District in Search of Progress* (with Mary F. Doughty). Ithaca, NY: Cornell University Press.
    1969   "La cultura del regionalismo en la vida urbana de Lima, Perú." *América Indígena* 29:949-982.
    1970   "Behind the Back of the City: 'Provincial' Life in Lima, Peru." In *Peasants in Cities.* William Mangin, editor, pp. 30-46. Boston: Houghton Mifflin.
    1972   "Peruvian Migrant Identity in the Urban Milieu." In *The Anthropology of Urban Environments.* T. Weaver and D. White, editors, pp. 39-50. Washington, DC: Society for Applied Anthropology Monograph, 11.
    1976   "Social Policy and Urban Growth in Lima." In *Peruvian Nationalism.* D. Chaplin, editor, pp. 75-110. New York: Transaction Books.
    1978   "El caso de las asociaciones provinciales voluntarios de Lima: Algunos problemas metodológicos y de interpretación." In *Urbanización en América Latina.* Jorge Hardoy, Richard Morse, and Richard Schaedel, editors, pp. 295-313. Buenos Aires: Ediciones SIPA-CLASCO.
    1979a   "The Social Lives of Migrants: The Case of Provincial Voluntary Associations." *XLII Proceedings of the International Congress of Americanists* (Paris) 10:321-332.
    1979b   "A Latin American Specialty in World Context: Urban Primacy and Cultural Colonialism in Peru." *Urban Anthropology* 8:383-398.
    1983   "Comments on Notes for a History of Peruvian Social Anthropology." *Current Anthropology* 24:351-353.
    1987   "Engineers and Energy in the Andes: An Update." In *Technology and Social Change.* H. R. Bernard, and P. Pelto, editors, pp. 11-36; 369-373. (Second edition). Waveland Press.

Doughty, Paul L., Elizabeth Burleigh, and Michael Painter
    1984   *Peru: An Evaluation of P.L. 480 Title II Food Assistance.* Washington DC: Agency for International Development.

Flaherty, Joseph A., Susan Birz, and Ronald M. Wintrob
    1987   "The Process of Acculturation: Theoretical Perspectives and an Empirical Investigation in Peru." *Social Science and Medicine* 25:839-847.

Ghersi B., Humberto, and Henry F. Dobyns
    1963   "Migración por etapas: El caso del Valle de Virú." In *Migración y integración en el Perú.* Henry F. Dobyns and Mario C. Vasquez, editors, pp. 152-159. Lima, Perú: Editorial Estudios Andinos.

Glewwe, Paul
    1988   *The Distribution of Welfare in Peru in 1985-86.* Living Standards Measurement Study Working Paper, No 42. Washington, DC: World Bank.

Gonzalez Prada, Manuel
    1960[1894] *Pájinas Libres.* Lima, Perú.

Hamilton, Gary
    1979   "Regional Associations and the Chinese City: A Comparative Perspective." *Comparative Studies in Society and History* 21:346-361.

Hirabayashi, Lane Ryo
    1986   "The Migrant Village Association in Latin America: A Comparative Analysis." *Latin American Research Review* 21:7-29.

Isbell, Billie Jean
    1978   *To Defend Ourselves: Ecology and Ritual in an Andean Village.* Austin: University of Texas Press.
Jongkind, Fred
    1971   "La supuesta funcionalidad de los clubes regionales en Lima, Perú." *Boletín de Estudios Latinoamericanos* (Centro de Estudio y Documentación Latinoamericana, Universidad de Amsterdam, Holland) 11:1-12.
    1974a   "A Reappraisal of the Role of Regional Associations in Lima, Peru: An Epistemological Perspective." *Comparative Studies in Society and History* 16:471-482.
    1974b   *Regional Clubs in Lima, Peru.* Ph.D. dissertation, CEDLA, Amsterdam.
    1986   "Ethnic Solidarity and Social Stratification: Migrant Organizations in Peru and Argentina." *Boletín de Estudios Latinoamericanos y del Caribe* 40:37-48.
Kerri, James Nwannukwu
    1976   "Studying Voluntary Associations as Adaptive Mechanisms: A Review of Anthropological Perspectives." *Current Anthropology* 17:23-35.
Lewis, Oscar
    1959   "Urbanization without Breakdown: A Case Study." *Scientific Monthly* 75:35-41.
Lloyd, Peter
    1980   *The Young Towns of Lima: Aspects of Urbanization in Peru.* New York: Cambridge University Press.
Long, Norman
    1973   "The Role of Regional Associations in Peru." In *The Process of Urbanization.* M. Drake, editor, pp. 173-188. Bletchley, Buckinghamshire: The Open University.
Long, Norman, and Bryan Roberts, editors
    1984   *Miners, Peasants and Entrepreneurs: Regional Development in the Central Highlands of Central Peru.* New York: Cambridge University Press.
Lobo, Susan
    1982   *A House of My Own.* Tucson: University of Arizona Press.
Lowenthal, Abraham F., editor
    1975   *The Peruvian Experiment: Continuity and Change under Military Rule.* Princeton: Princeton University Press.
Mangin, William
    1959   "The Role of Regional Associations in the Adaptation of Rural Populations in Peru." *Sociologus* 9:21-36.
    1963   "Urbanization Case History in Peru." *Architectural Design* 8:366-370.
    1965   "The Role of Regional Associations in the Adaptation of Rural Migrants to the Cities in Peru." In *Contemporary Cultures and Societies in Latin America.* Dwight Heath and Richard N. Adams, editors, pp. 311-323. New York:
    1967   "Latin American Squatter Settlements: A Problem and a Solution." *Latin American Research Review* 2:65-98.
    1970   *Peasants in Cities.* Boston: Houghton Mifflin.
Mariategui, José Carlos
    1928   *Siete ensayos de interpretación de la realidad Peruana.* Lima, Perú: Biblioteca Amauta.
Martínez, Hector
    1980   *Migraciones internas en el Perú: Aproximación crítica y bibliografía.* Lima, Perú: Instituto de Estudios Peruanos.
Matos Mar, José
    1961   "Migration and Urbanization: The 'Barriadas' of Lima, an Example of Integration into Urban Life." In *Urbanization in Latin America.* P. Hauser, editor, pp. 170-190. Paris: UNESCO.
    1986   *Taquile en Lima: Siete familias cuentan....* Lima, Perú: Fondo Internacional para la Promoción de la Cultura, UNESCO y Banco Nacional del Perú.
McDougal, M. S., H. D. Lasswell, and L. Chen
    1980   *Human Rights and World Public Order.* New Haven: Yale University Press.
Myers, Sarah K.
    1973   *Language Shift among Migrants to Lima, Peru.* Chicago: University of Chicago Department of Geography Research Paper, 147.
Millones, Luís
    1985   "Tugurio, the Culture of Peruvian Marginal Population: A Study of a Lima Slum." In *Peruvian*

Contexts of Change. William W. Stein, editor and translator. New Brunswick: Transaction Books.

Osterling, Jorge
1980   *De campesinos a profesionales: Migrantes de Huayopampa en Lima.* Perú: Pontificia Universidad Católica del Perú.

Osterling, Jorge, and Hector Martínez
1983   "Notes for a History of Peruvian Social Anthropology." *Current Anthropology* 24:343-360.

Patch, Richard
1967   *La Parada: Lima's Market, Part I: A Villager Who Met Disaster.* West Coast South America Series. Volume 14.

Peru
1932   *Censo de las provincias de Lima y Callao levantado el 13 de noviembre de 1931.* Trabajo Ejecutado por la Junta Departamental de Lima Pro-Desocupados, Imprenta Torres Aguirre. Lima.

1965   *VI Censo nacional de población 1961.*

1974   *Censos nacionales VII de población, 1972.*

1981   *Censos nacionales VIII de población, 1981.* Resultados provisionales del censo de población, 12 de julio de 1981. Lima: Instituto Nacional de Estadística.

1984a   *Censos nacionales VIII de población–III de vivienda, 1981.* Lima: Dirección General de Demografía.

1984b   *Proyecciones especiales de población.* Boletín Especial No. 8. Lima: Dirección General de Demografía.

Roberts, Bryan
1974   "The Interrelationships of City and Provinces in Peru and Guatemala." *Latin American Urban Research* 4:207-236.

1975   "Center and Periphery in the Development Process: The Case of Peru." *Latin American Urban Research* 5:77-108.

1978   *Cities of Peasants: The Political Economy of Urbanization in the Third World.* Beverly Hills: Sage Publications.

Sassen-Koob, Saskia
1979   "Formal and Informal Associations: Dominicans and Colombians in New York." *International Migration Review* 12:314-332.

Schaedel, Richard P.
1979   "From Homogenization to Heterogenization in Lima, Peru." *Urban Anthropology* 8:399-420.

Skeldon, Ronald
1974   *Migration in a Peasant Society: The Example of Cuzco, Peru.* Ph.D. dissertation, University of Toronto, Canada.

1976   "Regional Associations and Population Migration in Peru: An Interpretation." *Urban Anthropology* 5:233-252.

1977   "Regional Associations: A Note on Opposed Interpretations." *Comparative Studies in Society and History* 19:499-505.

Tulles, F. Lamond
1970   *Lord and Peasant in Peru: A Paradigm of Political and Social Change.* Cambridge, MA: Harvard University Press.

Turner, John F.C.
1965   "Lima's Barriadas and Corralones: Suburbs versus Slums." *Ekistics* [Greece] 19:152-156.

University of Florida Foundation
1990   *Florida Today.* Gainesville, Florida.

Ursinus College
1990   *Alumni Bulletin.* Collegeville, Pennsylvania.

Valcarcel, Luís E.
1914   *La cuestión agraria en Cuzco.* Cuzco, Peru: Editorial Minerra
1927   *Tempestad en los Andes.* Lima, Peru:

Wallace, James M.
1984   "Urban Anthropology in Lima: An Overview." *Latin American Research Review* 19:57-86.

Wilson, Patricia A., and Carol Wise
1986   "The Regional Implications of Public Investment in Peru, 1968-1983." *Latin American Research Review* 21:93-116.

CHAPTER SIX

Indians of the Sierra in Quito and Guayaquil: Interethnic Relations and the Urbanization of Migrants

Hernán Carrasco M.
Institute of Ecuadorian Studies

Translated by Lane R. Hirabayashi[1]

INTRODUCTION

The concentration of a significant percentage of the population in a single urban center has been one of the outstanding characteristics of the urbanization process in the majority of Latin American countries.[2] In such cases, internal migration has been directed to one city in particular, usually the capital of the respective nation, in virtue of its capacity to concentrate economic activities and the political-administrative apparatus. The cities in question have experienced increased demographic growth that is a product of the displacement of the population from the rural areas and small provincial cities.

As a result, studies concerning the migratory process to urban areas have been carried out within a restricted universe of analysis insofar as they consider only one urban point of destination in each country where groups from diverse origins congregate. While this approach has stimulated comparisons between migrants who come from various cultural backgrounds, or out of different structural situations, located in the same point of destination, it has also hindered the emergence of comparative approaches in which variable factors are identified and examined in terms of the specificities of each city.

An effect of this approach to the study of rural/urban migration is the tendency to underscore the role that migrants' sociocultural characteristics play in processes of urbanization. Although the majority of studies consider this factor in relation to the urban context in which the lives of migrants unfold, there are few comparative analyses available that allow the more precise documentation of the effect of urban conditions upon sociocultural phenomena.

The Ecuadorian case presents an opportunity to address this problem. In Ecuador the urbanization process does not exhibit the same tendency, noted above, toward an urban structure characterized by a single dominant city. On the contrary, since the nineteenth century, two important urban centers have emerged–Quito, the capital of Ecuador, and Guayaquil, the principal port–and during the second half of this century the relative importance of a group of intermediate cities has been growing. Rural-urban migration has been directed toward diverse cities, principally Quito and Guayaquil, and there are a number of areas in the country, among which the central-south sierra stands out, that have sent peasants to both urban destinations. Additionally, there is a comparative advantage in that the two primary cities have a more or less similar number of residents[3], and they are in regions that can be clearly differentiated in terms of their ecological, economic, political, and cultural characteristics. Because of such differences in the two points of destination, peasant migrants face contrasting urban conditions.

By means of a case study–that of migrants originating from the sierran village of Puesetus–I will illustrate how significant differences emerge in Quito, as opposed to Guayaquil, on the part of indigenous peasant migrants who share similar historical and cultural backgrounds. To accomplish this, I first characterize the point of origin, and the nature of out-migration, in order to proceed to a description of the most relevant aspects of the insertion of the migrants into each of the two cities–specifically, in terms of their occupations, residential patterns, and formal/informal associations. On the basis of these primary data I will show the importance of interethnic relations as the central variable in explaining why the migrants from Puesetus in Quito have succeeded in organizing an association that has formal legal status as well as a wide range of functions. By comparison, migrants from Puesetus in Guayaquil tend to keep their social networks on an informal basis, largely as a result of their commitment to ethnically undifferentiated religious groups.

Insofar as the Association of Indians Resident in Quito Álejo Saes (the official name adopted by migrants from Puesetus in the capital) represents a pioneering form of institutionalization, it is also necessary to explain why migrant associations have not proliferated in the Ecuadorian context. As of a very recent date, informal networks among indigenous peasant migrants, based primarily on kinship and common origins, have sufficed for the processes of urbanization. Nevertheless, for the last few years, and to a growing extent over recent months, there has been a concerted effort to formalize these networks, always taking the local indigenous community as a key point of reference. Like the Association Álejo Saes, the new migrant associations that have appeared on the social scene are a response to a discourse with a strong ethnic content. But even as this is occurring in Quito, the indigenous migrants from Guayaquil seem to be heading in the opposite direction.

AGRARIAN TRANSFORMATIONS AND MIGRATION: THE CASE OF PUESETUS

Until the twentieth century, the agrarian structure of the Ecuadorian sierra was dominated by the *haciendas*–great landed estates that, by means of a strict command over resources, controlled the conduct of the rural populace. Such control permitted a class of landlords to obtain rents (in labor, or in kind) from a large part of the peasant population, the majority of whom were indians (see Barsky 1985; Corporate Author 1984; Guerrero 1975).

Even though a sector of indigenous peasants worked small landholdings, another large percentage used the lands of the large estates (or *huasipungos*) in usufruct, in exchange for which they would deliver a set number of days of labor to the patron. As late as 1960, some 32 percent of the peasant families belonged to the category of *huasipungueros*, or those who worked on the *haciendas* of the sierra (see Velasco 1983). The "free" peasantry who owned their own land also depended on the *haciendas* in order to establish relationships based on partnership, or else for access to pasture, water, and even roads. Thus, they were also obliged to contribute work for the benefit of the landholder's enterprise.

The domination of the *hacienda* and its form of functioning–that is, characterized by a predominance of noncapitalistic relations of production, and the appropriation of rent in labor or "in kind"–shaped a characteristic situation in relation to local population dynamics. The logic of renting demands the availability of large amounts of manpower in order to sustain the process of accumulation. The system of *haciendas* implied, for this reason, the maintenance of a large population, and the system greatly limited the movement of peasants, thus generating a "captive" population (see Pachano 1988).

On the other hand, the creation of a broader market for labor met with obstacles not only because of the lack of supply but also because of the lack of demand for a work force given the limited development of the capitalist sector of the economy. Under such circumstances, even the most independent members of the peasant sector, as well as the mestizo population of the communities located on the *hacienda* lands, were forced to resort to the *hacienda* each time they needed additional resources.

Under such conditions, migratory movement, and in particular that of the indigenous peasants from the sierra, was almost nonexistent or, at the least, did not reach large numbers. However, the profound transformations that the farmers of the sierra experienced since the 1950s resulted in the liberation of the peasant work force previously bound to the *hacienda* system and created the conditions for the growth of massive migratory movements of a diverse nature.

The dissolution of the grand estates, which is verified through a number of sources (see Barsky 1985; Guerrero 1984), translated into problems for a large sector of small-scale peasants. The latter enlarged the group of "free" peasantry, but at the same time a significant proportion of the rural population was left without access to agrarian resources. As a result, peasants caught in this situation were displaced in a definitive manner toward other parts of the country. In the beginning of this process of transformation, mestizo and indian ex-farmers, as well as mestizos in general from the rural communities, moved to the urban centers as well as to zones of "colonization" in the interior, redefining their position in the national society in the process. But once the new structural situation became consolidated, creating a vast sector of small-scale peasants, temporal migration became the predominant type. The peasants facing the agrarian transformations described above had to survive on very reduced bases for autonomous reproduction, and, in order to manipulate limited agricultural resources, many peasant families were forced to sell wage labor or to pursue diverse activities in the informal sector of the urban economy. The entrance and exit of the small peasant landholder into the work force is currently the most characteristic reproductive strategy of the peasant families of the sierra today (see Farrell et al. 1988).

This global view of the processes of change experienced by the farmers of the sierra, and the impact that these processes have had on migratory movements, does not imply a uniformity among the diverse mountain provinces. Nonetheless, it is a synthesis that is very close to what occurred in the microregion encompassing the community of Puesetus.[4] Before the processes of agrarian transformation, the community of Puesetus was made up of small, but "free," indigenous landholders. They were, however, still dependent on the *hacienda* of the same name, whose holdings encompassed the entire valley of the microregion and even extended into parts of the surrounding highlands. The *hacienda* of Puesetus belonged to the church until the beginning of the twentieth century. Subsequently, there was a gradual process of fragmentation as lands were obtained by white families from the provincial capital. Notwithstanding this initial fragmentation, the resulting division of the land was carried out in such a way as to maintain control over local indigenous peasants, in terms of the latter still needing access to the resources of the *haciendas*, or furnishing the landowners with temporary wage labor. By the beginning of the 1960s, there were even some middle-sized holdings that required wage labor, but the fragmentation of holdings has intensified due to inheritance and through the sale of small parcels of land.

Since then, the community of Puesetus has changed, in the sense that some families— both local mestizos and indigenous peasants—obtained access to additional parcels that were originally part of the ex-estate and were thus able to increase their holdings. At the same time, they lost some of their territorial integrity, in part because of the relative dispersion of the recently acquired lots, the creation of new communal lands, and, above all, because of the inclusion of mestizo landowners on the outskirts of the village. The indigenous families of Puesetus who participated in the local land market are, in all, a small number. The great majority of them hold on to their old parcels of land, which have gone through a process of further fragmentation because the extant rules of inheritance stipulate that property be divided into equal parts among each child of the landowner. In this fashion, beginning in the 1960s, the community has become more diverse, although the majority of the families continue to hold small parcels. For such families, their social reproduction is possible only to the extent that they are able to obtain additional resources.

These conditions stimulate out-migration. In contrast to what happens in other parts of the sierra, and even what happens within the larger province of Chimborazo, agrarian transformations in the microregion where the community of Puesetus is located do not involve the total expulsion of the population. The extent to which the large estate was divided made it possible for some peasant families to augment their property by annexing new lots. Thus, the early migrants from Puesetus were not permanent migrants but, on the contrary, usually temporary sojourners.

For the most part, the early migrants from Puesetus were young men who preferred to go to the city of Guayaquil; only a few decided to go to Quito. This reveals a certain knowledge of the labor market on the coast—a product of the fact that indigenous peasants from communities in the neighboring parish of Licto have had a strong migratory pattern since the 1940s that has been directed toward both rural and urban destinations on the coast. This tendency was maintained during all of that decade, but beginning in the 1970s the situation began to become more complicated when some families undertook a permanent move to Quito. Subsequently, by the middle of the 1980s Quito became the principal urban destination.

This change in the preferred urban point of destination indicates a clear correlation with an increased complexity in the modes of migration. There is a correspondence, that is, between the predominance of temporary migration and the selection of the city of Guayaquil as the preferred destination and, in turn, the replacement of Guayaquil by Quito, accompanying the gradual diversification of peasants' strategies of social reproduction. The appearance of a growing number of family units that undertook permanent migration was largely a response to the ongoing division of small lots. Nevertheless, cultural and ideological factors also played a role, and the latter enable us to better appreciate the fact that the diversification of migration patterns appears in association with a change in decisions relative to a given point of destination.

By means of a "trial and error" method, initiated by the pioneers in both cities, the selection of a given urban point of destination responds not solely to the dynamics of capitalist accumulation but also to demonstrated outcomes emerging from the experiences of the initial migrants. Specifically, the nature of interethnic relations that are extant in one or the other city influences the evolution of initial options.

Actually, there are about thirty nuclear families in Quito who were originally from Puesetus; some of them maintain small parcels in the point of origin, while others–generally young couples–hope to inherit a parcel in the future. Only a few families have detached themselves completely from farming as an option. Thus, it is somewhat ambiguous as to whether Puesetus families in Quito are in fact permanent migrants or not, although it is probable that some of them are. Patterns of temporary migration occur as often in nuclear families that come to live in the capital for a more or less indefinite period, but this is frequently conditioned by the requirements of farming small parcels, as it is for about thirty or more individuals–heads of households, or young, single, men, for the most part–who come into the city during the slack periods of the agricultural cycle while their wives and children remain at home.

In Guayaquil, on the other hand, there are fewer migrants overall. There are only about ten families from Puesetus that live in Guayaquil permanently, while the number of temporary migrants, most of whom are young, single, men, fluctuates between thirty and forty in the best of times.

INFORMAL NETWORKS, OCCUPATIONS, AND RESIDENTIAL PATTERNS

Both in Quito and Guayaquil, migrants from Puesetus reconstitute an aggregate of effective social networks based on kinship and principles of mutual aid, reciprocity, and redistribution, all of which govern the lives of the indigenous peasants of the sierra. The reconstitution of these informal networks in a new setting appears to be an exigency of the urbanization process, and clearly they have proven to be effective. Although informal networks have contributed to the material survival of the migrants in both cities, one becomes immediately aware of certain differences that have appeared in each locale as a result of the interaction with other social groups, and the response of the indigenous migrants to the greater or lesser degree of conflictive interethnic relations.

It is an established fact that peasant migrants coming from the same point of origin tend to pursue a limited range of occupations, and that a good number of migrants concentrate in one or two areas of endeavor. More than a reflection of special abilities in an occupational field, this tendency can be attributed to the assistance given by the "older" migrants in the city, who help the recent arrivals to find a job. Likewise, informal networks facilitate the acquisition of housing, with the frequent result that the migrants form residential clusters and tend to be concentrated in two or three neighborhoods in the urban point of destination.

In these respects there are few differences between the migrants from Puesetus in Quito and Guayaquil. Thus, in terms of the acquisition of employment, about 50 percent of the migrants in Quito and about 60 percent of the migrants in Guayaquil said that they had received help from kin. It should be noted that these percentages would actually be higher if one considered only those occupations that involve a salary: construction workers and employees in Quito, and dock workers and workers in agro-industrial businesses (for example, those who run rice hulling machines) in Guayaquil. Global percentages are pushed downward by the fact that many of the street vendors–an important occupation in both cities–said that they entered in commercial pursuits through their own initiative.

This kind of aid, provided via informal networks, is reflected in the strong occupational concentration that exists in the two cities. In Quito almost 50 percent of the migrants carry out duties as construction workers, and about 25 percent work as businessmen, the majority of whom are street vendors, with some simultaneously involved in the delivery of foodstuffs to restaurants. Approximately 12 percent are workers and relatively stable employees, and a similar percentage carry cargo in the markets. In Guayaquil around 55 percent of the migrants have developed commercial activities–the majority of them street vendors, and a few in established businesses. Twenty-five percent have jobs as members of work crews loading and unloading cargo, and about 15 percent work in the rice hulling industry. Inasmuch as my data refer only to the heads of households, the numbers are susceptible to a certain variation if one considers the work of other members of the domestic unit in the city. In both cases, the tendency toward occupational concentration is accented. This occurs because almost all of the wives carry out some economic activity work as street vendors.

None of the activities considered here produce an income that would permit significant economic differentiation among the migrant population. Nevertheless, in Quito as in Guayaquil, there are a few families in business who have achieved a certain level of accumulation.

From an occupational point of view, it does not seem that there are significant differences between the migrants in Quito and in Guayaquil, even though they themselves think that in the latter city it is "easier to earn money." But this similarity is only superficial, in that it does not encompass the character of social relations and interethnic relations that are present in the occupational setting. It is therefore appropriate to examine this dimension in more depth, in order to see the factors that have led the migrants in each city to develop different adaptational responses.

In Quito, the majority of the heads of migrant households work as construction workers. This is an area of the labor market that is nourished almost exclusively from the labor of peasant migrants. This even has a spatial dimension. Migrants gather in a specific part of the city–Avenida 24 de Mayo–to seek employment. There they are joined by master bricklayers, many of whom are also indigenous migrants, who subcontract teams of hired laborers for a job they are supervising, for a period established by common agreement. It is not unusual that many of these arrangements are made in Quechua, and that migrants who come from the same place of origin, and are at times even related through kinship, are contracted for the same job. This creates a situation where the everyday work environment facilitates the use of the migrants' native language. This same practice permits indigenous migrants to feel among equals as well as to maintain, without feelings of inferiority, regional customs and forms of interaction.

The interaction of migrant workers with people in other levels of the construction businesses per se is minimal; when they do establish contacts, these are mediated by a set of common codes between the bosses and the workers. Supervisors and foreman utilize, at least in the work context, a "Quechuized" version of Spanish that facilitates communication with the workers. This reveals a point of transcendental importance from the perspective of the nature of the interethnic relations: in Quito, and in the sierran cities in general, whites and mestizos have assumed a paternalistic role in relation to indigenous migrants, familiar to the latter insofar as it has a resemblance to interethnic relations found in the rural areas. In turn, migrants know how to utilize this practice for their own ends, even though it is evident that Indian-mestizo relationships continue to be asymmetrical.

Interethnic relations in the sierran cities are also expressed in the pursuit of other occupations. For example, the street vendors have to engage in daily interaction with the bigger merchants in the markets. Because many of the merchants come from small sierran villages, they act in accordance with rural conventions familiar to their customers. Even if the merchants were born in the city, however, they have to assimilate to the behavior and forms of interaction typical of the rural setting, and even adopt indigenous dress, to the point that the markets in the center of the city and even the residential neighborhoods are areas that appear to be strongly indigenous.

At other levels, the migrant street vendor has to interact daily with a varying clientele that, in general, tend to reproduce the paternalistic style. Expressions like *caserito* (little housewife) and *hijito* (sonny), as well as others, are frequently heard between the buyer and the seller. In addition, it is worth noting that the practice of bargaining, which the migrant businessmen carry out with great ability and an Andean patience, facilitates a respectful treatment that is consistent with rural conceptions of time. Only two situations create conflict for the indigenous migrants who become street vendors, especially if they are women: to be the victim of theft or abuse—both of which tend to be perpetrated by people from the coast—or the victim of harassment on the part of the municipal police.

The contrast between this situation and the one extant on the coast, specifically in Guayaquil, is marked. The traditional rivalry between people from the coast versus the sierra, based on a strong sense of regional identity, is transformed with frequency into contempt if the "other" is, in addition to coming from the sierra, an Indian. On the occupational plane, this is expressed in a variety of ways: we have observed, for example, that in the work of loading and unloading on the docks, the Indians from the sierra have the heavier jobs, involving carrying things on their shoulders, while the other workers, from the coast, "*hacen cargar*"—that is, push the cargo onto the shoulders of the sierran migrants. Even though this ethnic discrimination is not extremely rigid, inasmuch as there are workers from the coast who also carry cargo, it is very rare that an indigenous migrant would be assigned one of the less menial jobs. Similarly, the treatment that door-to-door salespersons receive is very discriminatory and frequently insulting. Nevertheless, the fact that two of the "oldest" migrants from Puesetus started in this fashion, and are now both large businessmen, encourages street vendors to pursue this occupation.

Residential patterns of both groups of migrants shows the efficacy of these informal networks; in their appearance they again do not show considerable differences. In Quito, there are three areas of residential concentration, each one of which involves a similar number of families. The most traditional, El Panecillo, brings together the older, more established migrants and shows a great difference in terms of housing and the provision of services. El Panecillo is a central barrio with a high percentage of indigenous residents that, until the beginning of the 1980s, was the initial destination of many of the migrants from Puesetus. In this neighborhood, however, there is not one family that owns its own housing.

The two more recently formed residential clusters emerged from the acquisition of urban lots on the part of some of the migrant families. Both clusters have been pivotal in facilitating the transfer of the old residents from El Panecillo, and attracting new migrants. Both clusters, located in the sectors of La Libertad Alta and Toctiuco Aldo, also form part of what has been called "clandestine subdivisions"–that is to say, non-urbanized subdivisions at the edge of the city–that are formed on the lands of ex-*haciendas*. On the other hand, they involve a heterogeneous ethnic composition, given that access operates in terms of the purchase/sale of lands. Thus, indigenous and mestizo migrants live together there, as well as people born in the city.

In each of the clusters, neighborly relations are fairly fluid, and the precariousness of the provision of urban services (assuming the latter are present to begin with) obliges the residents to join together in order to slowly begin urbanizing their respective sectors.

The three clusters are relatively close to two important areas of migrant activity: Avenida 24 de Mayo, the place where the construction workers are contracted, and the Mercado San Roque, where salespersons go to purchase their merchandise. Nevertheless, two of the clusters manifest certain rural features–as much a reflection of the lack of provision of urban services as a matter of ecological location that makes it possible for residents to plant small gardens and to raise smaller domestic animals.

In Guayaquil, the migrants from Puesetus live primarily in neighborhoods that border on the Mercado Central and the Mercado Machala. They rent rooms in deteriorated slum housing (*tugurios*). Not surprisingly, the area shows signs of density many times those found in the rest of Quito. The neighboring sector in the Central Market is practically an "indigenous zone." Apart from the rooms in the slums, one finds restaurants, bars, amusement parlors, and the storefronts of religious sects. Nevertheless, although this "indigenous zone" is clearly delimited and recognized by the local population, it is also subject to "invasion." During the day there are many street vendors from diverse ethnic backgrounds. During the night its streets become dangerous because of the presence of delinquents and youth gangs, largely made up of young men from the coast. This involves, then, a zone that is simultaneously "familiar" as it is "foreign"–in other words, indians are only able to exist peacefully behind closed doors. In addition to the migrants in the rooms of the *tugurios*, there is another residential pattern that has now disappeared among the migrants from Puesetus in Quito. Many of the temporary migrants used to stay, for limited periods of time, in the Casa Posada San José, an institution administrated by Catholics that is located in the neighborhood of the Mercado Sur.

Although the residential patterns of the migrants in Guayaquil do not seem substantially different from those observed in Quito, at least two aspects merit further consideration.

In the first place, the setting of Guayaquil consists only of renters and those who stay in the Casa Posada, while in the case of Quito there are some migrants who have obtained access to urban lots; with recourse to mutual aid, they have also been able to build their own housing. This is quite notable because, in Quito, urban expansion is carried out via clandestine subdivision–that is to say, through economic means. In Guayaquil, a good part of the process of expansion has occurred through land invasions–that is, through political means.

The differential that presents itself is clear: despite low incomes, migrants in Quito achieved access to urban lots through economic transactions; by contrast, the migrants in Guayaquil have not become property owners even though they have participated in land invasions. How can this be explained?

A response to this question can be found in the political character of urban expansion in Guayaquil, as well as in the nature of interethnic relations. In effect, the massive invasions of land in Guayaquil are the result of the arrangement of groups organized and led by local political leaders who then established patron-client relationships with the families that participated in each invasion. This created the bases for the appearance of populist political movements, characteristic of the social scene in Guayaquil. The configuration of these organizations is driven by cultural codes that are not controlled by the indigenous population of the sierra. This adds up to the fact that, politically speaking, the indigenous population is seen as difficult to manipulate– "traitorous," in the language of the political leaders from the coast–which signifies that they are frequently not taken into account as potential clients.

Indigenous migrants have their own version of this that alludes, fundamentally, to interethnic conflict. Indigenous migrants think that even when they offer to integrate into the organizations that carry out the land invasions, it is very difficult for them to live in the same space with other *serranos*, Blacks, and people from the coast in general. They think that to belong to an organization and a neighborhood with such persons only exposes them to greater scorn, ultimately intensifying interethnic conflicts.

Migrants also raise a variety of practical considerations. The invasions are carried out, for the most part, on swampy lands on which the participants–making use of cultural notions of architectural design that come out of their peasant coastal background– construct extremely precarious housing. Evidently, such housing patterns are not agreeable to the indigenous migrants from the sierra, who are accustomed to a style that emphasizes the privacy of the individual house. They also consider that the ecological character of the land invasions exposes them to diseases they are unfamiliar with. Also, they view as inconvenient the fact that the invasions are far from the markets where they carry out their economic activities. The problem of distance is not only physical; it also means that they have to compete for scarce means of transportation, a situation in which they feel at a disadvantage. They also see potential conflicts with their neighbors. Finally, they feel that even if and when they own a lot, it could be snatched away from them, given the need to "abandon" it during the working day. They fear that their homes can be easily ransacked, a fact that has occurred even in the relatively protected area in which they live.

A second concern is the impact of religious organization on the lives of indigenous migrants in Guayaquil, a situation that is much less significant in Quito. In Guayaquil, the evangelical sects have developed an intense style of proselytization, aimed specifically at the conversion of indigenous migrants from the sierra, an enterprise that has had notable success. To a certain extent, the work of conversion generates interethnic conflict, yet it offers migrants who join a moral status that puts them above the rest of the population from the coast of Ecuador. In order to better understand the implicit dimensions of this phenomenon, it is necessary to know about the stereotypes attributed to the population from the coast. Although migrants from the sierra feel a strong sense of inferiority in their relations with the people from the coast, the *serranos* disapprove of their sexual behavior and believe they lack solid moral principles. Thus, the *costeños* are assigned a series of negative characteristics: the tendency toward delinquency, violence, idleness, a preference for living the easy life, and wastefulness.[5]

Within this context, the functions of a discourse, strongly sustained by notions of moral development and the condemnation of sin, is apparent. The migrants from Puesetus in Guayaquil have joined the evangelical churches in growing numbers. This is in spite of the fact that, traditionally, the members of the community identify with the Catholic religion, and most of the principal leaders were brought up within the context of Catholicism. In the evangelical church, and in terms of their everyday religious practices, indigenous migrants can find a social space in which they are the equals of migrants from the coast, and with whom they share a sense of evangelical militancy. This puts them above the rest of the local population. In the context of the cult, it also becomes possible for indigenous migrants to develop broader ties of cooperation and social solidarity, including a feeling of respect accorded to "brothers" of different origins. All of this helps to smooth out interethnic tensions and conflicts.

The moral development of migrants from Puesetus who have joined evangelical sects is accepted by those who maintain the Catholic tradition, including migrants to Quito and those who have stayed in the community of origin. All acknowledge the fact that the evangelical families have improved themselves. They have been able to wipe out drunkenness, they do not fight with their relatives, they do not mistreat their women, and they have been able to succeed economically. As can be appreciated, various of these areas of achievement stand in direct contrast to the stereotypes that are generally attributed to people from the coast. Nevertheless, parallel to this realization, the indians of Puesetus keep their Catholic tradition. Nonetheless, they (especially those that belong to the Association Álejo Saes) believe that their evangelicized *paisanos* (that is, fellow villagers) are suffering from a process of "de-indigenization" in that they tend to distance themselves culturally from their background.

Without a doubt, this evaluation appears to be accurate. The character of interethnic relations in Guayaquil has influenced the migrants living there to deliberately try to hide their indigenous background, and this strategy has definitely been reinforced in the context of militant evangelism. It is convenient to dwell here on some of the opinions of the migrants themselves in this regard, especially those who have resided in both cities.

Such migrants think that Quito is "a city with a life style similar to that of the entire inter-Andean region," and that "the climate is the same as at home." "The indigenous migrants there do not feel the stigma of being indian; they do not need to change their clothes or speak a very different language." In this fashion, they are quite positive about the fact that there are indigenous people in the city. Thus, migrants recognize that from the very moment of its foundation, Quito was the site of an indigenous Andean culture that is constantly renewed by new migrants.[6] This permits new migrants in Quito "to leave the house feeling quite at home."

Opinions in regard to Guayaquil stem from the general recognition that the latter involves "a region that is very distinct from the inter-Andean one" with a climate that immediately makes people change their everyday lives; for example, in the use of fans, refrigerators, and so forth. But emphasis is always placed on the conflictive interethnic relationships in Guayaquil and the consequences that this unfavorable situation brings. Migrants observe that on the coast the local population treats indians like "hicks," in that the indians are easily frightened and intimidated, and think of them generally as "persons without any training or preparation–like animals." Not surprisingly, this creates "an inferiority complex about being indian" in the minds of migrants. The consequences of feelings of inferiority find expression in the need to "change one's dress and speech." This can go to such extremes that, at home, "some families no longer want to speak in Quechua," with the result that "on the coast, indigenous migrants are almost the same as the coastal population in terms of their clothes, speech, and customs."

Selected external aspects, involving clothes and language, acquire a special relevance in the perceptions that the migrants themselves have about their situation in different urban contexts. The attitudes of those who go to Quito are very distinct from those who go to Guayaquil. Thus, while indigenous migrants feel free to leave their homes in Quito as they please, they view the migrants to Guayaquil with a mixture of amazement and surprise. For example, they note that some of the women from the village "change their clothes in the bus terminal bathroom in Riobamba, in order to arrive in Guayaquil without seeming to be indians." This procedure is repeated on the return trip when, in the same place, the women put their traditional clothing back on. In a similar fashion, when some of the migrants return from Guayaquil, "they return talking like costeños, and some refuse to speak Quechua even in the local community."

The contrast between these two cities appears, above all, to be the nature of the relationship between the migrants and the native-born urban population, particularly in terms of a cultural conflict. In my view, this element explains the different responses that the migrants from Puesetus express in the two points of urban destination–Quito and Guayaquil. Beyond the specific details presented above, these same differences are the product of distinct settings, decisions and outcomes. In Quito we see a process of ethnic revitalization in the context of a marked process of politicization. In contrast, adaptation in Guayaquil has been characterized by a gradual process of de-indigenization, mediated by the affiliation of migrants with nonethnic evangelical sects.

INFORMAL NETWORKS AND PROCESSES OF ORGANIZATION

In both cities informal networks based on relationships of kinship and common origins have been efficacious in attaining a series of objectives. We have seen, for example, that such networks play a crucial role in helping migrants obtain employment and housing. They also stimulate the evolution of migratory movement, insofar as the presence of kin in certain points of destination facilitates the insertion of new migrants into city life. In turn, patterns of concentration, in relation to the labor market and in urban residential settlement, act to reinforce extant social networks.

On the other hand, one of the outstanding characteristics of the migratory flow toward both destinations is the presence of resident families, yet there is continuity of patterns of temporary migration. The latter permits the maintenance of constant communication with the countryside, without requiring more than the agricultural interests still held by a majority of the migrant families and individuals, via the constant coming and going of temporary migrants who are frequently the carriers of messages, errands, and products.

One must also consider that the physical distance between the community and the urban points of destination is relatively small. The route between Puesetus and Quito is approximately 210 kilometers, and some 250 kilometers separate the former from Guayaquil. Ground transportation between Riobamba–the provincial capital, no more than 20 kilometers from Puesetus–and between both of the two principal cities of Ecuador, is continual, at half-hour intervals throughout the week.

Weak linkages that indigenous migrants have with urban labor organizations, whether political or trade-oriented, and also to organizations of the administrative apparatus, whether state or municipal, are yet another set of factors that favors the migrants' participation in informal networks.

This general configuration of factors characterizes not only the migrants from Puesetus but also the bulk of the rural-urban migrants coming from indigenous communities in the province of Chimborazo and and similar provinces in the Ecuadorian sierra. The particularities and commonalities that can be found do not affect what has been one of the distinctive characteristics of the situation of the indigenous migrants in Ecuadorian cities: they have maintained the operation of informal networks before undertaking efforts to build formal organizations. The recent growth of indigenous migrant associations, specifically in Quito, ought to be explained in relation to their notorious slowness to develop if one considers the fact that migratory processes were initiated around 1960, in the present case, and even before that in other areas of the sierra.

A tentative explanation for the absence of indigenous migrant organizations in Ecuadorian cities stems from the fact that, in many of the rural areas in the sierra, and in those of the province of Chimborazo in particular, an active peasant movement dates back to the previous era of agrarian transformation. The members of this movement engaged in protracted struggle–at times openly, and at times in secret–for access to land (see Guerrero 1984). A good part of this struggle did not transcend the local scene and yet was often successful in accelerating the process of transformation. At their peak, organizations with a national character, such as the Indian Federation of Ecuador (Federación Ecuatoriana de Indios, or FEI), and the National Federation of Peasant Organizations (Federación Nacional de Organizaciones Campesinas, or FENOC), took on the responsibility of representing local conflicts on the urban and national scene vis-à-vis the state apparatus, with a discourse centered around the issue of indigenous peasants' access to land. Despite the relative neglect of the cultural and ideological aspects of this same peasantry, the federations were able to tap into part of the peasant masses and their communal organizations; that is, the federations were able to make more of these issues than the country's main political parties–indigenous peasants' more natural representatives–were able to.

Besides the presence of these organizations, Chimborazo has a special interest in the work carried out by the Diocese of Riobamba. Under the direction of Bishop Leonida Proaño, known as the "Bishop of the Indians," the Catholic Church has developed a position with a strong ethnic dimension, based on the general framework of the Theology of Liberation and a preferred orientation toward the poor. By means of various institutional apparatus, the Diocese of Riobamba came to dedicate itself to the formation and facilitation of indigenous leadership, among them the most notable leaders of Puesetus. The work of the Church strengthened the communal organizations and motivated the affiliation of these into larger organizations of a communal character, such as the Indigenous Movement of Chimborazo (Movimiento Indígena de Chimborazo), and nationally as well.

When the migratory flows reach a massive character, the more politicized migrants join these and other organizations that have a national or regional character, most of which focus on rural conflicts and channel local interests by way of a greater institutionalization. While this channel is effective, the creation of separate migrant organizations to assume the representation of communal affairs seems unnecessary. On the other hand, from the perspective of many of the peasant leaders, this type of initiative can be classified as "divisionary," given the processes of fragmentation that the peasant movement has experienced since the agrarian transformation.

An emphasis on the peasant dimension of political discourse, as opposed to ethnic dimensions, appears to have been effective, insofar as the urban interests of the migrants do not appear to be well defined. Moreover, the motives for migration still pertain to objectives tied to the maintenance of agricultural life that, over the subsequent years, were made more viable by increasing access to land, whether by means of mercantile transactions or by means of political struggle.

In the case of Puesetus, we have demonstrated that a significant proportion of the migrants have reinvested savings that were realized in the city in order to supplement their rural resources, for example, the purchase of land, the construction of additional housing in the fields, and the incorporation of new technologies. Among the migrants in Quito, about 85 percent have been able to unite sufficient savings in order to realize some kind of investment. Of these, about 82 percent show a clear tendency toward reinvestment in agricultural resources or, at the least, to conserve minimal bases for peasant reproduction. Only some 15 percent prefer to acquire urban lots and construct their own dwellings in the city (see Carrasco 1989; Farrell et al. 1988). Even though we do not have equivalent data for Guayaquil, we can affirm that two of the families who have gone to this city are among those migrants who have been able to acquire the most land in Puesetus in the 1980s.

Peasant organizations with a national character, at least those that assume the task of representing the peasants of the sierra, prefer to operate out of Quito because it is the capital of the republic and houses most of the decision-making bureaucracies that focus on agrarian issues. The actions of these organizations, which have been more or less effective, inhibits the alternative possibility of institutionalizing the informal networks of the migrant groups.

Migrants in Guayaquil, for their part, have not been interested in formalizing their informal networks. In reality, part of their strategy of insertion into the urban environment consisted in hiding their indigenous background and maintaining informal networks only in their private lives. In such a setting, a formal organization would be a detriment to the necessity of lessening interethnic conflict. It should be evident that the inferiority complex that the indigenous migrants have in the urban coastal setting is a negative constraint, blocking any initiative that might allow identification or formalization based on migrants' indigenous background. Besides, the institutionalization of the informal networks lacks a strong rationale in that Guayaquil is not the center of political decisions relevant to the peasants of the sierra.

In the 1980s there were two parallel phenomena that help explain the recent emergence of migrant associations in Quito. On one hand, the peasant movement is experiencing increasing crisis and fragmentation–a process that was already underway in previous years. On the other hand, ethnic organizations evolved simultaneously that sought to redefine the position of the indian in national society and to revitalize indigenous identity. Even though such organizations, and the indigenous movement as a whole, raised questions about land, education, health, and other topics, the center of their discourse aims at the revitalization of identities and of the culture of each ethnic group.

At the end of the 1980s, the ethnic movement presents a very favorable balance in terms of achievements. Nevertheless, the preferential attention given to the defense of the lands threatened by the expansion of the national economy of ethnic groups of the Amazonia has resulted in the relative neglect of some of the principal conflicts that confront the sierran communities, among which is growing demographic pressure on limited arable land. Neither has the ethnic movement been able to incorporate specific problems that face indigenous migrants into its agenda, in spite of the fact that the latter constitute an important constituency.

Some ethnic organizations of the sierra clearly show the difficulty of conjugating an ideological discourse, centered on cultural identity, with concrete struggles related to land, and thus have begun to experience internal struggles between those who elevate one or the other priority. Even though there is a natural correlation between these projects—in that, without land, cultural projects can be brought to ruin, or at least are seriously impeded—in practice ethnic organizations have not developed defined political positions around the land issue.

The scene of this debate encompasses both the sierra and the Amazon, as well as Quito, the traditional seat of power. The political parties that have strong roots in the sierra have not reached an interpretation of the current ethnic revitalization, as the greater part of this issue has scant credibility when it is contrasted with the peasant problem. In the coastal region, and Guayaquil in particular, the ethnic question and the debate concerning the indian does not occupy a central place. The preoccupations of the coastal farmers have a clearly local matrix that, given the ecological differences between the regions, results in neglect of the specific difficulties faced by the peasants of the sierra.

As a result, the sierran communities face a crisis of representation in respect to certain concrete problems, and this gap has created the conditions for the appearance of migrant organizations. Among the pioneers, the migrants from Puesetus in Quito have taken up these kinds of initiatives. A short summary of the explicit objectives pursued by the Asociación Álejo Saes helps to clarify their orientation.

The statutes of the organization propose the following ends, among others:
• To seek the well-being of associates, giving them whatever help might be necessary
• To seek the moral, physical, and intellectual development of associates
• To channel economic resources, obtained from both state and private institutions, for the benefit of associates
• To promote the organization of community businesses oriented toward the production and commercialization of agricultural, industrial, and craft products, in conjunction with Puesetus
• To organize educational centers, both for associates as well as for their children
• To promote the investigation, diffusion, and assimilation of indigenous science, technology, and culture
• To struggle to defend the Quechua nation in terms of peaceful dialogue with the diverse ethnic groups that live in Ecuador
• To promote cultural interchange.
Such objectives reveal the character of these new organizations that emphasize, in

particular, a preoccupation with the well-being of migrants, as well as the community of origin, based on the explicit recognition that those who belong to the association share a common identity and cultural heritage.

Meanwhile in Guayaquil, ethnic awareness of the migrants is weakened by (1) the cultural siege that they are subject to, (2) their own sense of inferiority, and (3) the militancy of the evangelical sects that put traditional beliefs and practices into question. In a parallel fashion, the indigenous migrants suffer from a process of depoliticization that, added to the rest of the factors, allows a prediction: it is unlikely that initiatives will occur that will lead to a formal migrant association. Nevertheless, the informal networks maintain their efficacy, and ties of solidarity and cooperation are amplified in the context of the religious cults. This is so, even to the point that solidarity is extended, in addition to fellow countrymen, to evangelical "brothers" from other parts of the country.

For its part, the rural community is exposed to the influence of both groups of migrants. While the Asociación Álejo Saes promotes community development, is able to revitalize traditional cultural practices, and seeks to augment a sense of ethnic identity and pride in being indian, the evangelical migrants in Guayaquil undertake a mission of proselytization designed to capture adherents among the peasant families. There is no direct confrontation between the adherents of these two positions, nor is there discrimination among the members in terms of religious orientation, in spite of the fact that the leaders of the migrant association in Quito hope to reconcile the two orientations. It is possible, however, that the different responses developed by the migrants from Puesetus in Quito and Guayaquil will begin to create difficulties for the continued unity of the provincial and migrant communities.

NOTES

1. The editors note that this chapter was written in early 1990, months before the major indigenous uprising in June. Nonetheless, direct lines of continuity run between the variables and organizations discussed in this chapter and the June uprising period. This is a topic Dr. Carrasco will address in future publications.

2. Mexico City in Mexico, Lima in Peru, Santiago in Chile, Buenos Aires in Argentina, and Montevideo in Uruguay are some illustrative examples of this process. Only the urban centers of Brazil, Colombia, and Ecuador exhibit a somewhat different dynamic.

3. In 1990, Guayaquil had a population of approximately 1,800,000, and Quito, 1,400,000, according to recent projections.

4. The community of Puesetus pertains to the province of Chimorazo, which is located in the southern central part of the sierra.

5. Lobo (1982) states that, in the case of Lima, migrants from the sierra have similar opinions in respect to the creole population. This does not exclude the fact, nonetheless, that migrants from the sierra and the creoles frequently establish cordial relationships, or at least they avoid each other if not, which does not tend to happen in the setting of Guayaquil.

6. Albó et al. (1982) have advanced a similar perspective in relation to the presence of Aymara indians in La Paz.

REFERENCES CITED

Albó, Xavier, Tomas Greaves, and Godofredo Sandoval
    1982   *Chukiyawu: La cara Aymara de la Paz. Tomo II: Una odisea: Buscar "pega."* La Paz: Cuadernos de Centro de Investigación y Promoción Del Campesinado (CIPCA), 22.

Barsky, Osvaldo
   1985   *La reforma agraria ecuatoriana.* Quito, Ecuador: Corporación Editora Nacional.
Carrasco, Hernán
   1989   "Migración temporal en la Sierra Ecuatoriana: Una estrategia de recampesinización." Paper presented at the seminar "Transformation in the Peasant Economy of the Andean Area, 1960-1988," Bogotá, Colombia.
Corporate Author
   1984   *Ecuador agrario.* Quito, Ecuador: Editorial El Conejo.
Farrel, Gilda, Simón Pachano, and Hernán Carrasco
   1988   *Caminantes y retornos.* Quito, Ecuador: Instituto de Estudios Ecuatorianos.
Guerrero, Andrés
   1975   *La hacienda precapitalista y la clase terrateniente en América Latina y su inserción en el modo de producción capitalista: El caso Ecuatoriano.* Quito, Ecuador: Universidad Central.
   1984   *Haciendas, capital y lucha de clases Andina.* Quito, Ecuador: Editorial El Conejo.
Lobo, Susan
   1982   *House of My Own.* Tucson: University of Arizona Press.
Pachano, Simón, editor
   1988   *Población, migración y empleo en el Ecuador.* Quito, Ecuador: Instituto Latinoamericano de Investigación Social.
Velasco, Fernando
   1983   *Reforma agraria y movimiento campesino indígena de la Sierra.* (Second Edition). Quito, Ecuador: El Conejo.

CHAPTER SEVEN

La Paz/Chukiyawu: The Two Faces of a City

Xavier Albó
Center for the Investigation and Promotion of the Peasantry, La Paz, Bolivia

Translated by Lane R. Hirabayashi

INTRODUCTION

The capital of Bolivia has two names: in Spanish, La Paz; in Aymara it is still known as Chukiyawu (or, Chukiyawu Marka, derived from *Chuki Yapu marka*, "Parcel of Precious Metal"). Beyond this, I note the allegory of a symbolic dualism that is much more socially and culturally profound than a simple linguistic parallel. The double name of the capital also reflects two sets of features and two essences. One is the notorious La Paz that is the center and the life force of the country. The other, hidden but nonetheless extant–Chukiyawu–is the heart of the Aymara world. Here I will use the city's two names in this allegorical sense.

Each dawn, Chukiyawu speaks on the radios; La Paz comes alive around 7 a.m. La Paz celebrates the sixteenth of July; Chukiyawu, the *Entrada del Gran Poder* in May. La Paz has its center in the Murillo plaza; Chukiyawu's is at the corner of Tumusla and Buenos Aires streets.

These are not parallel cities but rather two faces of the same dialectical reality. La Paz would like to erase Chukiyawu from the map, but it nonetheless lives off its work. Chukiyawu continues to be fed by thousands of migrants from the highlands–known as "residents"–who need La Paz.

In this chapter I present some fundamental aspects of this complementary reality.

First, I provide a global overview of its historical, geographical and cultural bases, in order to concentrate on the dialectical relationships that this reality presents, with special emphasis on the diverse sociocultural roots of its principal human populations.[1]

GENERAL PANORAMA

A Unique Landscape

With its unique geography, La Paz/Chukiyawu is a fascinating city not only to the tourist but also to the social geographer, the anthropologist, the sociologist, the linguist, and other scholars.

Geographically speaking, La Paz's locale makes it the highest capital city in the world; it is also an urban agglomeration with tremendous internal variation in elevation, ranging from more than 4,150 meters in El Alto to 3,180 meters in the residential neighborhood of Aranjuez. Outside of the flat portion of El Alto, an area that is constantly growing, the city is located in an impressive canyon–sheltered but with limited possibilities for growth–whose unstable hillsides are covered with ever-increasing numbers of precariously situated houses. This canyon, also known as La Hoyada, is divided by a total of 185 rivers and ravines that make a giddy descent through the mass of people from the Altiplano and the counterforts of the Andes to the final funnel by the principal avenue that crosses the city. When it rains, any street can be transformed into a large and powerful river in a matter of minutes. The largest distance from the edge of the built up part of El Alto to the other side of the Valley of Calacoto-Los Pinos is about 18 kilometers in a straight line, but about 40 kilometers in terms of the main road. In La Hoyada there are many parts of the city in which the unevenness can be as much as 400 to 500 meters within a distance of only 2 kilometers, that require 10 or more kilometers to travel in a vehicle.

The city's urban sociology is shaped within this exceptional ecological setting. In synthesis, it can be said that the "higher" (sociologically speaking) neighborhoods are in the geographically lower portions of the city, and that the lower socioeconomic classes live in the "upper" neighborhoods. The less extreme and more comfortable the climate of a given portion of the city is, the more wealthy and better serviced are its residents, and the more they identify themselves with "La Paz." At the other extreme are the homes of the impoverished sectors, easily identified with "Chukiyawu."

An urban geography so fragmented by unevenness and ravines makes it easy for wards to become like towns or villas, especially in the "popular" neighborhoods, in a kind of urban adaptation of the ancient rural community: each town has its own board of directors, public works, actions, and communal celebrations, as well as a good measure of self-governance.

Historical Development

The Aymara name for the city of La Paz–Chukiyawu, or *Chuki Yapu*–brings to our attention the origins of the city, sitting among the highlands that cover a large part of the ancient *Qullasuyu*. Before the Colonial era, *Chuki Yapu* was comprised of corn-producing communities, made up of people from diverse Aymara *ayllu* (kin-groupings), within a framework of vertical access to a range of ecological niches (Murra 1972).

In 1548 a new Spanish city, *Nuestra Señora de La Paz*, was added to the diverse indigenous population. La Paz fulfilled a variety of functions: it was the center for the exploitation of gold production (recalling the significance of the Aymara name, "parcel of precious metal"); it was the door for the exploitation of coca in the neighboring subtropical *yungas*; and it was a convenient stop on the routes between Lima and Potosi. Since then, in this fashion, the city has maintained a dual structure from an ethnic, linguistic and social point of view. It was, and is, a city of Indians, as well as a city of Spaniards–Chukiyawu and La Paz.

This duality, already evident by the sixteenth century (Saignes 1978), persisted throughout the colonial period with a clear ethnic division in the city's residential areas. We find this, for example, in 1781 during the celebrated siege that occurred as a result of the indigenous uprising led by Tupaq Amaru and Tupaq Katari. Consequently, by conscious design, the Spanish population who were under attack decided to fortify only their own neighborhoods, whereas the Indian parishes decided to join the side of the besiegers. In addition, when general hunger caused by the siege increased, the Spanish-Creole population decided to fire their indigenous servants. Many of the latter also joined the uprising (Siles 1980).

Already by the epoch of the Republic, the persistent importance of ethnic categories in order to understand the social and even geographic dimensions of the city becomes even stronger, as is evidenced in studies by Guardia (1971), Leonard (1948), Lindert and Verkoren (1982) and Schoop (1981).

After the confiscation of various *haciendas*–stemming from the Agrarian Reform of 1953 as well as the subsequent Urban Reform–allowed urban growth, the city began to climb the hillside toward the highlands, finally stopping in what came to be called "El Alto" of La Paz. In 1988, owing to a constant pattern of expansion in the old valley of Chuki Yapu, El Alto broke off from La Paz and was declared an official city, converting it into the third largest city in the nation after La Paz and Santa Cruz.

Here, for the purposes of this chapter, we will dispense with this recent administrative division and speak of La Paz and El Alto as a continuous urban conglomeration.

Demographic History

The most recent demographic census carried out in the city of La Paz (which then encompassed El Alto) was carried out in 1976. It produced the following data that are of special interest for our concerns (INE 1980):

• Total urban population	654,713
• Immigrants from other places	250,313 (38 %)
• Immigrants of Aymara provinces from the same department	160,487 (25.3 %)

The annual rate of growth between 1950 and 1976 was:

• La Paz	3.5 %
• Bolivia as a whole	2.1 %
• Rural areas as a whole	1.0 %

La Paz/El Alto was the largest urban agglomeration in the country. It was second in terms of its rate of growth, outstripped by Santa Cruz in the subtropics, even though, in absolute numbers, it constantly received the largest annual contingent of in-migrants.

It is estimated that the annual rhythm of urban growth has accelerated between 1976 and 1990, above all in El Alto, where the yearly rate of growth is probably well over 10 percent; as of 1986, in-migrants were on the order of 47 percent of the total (Franqueville and Aguilar 1988:25). Unfortunately, there are no available census materials for the years after 1976. On the basis of surveys and the projections of the National Statistical Institute (INE), I can affirm that currently, La Paz, as the primary urban center of the nation, has easily accumulated a million residents, with perhaps some 850,000 in the valley of La Paz and some 350,000 in the new city of El Alto (which, in 1950, had only 11,000 residents).

Because of the above-noted statistical limitation, I will continue to refer to the data generated by the 1976 census as well as a survey that was carried out by my colleagues and myself in 1976, concerning Aymara immigrants from rural points of origin (Albó et al. 1981).

CULTURAL AND LINGUISTIC DISTRIBUTION

Basic Data, 1976

Linguistic data provide one of the best quantitative indices that I can utilize to study the sociocultural duality of the city. According to the 1976 census, it was difficult to survive in the city without being able to command the dominant language–Spanish. About 96 percent of the population over five years of age reported knowing Spanish, with some 88 percent of the heads of households reporting that Spanish was the predominant language used in the home. Even more significant are the figures concerning the various languages known. In rounded percentages, the figures are as follows for the population over five years of age:

Monolingual:	Spanish	44%	(-)
	Aymara	3%	(+)
Multilingual:	Spanish-Aymara	42%	(+)
	Spanish-Quechua	7%	
	Spanish-Quechua-Aymara	3%	

The plus or minus sign next to the percentages indicates my estimate of the principal exaggerations (- sign) or underestimates (+ sign) on the part of the 1976 census owing to distortions that the factor of prestige creates.[2]

Beyond the degree of confidence I can assign to census data, the most impressive figures reflect the imposition of Spanish on the residents of La Paz, in that it is imperative for survival; nonetheless, the predominant condition is one of multilingualism, which is in turn an indication of an intercultural reality.

In La Paz, access to Spanish is easier not only because there are more and better educational services but also because there are many more opportunities that facilitate, and even demand, the functional use of Spanish. Because of this (and limiting ourselves to those who have had no formal instruction, and only to those parts of the country where there are significant numbers of Quechua and Aymara), one notes a clear correlation between the increase in monolingualism involving Spanish as well as a concomitant decrease in monolingualism involving indigenous languages and rising levels of urbanization.

MONOLINGUALS

	% of Spanish		% of Indian	
	men	women	men	women
•Rural areas (<2,000)	4	3	78	84
•Intermediate urban areas	38	17	24	32
•La Paz/El Alto	44	18	17	23

Language, Age, and Gender

Figure 7.1 indicates the distribution of languages according to age cohorts in 1976. The most notable feature is the growth of Spanish monolingualism in the youngest cohorts, probably born in, or at least brought up and educated in, La Paz.

This pattern begins to reverse itself, however, in the cohort between 15 and 20 years of age. The reason is that this age group is heavily composed of labor immigrants who originate, above all, from the rural sectors of the rest of the department of La Paz. Among these immigrants are many women who arrive at a tender age primarily in order to work as domestic servants.

Also note that it is precisely the age group between 15 and 40 who are most economically active, and that the number of monolingual speakers of indigenous languages all but disappears, but primarily among the men. It is easier for the women to remain monolingual, even in this age range, if only because they have no other job besides that of "housewife." For both genders among those less than 15 years old, there is also a residual number who do not know Spanish; this probably represents "passive" migrants who came with their families and who work as servants or at other low skilled jobs, who have not had the opportunity to attend school in La Paz.

Language, Culture, and Immigration

As a consequence of the historical overview presented above, the Aymara population and culture has been fed by three sources over the last few decades, namely (1) Aymara who were born and raised in the city, and whose antecedents may also have been in La Paz for generations; (2) the sectors who have recently come to the city, formed by rural communities that have been absorbed by the ever-expanding boundaries of the city; (3) Aymara born in the provinces who have come to La Paz. At the same time, the population affiliated with the Spanish language and cultural orientation are also fed by three sources: (1) people of this background who were born and raised in La Paz; (2) immigrants from the interior of the country (but outside the Department of La Paz) and, above all, from other smaller,

FIGURE 7.1 AGE PYRAMID AND LINGUISTIC PROFILE: LA PAZ, BOLIVIA

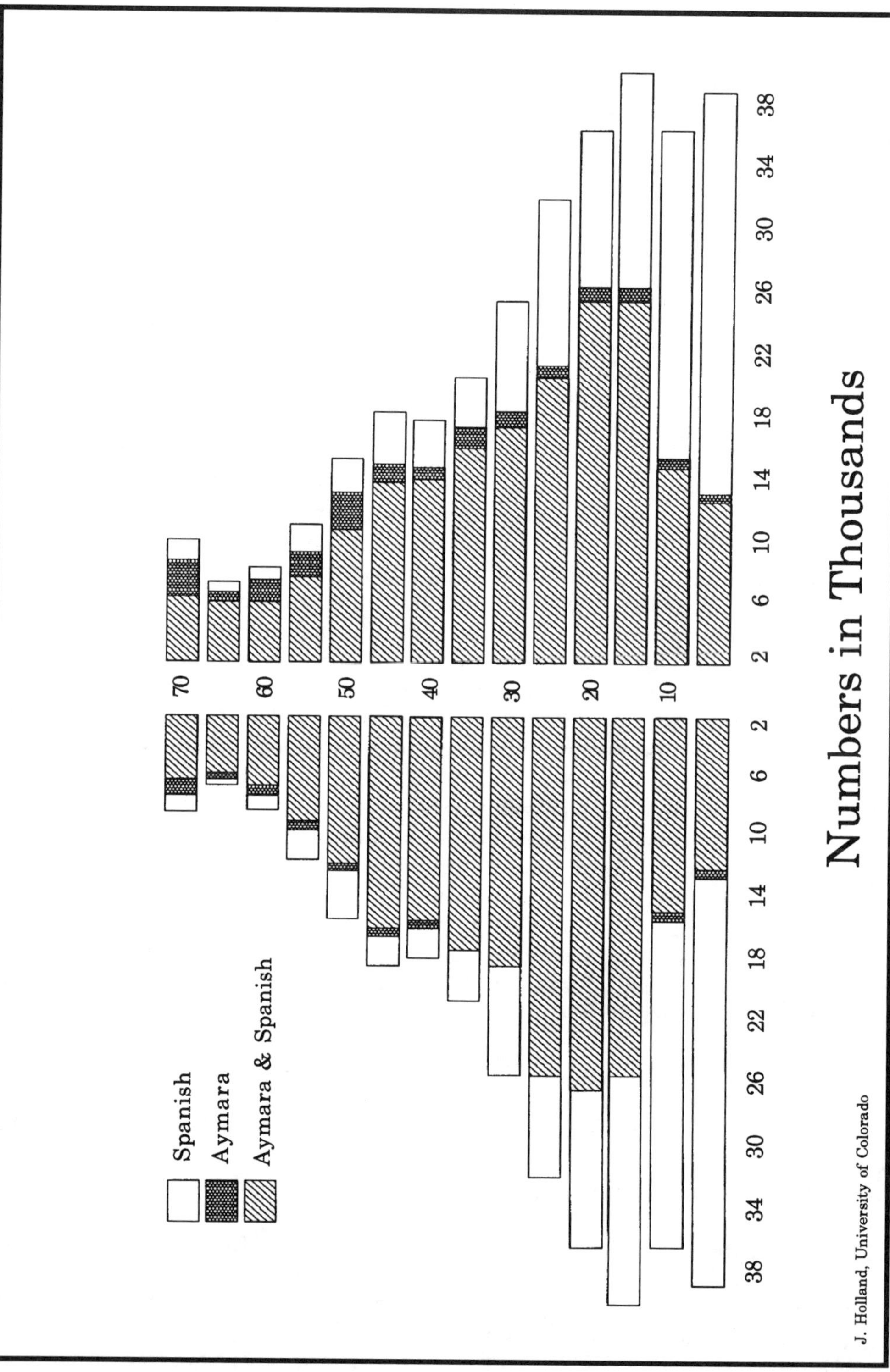

(Based on 1976 Census)

urban centers; (3) the descendents of Aymara born in the city (and, to a lesser degree, those who were brought up in La Paz from an early age) who have lost their initial cultural identity and who have clearly passed into the dominant cultural group.

The 10 percent who know Quechua correspond almost exclusively to recent immigrants from diverse urban and rural areas of the country where Quechua is spoken (including a small sector to the north of the Department of La Paz). We should not forget that, at the national level, Quechua is the largest of the indigenous languages, with its speakers comprising some 38 percent of the national total, as opposed to about 28 percent who speak Aymara, according to the 1976 census.

I do not consider the very small group of foreign immigrants here. In the twentieth century neither La Paz nor Bolivia in general has had massive European immigration. There have only been small groups of such immigrants, who have had an undeniable influence on the economy of the country, but who have had little impact on the linguistic and cultural configuration of the city.

The 1976 census offers other data of interest concerning the importance of immigration on the sociocultural and linguistic composition of La Paz. This will be clear if considered in terms of three distinct groups, namely those that were born in the city (among whom are also Aymara), who make up some 64 percent of the total; immigrants from the rest of the Department of La Paz (very often, of Aymara origin), that comprise 25 percent of the total; and immigrants from the rest of the country (the majority of whom are from cities of intermediate size) that make up only 11 percent of the total.

The distinction between the second and third groups is fundamental. In contrast to expectations, the third group actually has the highest proportion of professionals, much greater than among the population actually born in the capital. On the other hand, the second group has the lowest level of professional representation among the three, with the first group occupying an intermediate position. (See Table 7.1., which further delineates these groups by occupation and by gender.)

In addition, among those who have arrived in La Paz from other departments in the country, the group that is most professionalized and oriented toward the Spanish language, there are actually a majority (53 percent) who also speak an indigenous language—above all, Quechua (46 percent)—although they may only use it occasionally. Nonetheless, this bilingual and bicultural background is much more predominant in the two other groups described above who together make up some 89 percent of the urban population.

Origins and Waves of the Residents

The case most worthy of analysis is the second group, immigrants born in the Department of La Paz. Both in the city and in their points of origin, these immigrants form a social group that is clearly recognized and that is given the name "residents" in both Spanish and Aymara.

Within this group there is a small minority that comes from the villages and from the mining towns. There are also a few that come from communities and villages located in a Quechua enclave in the north of the Department of La Paz. The great majority, however, have emigrated from rural Aymara communities. Because of this, 89 percent of this group knows an indigenous language, particularly Aymara (87 percent).

There have been many migratory "waves" of residents. Limiting ourselves to the

TABLE 7.1 CITY OF LA PAZ, OCCUPATIONAL DISTRIBUTION BY SEX AND BY PLACE OF ORIGIN (1976 CENSUS).

	Men				Women			
	TOTAL	Born in La Paz	Born in the rest of the department	Born in the rest of the nation	TOTAL	Born in La Paz	Born in the rest of the department	Born in rest of the nation
0. Professionals	8.2	8.3	3.0	20.3	12.1	10.7	2.5	28.2
1. Managers	2.0	1.8	0.6	3.8	1.0	0.9	0.8	1.2
2. Office Workers	12.0	12.9	5.9	21.5	13.3	16.7	2.1	20.4
3. Businessmen	7.2	6.2	7.0	6.7	23.6	23.3	20.4	12.6
4. Farmers	2.5	11.6	3.8	0.6	1.0	10.7	2.1	0.1
5. Transportation workers	6.5	7.3	5.9	4.8	—	—	—	—
6. Artisans I	32.5	29.2	39.5	16.9	7.2	8.8	6.2	5.7
7. Artisans II	6.4	5.2	9.3	3.1	2.3	2.8	2.1	1.1
8. Wage Laborers	6.1	4.3	8.8	2.1	1.2	1.3	1.6	0.7
9. Service Providers	10.8	7.6	11.4	15.6	34.8	20.8	51.4	27.2
Unemployed	5.3	5.6	4.6	4.4	3.5	3.8	2.9	2.7
Total %	100.0	100.0	100.0	100.0	100.0	100.0	100.0	100.0
Thousands	1502	674	625	203	689	317	243	129
% of Total	100.0	44.9	41.6	13.5	100.0	46.0	35.3	18.7

relatively recent past, the great boom occurred starting from the Reform *and* the Agrarian Revolution of 1953. Both developments substantially modified the socioeconomic structure of Bolivian agriculture, insofar as they abolished the feudal hacienda system that comprised the greater part of the valleys and *yungas* (which are very fertile and productive) and the best areas of the highlands (which are more arid).

Prior to this period of social change, Chukiyawu was primarily made up of Aymara residents in the city, some of whom had been there for a number of generations. The principal permanently resident immigrant Aymara group was made up of the surplus population from the rural communities–people who had been able to escape, or were thrown out of, the haciendas. The majority of Aymara were concentrated in the slopes of Villa Victoria, Callampaya, and, above all, Chijini, which was closer to the highlands where the Aymara come from, and where the residents dedicated themselves primarily to commercial and artisan activities. Chijini was specifically the locale where the fiesta of the *Señor del Gran Poder* was established, which, as we will see below, has now become one of the most important symbols of the actual persistence of Chukiyawu (Albó and Preiswerk 1986).

During this same period, during any part of a given year, but most specifically after the harvest, there was another significant but transitory group. Originating from numerous haciendas in the area, these migrants came from the fields into the city to work in the homes of their bosses. Some came transporting foodstuffs, providing the fundamental basis for urban provisionment. Other men and women arrived for short-term periods in the city to complete diverse obligations relating to *pongueaje*: that is, free domestic service for the households of their *patrones*. These situations explains why, during this period, there was such a high level of bilingualism, including among the white middle- and upper-class population. Knowing Aymara could even have been a sign of status, insofar as it was a correlate of hacienda ownership, implying regular access to these kinds of *pongos*, or servants, in both the province and in La Paz.

After the Agrarian Reform of 1953, this arrangement was drastically modified. Subsequently, the first major wave of migration to La Paz took place, principally involving nonpeasants–that is to say, *patrones*, labor bosses, and people with other jobs linked to the hacienda system such as lawyers and other functionaries from the intermediate towns whose livelihood depended to a great extent upon the prevailing socioeconomic order. Many of these people left the provinces because of concerns about agitation taking place in many agricultural areas, or simply because they were no longer constrained by the ancient regime.

These new immigrants were the first to make up the organized groups of "residents," whose primary point of reference had to do with their villages of origin–normally, some village of *vecinos*, that is to say, of *mistis* (mestizos) or *q'aras* (non-Indians). This provided the roots for the formation of "cultural centers" on the part of those from a given village. Because of these same circumstances, however, the focus of migrants' cultural centers was not so much the point of origin as it was mutual aid among immigrants to facilitate their urban adaptation, as occurs in Lima and in other cities. The existence of businesses (such as hotels, workshops, and even including some public offices) with a high proportion of employees from a given provincial town can only be accounted for in this fashion.

This first kind of immigrant, a *vecino* from the provinces, was able to make a fairly easy transition into the professional and bureaucratic world of the middle class–a vast sector in the capital city. There is also a signficant economic sector made up of intermediaries and merchants that have established a new kind of relationship with the provinces, filling a gap that developed, momentarily, when the agricultural supply system tied to the haciendas began to fall apart. Apart from the latter entrepreneurs, who tend to be more bilingual and inter-cultural, these early residents have been able to adjust very rapidly to the urban cultural model associated with the Spanish language, even though it is not uncommon that certain ties to the village of origin are maintained, especially in regard to the fiesta of the village's patron saint.

The following wave came from the same provinces: that is to say, from the same communities of origin (that had never really stopped sending migrants to the city), and from the ex-haciendas, now reconstituted as peasant communities. In the first stage, the termination of the hacienda system reduced population pressure on arable land. But this provided only a few years of relief, above all because upon not having to provide free labor to the hacienda the available labor time of any single individual doubled. This wave has increased in size every year since the 1960s. The great urban expansion of La Paz is principally due to this phenomenon. In point of fact, this wave makes up the great majority of the so-called residents.

Occupationally, the immigrants from provincial communities of this second and current wave are dedicated to informal activities, above all tied to popular arts and crafts, construction, and, to a lesser extent, to small businesses and to low-paying jobs. Since the 1970s the participation of this group in the informal sector has greatly increased. They also tend to form centers related to their points of origin, but these—in contrast to the associations mentioned previously—are usually called "Action Centers" of this or that village or town, whose activities have much more to do with the point of origin.

In the following pages, if not otherwise specified, when we refer to the "residents" we are referring to all of them, even though because of both their importance and because of our greater familiarity with them the data are most applicable to those who originate from Aymara peasant communities.

Language

Culturally, the residents are characterized by an ambiguous situation, and oscillate between their provincial communities of origin and their new urban residence, La Paz. They are deeply concerned about their individual social mobility in the urban setting but, at the same time, their achievements in this regard can only be expressed vis-à-vis their compatriots, given that non-Aymara either do not care or ignore them. This is actually one of the fundamental bases for the persistence of Chukiyawu in the heart of La Paz.

The residents' linguistic behavior reflects this cultural ambiguity. Even though there is a tendency to switch to Spanish once they are established in the capital, more than a quarter affirm that they prefer to use their "mother" tongue in their homes, and in this case—more than in the other two groups—it is likely that the actual figure is very much higher but has been lowered in the census due to "impression management." The status quo is that, even at home, the use of two languages is intermingled, which intensifies the use of Aymara above all among adult women, but also Spanish, especially among school-age children.

In contrast to this group of residents, among those born in La Paz (representing about 64 percent of the total urban population), the tendency toward Castellanization is the most notable, but never to the level manifested by the more qualified immigrants from the interior of the country. It is significant that, including those persons born in the city, approximately one out of every six families prefers to continue speaking Aymara at home, and that two out of three families know this language. From this last statistic, it is probable that most families do not keep Aymara alive as a simple memory of a vanishing past, but rather as a fully functioning medium of communication in certain specific situations that we will analyze below.

Language and Occupation

According to the 1976 census, the residents, who at best constitute only 25 percent of the total population of La Paz, represent a much larger proportion of the city's work force: they are 42 percent of the economically active male population and 35 percent of the working women. As we see in Table 7.2, this group–in contrast to the third group–are situated by preference in lower-level occupations, above all in small-scale, familiar, craft and artisan pursuits, as well as in the less-skilled levels of the service and manual labor sectors of the occupational structure. In the case of women, the majority of jobs are held in the areas of domestic service and small businesses.

We will focus on the economically active population, fifteen years of age or more, whose linguistic correlates are detailed in Table 7.2. Unfortunately, the occupational categories utilized in the census have some limitations that impede greater analytic precision. On the basis of the data presented in the table, we can group occupations vis-à-vis three broad categories: Spanish, indigenous, and transitional.

The Spanish encompass the first three occupational categories in the table: professionals, those who occupy managerial positions, and employees in offices. These are the occupations that manifest, in a consistent fashion, Spanish language utilization, including monolingual emphasis in this language.

There is, overall, a curious situation: among the immigrant residents from a peasant Aymara background, there are some 12 percent female managers that continue to be monolingual Aymara speakers. This statistic might reflect, in part, a technical deficiency in the census in regard to the determination of categories. It also indicates, in part, the possibility of realizing certain levels of economic achievement without necessarily having to speak Spanish, in terms of reaching entrepreneurial status in certain commercial or artisan enterprises.

But, on the whole, a Spanish language orientation predominates in this group. Thus, it is quite illuminating, for example, that some 50 percent of the women office workers born in the provinces report that they do not know how to speak Aymara. Is it that they actually do not know, or that they do not want to know? I propose that office employees, specifically women, more so than those in other occupational pursuits, experience greater pressure to speak Spanish once they have reached certain levels in this profession–a profession characteristic of La Paz rather than Chukiyawu.

The most clearly indigenous occupational pursuit is that of farmer, an occupation that is practiced to some extent in areas on the edge of the city. In this occupational category one finds the highest percentages of those that know and use Aymara and, concomitantly, the lowest percentage of those that know and use Spanish. This characteristic is so well known that it leads many to the incorrect impression that an Aymara cultural and linguistic orientation is solely correlated with Bolivia's peasant class. The thrust of these data give lie to such a close correlation. Without a doubt, though, this is the occupational

TABLE 7.2   CITY OF LA PAZ, LANGUAGE ACCORDING TO OCCUPATION, PLACE OF BIRTH AND SEX. (ONLY THE ECONOMICALLY ACTIVE POPULATION IN THE DEPARTMENT OF LA PAZ, 1976 CENSUS).

PART 1

| | Daily Languages | | | Languages Known | | | | | | | |
| | | | | Men | | | | Women | | | |
Born in the rest of the department	Thousands of Families	Ay %	Sp %	Thousands	Only Sp %	Only Ay %	Both Ay-Sp %	Thousands	Only Sp %	Only Ay %	Both Ay-Sp %
0. Professionals	1.8	4	95	1.9	15		80	0.6	31	1	58
1. Managers[a]	0.4	12	87	0.4	14	2	80	0.2	9	12	77
2. Office Workers	3.1	6	94	3.7	15		81	0.5	50		38
3. Businessmen	6.3	22	77	4.4	6	3	89	5.9	4	14	81
4. Farmers	2.0	57	42	2.4	4	22	72	0.5		51	48
5. Trans. Workers	3.0	8	92	3.7	6		93	—	—	—	—
6. Artisans I	20.0	22	78	24.7	4	3	92	1.5	8	18	72
7. Artisans II	4.7	26	74	5.8	4	6	89	0.5	6	10	81
8. Wage Laborers	14.7	28	72	5.5	4	6	88	0.4	5	26	67
9. Service Providers	5.5	18	82	7.1	6	2	89	12.5	6	6	82
Unemployed	2.1	27	72	2.9	8	12	79	0.7	9	25	60
TOTALS	**63.6**	**23**	**73**	**62.5**	**6**	**4**	**88**	**24.3**	**7**	**10**	**78**

TABLE 7.2   CITY OF LA PAZ, LANGUAGE ACCORDING TO OCCUPATION, PLACE OF BIRTH AND SEX. (ONLY THE ECONOMICALLY ACTIVE POPULATION IN THE DEPARTMENT OF LA PAZ, 1976 CENSUS).

PART 2

	Daily Languages			Languages Known							
					Men				Women		
					Only Sp	Only Ay	Both Ay-Sp		Only Sp	Only Ay	Both Ay-Sp
Born in La Paz	Thousands of Families	Ay %	Sp %	Thousands	%	%	%	Thousands	%	%	%
0. Professionals	4.9	2	98	5.6	57		37	3.4	66		29
1. Managers[a]	1.0	1	98	1.2	60		35	0.3	38	1	58
2. Office Workers	6.9	1	99	8.7	57		39	3.3	81		15
3. Businessmen	5.3	10	89	4.2	36	1	61	2.4	17	5	76
4. Farmers	6.2	85	15	7.8	2	33	65	3.4	1	58	41
5. Trans. Workers	3.8	7	93	4.9	18		80	—	—	—	—
6. Artisans I	13.6	12	88	19.7	23	1	74	2.8	29	6	63
7. Artisans II	2.6	18	82	3.5	24	3	71	0.9	23	3	71
8. Wage Laborers	13.2	16	84	2.9	18	3	78	0.4	31	8	59
9. Service Providers	3.9	8	92	5.1	34	1	61	6.6	24	3	71
Unemployed	1.8	13	87	3.8	39	5	54	1.2	43	9	46
TOTALS	**63.4**	**17**	**82**	**67.4**	**30**	**5**	**62**	**31.7**	**35**	**9**	**53**

a. Includes some independent business persons, above all women.

pursuit that most favors the maintenance of indigenous language and culture.

What is of interest in this case is that farmers born in the city continue to be more attached to Aymara than their counterparts who arrive from the provinces. Among the former, there are more monolingual Spanish speakers but also many more who assert that they prefer to use Aymara at home. It is as if the residents arrived in the city as part of a process of social mobility, implying a certain degree of cultural ambivalence, as noted above. On the other hand, farmers born in the city are descendants of peasants from ancient communities that continue to be cut off (and even threatened) within the urban context as a result of the constant expansion of the city. The fact that they continue to pursue agriculture indicates their attitude of resistance, reinforced by the correlative linguistic attitude. Nor is this a matter of the peripheralization of a particular economic activity since its proximity to the city serves to provide a tremendous marketing advantage; rather, the potential of this pursuit is permanently threatened by urban expansion. This fact reinforces farmers' cultural and linguistic loyalties, at least among the adults, who are more preoccupied with economic survival.

The rest of the occupations are of a transitional nature. In all of these, what attracts one's attention is precisely the high number of bilinguals, although they have diverse occupational pursuits.

Some types of businessmen, drivers, and artisans represent those who most need bilingual abilities as a lifestyle, given that their occupational success depends to a great extent upon this ability in order to work in both cultural worlds with grace. At the same time, however, and above all for the drivers, urban occupational pursuits weigh heavily on the individual's personal attitude toward language. Because of this, the majority opt for Spanish as the language of preference in the home.

Among women, occupations involving business and domestic service are of particular importance. Businesswomen's levels of bilingualism are notably less than those of businessmen, basically because the former carry out less prestigious activities. These have either to do with contacts with the provinces or with the "popular" urban settings.

In contrast, the domestic servant, almost by definition, needs to know the language and culture of the *patrons*. Domestic service specifically involves young single women, who see the jobs as an entrance to the urban world. If a young male peasant comes into the city, among other things to learn Spanish ways, the parallel path for the young female peasant is to throw herself into the adventure of domestic service in the city, as difficult as this "adventure" sometimes turns out to be.[3]

Given that these are these general tendencies within each occupation, there are no significant differences between the linguistic behavior of the residents and those born in La Paz, except that the latter increase the proportion of those who speak Spanish an average of approximately 10 percent. This difference reflects, in good part, distinct strata within the same occupation. Note, however, that the census categories hide occupational variations that necessitate further separation in order to be properly analyzed. For example, the rubric of "services" encompasses everything from professional soldiers to draftees, door-to-door salespersons, and domestic servants; the rubric of "artisans" encompasses everything from sophisticated mechanics to housewives who sew in their homes.

Ethnogeographic Distribution

Leonard (1948) has already demonstrated a certain correlation between ethnic origins–

and therefore language–and residential neighborhoods that, at the time, encompassed only what is today the urban center (see Map 7.1). Even though the data are not fully comparable, the 1976 census indicates the concentration of the Aymara population in the higher portions of the valley (above all on the western side), and toward El Alto, which in Leonard's day was still not really urbanized (see Map 7.2). In 1990 these areas continued to have a very high Aymara presence, but the principal area of concentration, whether the Aymara are immigrants or not, was El Alto. According to surveys carried out there in 1987, some 65 percent of the population know Aymara, and another 6 percent know Quechua (SURPO 1988).

This process of ethnogeographic concentration can be better understood in light of general processes of urban growth, illustrated in the work of Guardia (1971) and, above all, in terms of interurban displacement, as analyzed by Lindert and Verkoren (1982). The advance of the urban perimeter is not due solely to the new waves of migration but to a combination of new migrants, plus the relocation of sectors of the population, including those who were born in La Paz and previously resided in other parts of the city. The latter are displaced toward the periphery primarily in their search for their own housing (probably of a very simple kind) that is more accessible toward the inhospitable edges of the city. During the 1970s the displacement was directed principally toward the higher edges of the valley; from the 1980s on it has been directed increasingly toward El Alto, located in the cold highlands, more than 4,000 meters above sea level.

In sum, as a result of this expansion and intra-urban migration, I can affirm that, currently, certain sectors of the city are largely Aymara, above all, on the edges of El Alto; in contrast to what would occur in a large megalopolis, however, in no case can we speak of large neighborhoods formed exclusively by a given social, ethnic, linguistic group. Rather, what is typical is that diverse social and cultural groups reside in the same neighborhood, although certainly the more "popular" classes tend to reside in the steeper and higher parts the neighborhood. In El Alto, the middle class (it is hard to find upper-class residents there) prefer to concentrate along the the major axes of communication for the most part. In some new parts of the city, such locations were even designed specifically to house the middle class. The most "Hispanicized" and exclusive neighborhoods–from Obrajes to Los Pinos, in the lowest part, geographically speaking, of La Paz–are accustomed to being surrounded by the more popular neighborhoods, made up of people who speak Aymara and, not surprisingly, work in a range of domestic occupations such as cooks, nannies, porters, and gardeners. It is worth noting that domestic employees are more abundant in such neighborhoods than in other parts of the city.

A clear concentration of Aymara residents does not occur in La Paz either, in a given community or zone of a single barrio. The trend is much more one of dispersion across many zones, in accordance with occupation and length of time in the city, with only a certain limited degree of concentration in some zones.

CULTURAL BOUNDARIES

The sociocultural base described so far indicates a clear discriminatory situation in which the institutions and the situations of greater social prestige acquire an *criollo* cultural contour and require the use of Spanish, while the Aymara language and culture, possibly in combination with Spanish, are restricted only to those sites of less social prestige.

MAP 7.1 DISTRIBUTION OF THE WHITE POPULATION OF LA PAZ, ACCORDING TO THE 1942 CENSUS

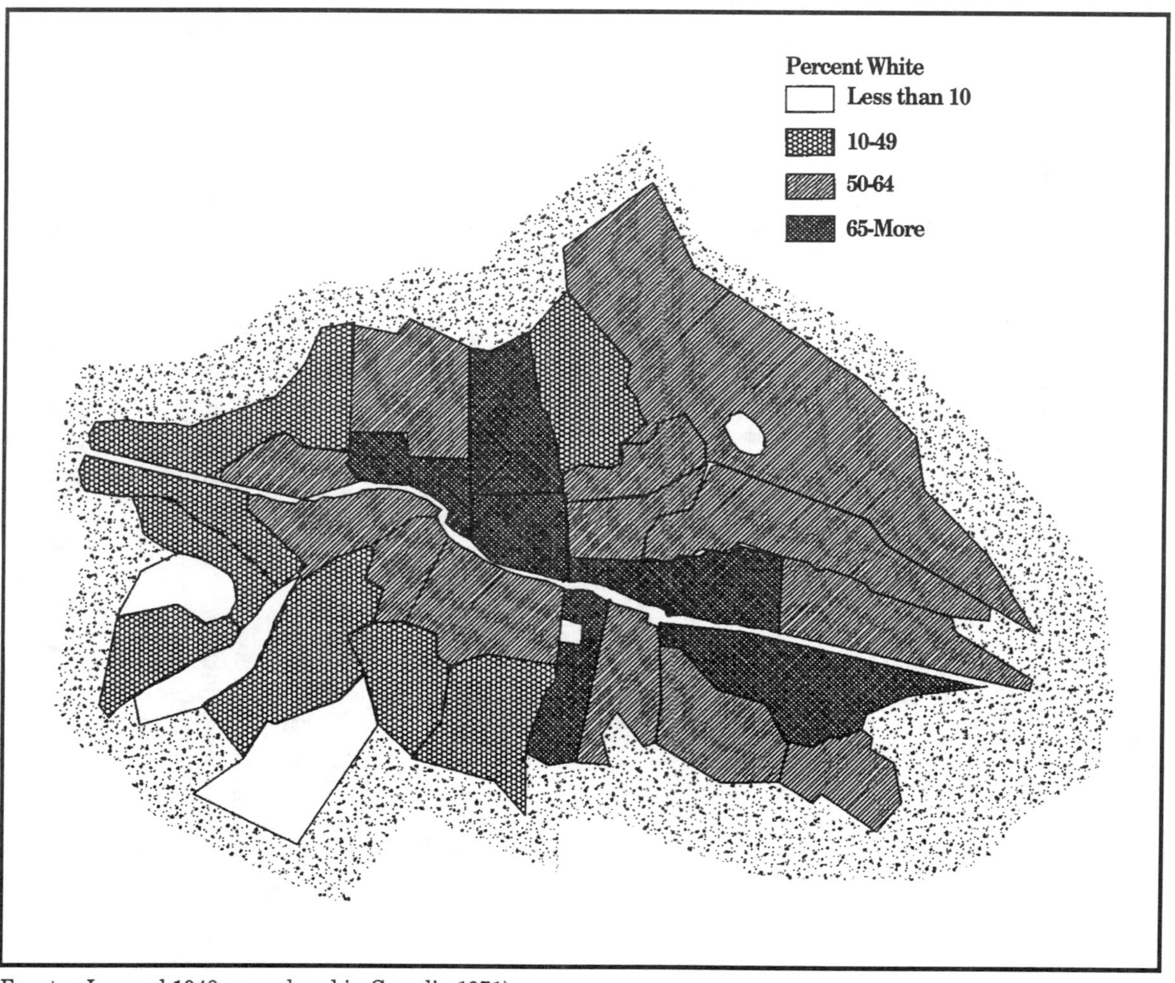

Fuente: Leonard 1948, reproduced in Guardia 1971).

MAP 7.2 DISTRIBUTION OF FAMILIES THAT REGULARLY USE THE AYMARA LANGUAGE IN THE HOME

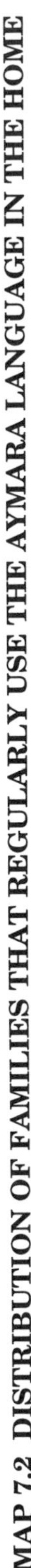

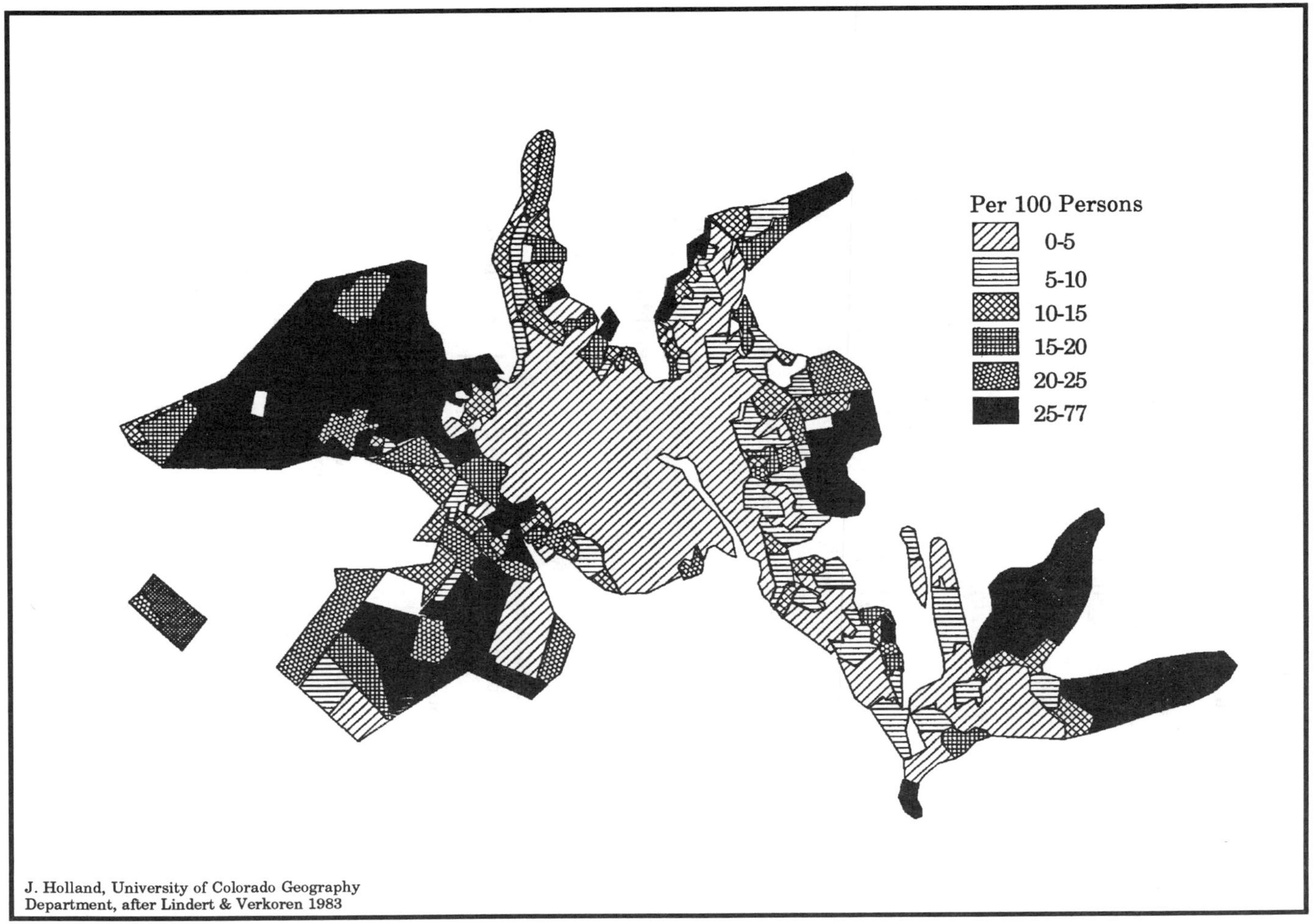
Per 100 Persons
0-5
5-10
10-15
15-20
20-25
25-77
J. Holland, University of Colorado Geography
Department, after Lindert & Verkoren 1983

(Segments of 1976 Census)

The linguistic term for this type of situation is "diglossia." It is typically found in any society characterized by one language (and cultural group) of high prestige and others of lesser prestige. From this one can surmise that, if there is no indication to the contrary, it is better to command the dominant language (as well as its concomitant cultural expressions)–in this case, Spanish. Correspondingly, the language and cultural expressions of lesser prestige become further debased and curtailed by those of the dominant group. Because of this, in consonance with other sociopolitical usages, it becomes very relevant to differentiate the language and the culture of the oppressor from the language and culture of the oppressed (Albó 1974).

Because this is a very generalized situation, it is not necessary to stop here in order to detail every case. We will only insist that this manifests itself in specific situations, including those outlined below.

Exclusive Boundaries of the Dominant Culture

There are situations in which the use of Spanish and the cultural forms of the dominant group are practically imperative even though this involves people who are obviously of Aymara origins. We can classify these into two broad categories: those situations that are appropriate only for "learned" people, and official, public situations.

The Academic World and Formal Education

Included in the first category are practically all academicians, from those in the universities and illustrious educational congresses to the lowest levels of the educational system, including preschools. In the city, it is assumed that these settings imply the sole use of Spanish and of "urban" comportment.

It is notable that, in many cases, including public academic functions dedicated to praising the Aymara language, only Spanish is utilized; if anyone starts using Aymara in order to illustrate a point, it is not done without first asking permission of, or offering apologies to, the audience. There is also a fundamental difficulty deriving from the secular discrimination against oppressed languages. The latter have not had the opportunity to evolve, or have had but have lost the appropriate terminology of a formal, conceptual nature that would be suitable for the academic world.

This exclusivity extends to all the lower levels of formal education. Let us imagine, for example, a peripheral school of El Alto, where a young student arrives–a recent immigrant from the provinces who is not familiar with Spanish. The use of Aymara on the part of the professor would be utilized only as an ultimate recourse, and probably carried out through the use of an interpreter. And if, in the same school, there was a girl in traditional dress, it is likely that she would be held back by the professor for her lack of "civilization," especially if she was already taking the more advanced courses. In one extraordinary case, when some years ago the wife of a poultryman showed up at a university entrance examination, her picture was published in all of the newspapers.

The Official, Public World

The other great exclusive boundary of the dominant culture involves official, public activities: spheres of government, the judicial system, public offices, the military, and so on. If in the provinces there may be occasions when public functionaries may accept the use of a native language in order to establish a minimal level of effective communication, this does not occur in the city.

In fact, this is one of the settings that most deserves denunciation insofar as it involves systematic discrimination against those participants who pertain to the popular classes. It is very typical for the latter to be condescended to; to be called "sonny" (no matter how old they actually are); to receive the slowest service, and to be served last; all this, of course, takes place in a language that the popular classes are the least familiar with (Yapita 1977).

Exclusive Public Places?

Are there any situations that overtly exclude the least prestigious social and ethnic groups? Up to 1952, around which time the dual state system known as "restricted democracy" was dismantled, the answer would be "yes." For example, in 1925, on the occasion of the first centennial of independence, a decree was declared in La Paz prohibiting any Indians from coming into the principal plaza of the capital in order not to give any illustrious visitors a poor impression. The formal repeal of this recent decree occurred simultaneously with the crisis of "restrictive democracy."

Since 1952, the situation has changed noticeably, and it has been confirmed that these kinds of discrimination are not acceptable. Generally, this is certain. But flagrant violations have continued; for example, in certain hotels and restaurants the entrance of prospective clients who appear to be Aymara is prohibited. And it occurs to no one that the stewardesses of the national airlines should dress as *cholitas* (i.e., in indigenous peasant clothes), or that only those who have a dark enough skin color be hired, or that the advice given to passengers also be offered in Quechua and Aymara if only because it is increasingly apparent that passengers are from these cultural and linguistic backgrounds.

But the most important aspect of what occurs in our city is not so much the exclusivity of these dominant sectors–the still-strong remnants of the colonial past–but rather the growing resistance of the urban Aymara. They will no longer tolerate the maintenance of this penumbra.

Traditional Boundaries of the Urban Aymara

In the face of the situation described above, the habitual boundary for the use of the Aymara language and its associated cultural expressions is–as occurs in all oppressed cultures–domestic life and its most natural extensions, such as certain traditional celebrations and rituals, purchasing and selling in the marketplace and in the streets, certain reunions and activities in the popular neighborhoods, and so forth.

This boundary is sufficiently broad to generate its own institutional settings. The most notable case has to do with the innumerable fiestas and celebrations along with the complementary institutions that these generate. For example, each barrio and almost every occupational trade union has its annual *fiesta patronal*, in connection with which there are numerous preparatory meetings, assignments and responsibilities, groups or fraternities of dance and practice, that can last for months at a time.

Another fundamental field has to do with the above-mentioned "residents' centers" that gather compatriots from a given community or village for diverse kinds of social activities. We have already mentioned the contrast between the "cultural centers" involving rural-urban migrants from villages, primarily dedicated to mutual aid between immigrants in order to facilitate their adaptation to the city, as opposed to the "action centers," composed of indigenous peasant immigrants who dedicate their efforts toward the point of origin. In addition, these organizations can assume different trajectories over time, according to how their membership becomes articulated to life in the city, as well as the degree of internal consolidation. But, considering them overall, the difference between these centers in La Paz/Chukiyawu and similar associations in other cities of immigrants, such as Lima, is that in La Paz the emphasis placed on maintaining ties to the point of origin is much stronger.

As in other places, one of the primary activities that attracts participants to these centers is the annual fiesta of the patron saint in the point of origin. Through their respective center, many residents can come together, participate in the fiesta, and, toward this end, also organize duties, meetings, assignments, and so forth, that occupy them in La Paz almost year-round. In addition, the center is the customary catalyst for the organization of support for whatever improvement is needed back in the community or village of origin, including any necessary political support activities. Even by the period of the Agrarian Reform, when the residents were not very well organized, the extent of activities having to do with the unionization of peasants was quite notable.

In a more intimate and familiar environment, we should also mention all of the traditional rituals that, given their adaptations to the new urban context, continue to be functional vis-à-vis various residents' needs. Thus, in the field of health, traditional (and very ritualized) forms of medicine may coexist with modern medicine (which at any rate is very lacking in the "marginal" neighborhoods). There are traditional doctors, termed *yatiris* and *kallawayas* in Aymara, that have migrated because there are actually more opportunities to practice their profession in the city, including the opportunity to treat middle and upper class patients.

Also, there are typically urban adaptations of traditional agricultural rites such as praying for the "fertility" of money. Frequently, on Mondays and Thursdays–days of the "Devil" (that is, of clandestine Andean divinities)–various businesses and other establishments will carry out traditional libations, or burn incense, to entreat "blessings" or economic success.

The world of bazaars and markets is another important extension of this familiar boundary. In this world, where women predominate, there is a permanent interchange between buyers and sellers or among the latter, who develop personal relationships over time that go far beyond an ordinary commercial relationship. Salespersons also form their own associations with directorial boards, led by the oldest practitioners, and have their own fiestas and dance groups.

Cultural Adaptation of Aymara in the Urban Setting

In all of these urban Aymara cultural expressions there is a systematic adaptation to the new urban situation. We have cited, for example, the adaptation of agrarian rituals. In the provinces, *Pacha Mama* (Mother Earth), is referred to above all in order to request the fecundity of fields and of animals; in the city, residents petition for the fertility of money, which also receives the symbolic designation *Phaxsi Mama* (Mother Moon), who is addressed as much as the Mother Earth. Similarly, residents can appeal to *Tio* (Uncle) lord of the underworld, as miners have since colonial days in order to request rich veins of precious metal, in an earlier form of adaptation of these same rituals.

One of the most important characteristics of such urban variations of Aymara culture is the importance that social stratification acquires. This appears, for example in terms of language, during fiestas, and in terms of dress.

Beyond the selection of one or the other language (Albó, in press), the importance of sociolinguistic matrices in other variations of a phonetic, grammatical, and lexical order are central. Thus, Briggs (1981) is able to identify a form of Aymara spoken by *patrones* as opposed to that spoken by the more "popular" sectors. A sophisticated system of social interaction has also evolved that combines aspects of Spanish (*tú / usted, don / doña, señor / señora*, etc.) with Aymara (*jilata, tata / mama, wiraqucha*, or its Spanish equivalent, *caballero*, etc.) or mixed forms, such as the uses with sociological connotations such as *compadre / comadre, padrino / madrina*, or *hijo / hija*.

Another typical adaptation that is utilized in order to emphasize social stratification occurs in the setting of fiestas. In the rural community, these serve above all to reinforce social mobility based on the generosity and the practice of reciprocity among all members of the community. By contrast, social mobility in the city reinforces prestige achieved by only a few on the basis of their greater individual economic success (Albó and Preiswerk 1986; Buechler 1980).

Finally, in a much more visible and permanent fashion, Aymara in the city have developed a sophisticated sense of women's fashion. Undoubtedly, the tendency of the younger generation to switch to Western clothing involves its novelty and variety, as well as the fact that it is more economical. But there continues to be manifest, in women's clothing, a gradation between the dress of the peasant women to the dress of the ex-peasant immigrant (both of whom are called "indians" by urban Aymara), to the *cholas paceñas* and *chotas* (women who have recently abandoned their traditional costume, although they continue to conserve certain features such as braids, loose hair, or carrying things on the back), in order to end, finally, as *señoras* mestizas, or *q'aras*.

These daily indications of stratification, including clothing, are manifested above all in the dress of women. This becomes even more obvious during fiestas, in terms of both street clothes and the costumes and disguises that play an important role and that are worn by the dance groups, all part of the symbolic Aymara cultural world, and that always evolve within a great spirit of creativity that continually introduces new innovations from year to year.

For the existence of this stratification, the urban use of traditional clothing and other features of traditional Aymara feminine dress continue to be important and generate a lucrative market. For the same reason, in La Paz, in contrast to what happens in Lima, it is common for domestic servants who have recently come from the provinces to continue wearing traditional dress. Moreover, through this practice they can presume among themselves, and above all among their compatriots in the village, concerning the variety of their wardrobe. This also explains why, in certain professions, especially that of salesperson, elegant traditional clothing can be a sign of greater prestige, signifying that the wearer has made the transition to being *chota*.

Some clearly Aymara cultural expressions have been part of La Paz's culture and identity for a long time. For example, on the first Tuesday of Carnival, all households in the city carry out the ritual of *ch'alla*, involving libations to favor good luck in the home and in business, and blessings throughout the year, or on the day of *iqiqu* (or *ekeko*), an Aymara divinity, now more well known in the city than in the provinces, characterized by a small figure with mestizo features loaded down with all sorts of articles and goods. Similarly, one of the fiestas most often frequented by everyone in the city is the *alasitas* fair (Aymara for "buy me"), the basis of which is the ritualization of the buying-selling relationship through the massive interchange of miniature objects and money. In spite of its clear Andean features, this fiesta was instituted in the eighteenth century, shortly after the denizens of La Paz were able to break the siege of the Aymara leader Tupaj Katari.

The Reconquest of Institutions by the Aymara

Overall, because of pressure exerted by the dominant society, it is evident that the general tendency of the city is toward increasing levels of castellanization and criollization. In the last few decades, the great demographic weight of the Aymara immigrants in La Paz, combined with their increasing access to education and even professional occupations, has generated a trend in the opposite direction. Thus, it is increasingly evident that Aymara are emerging from the semiclandestine status imposed by the dominant society. Specifically, Aymara are making their presence known in institutional circles that were previously the exclusive purview of the Spanish-speaking world. The following outline provides only a partial indication of the scope of this phenomena.

Peasant Unions

Since 1978, the unionization movement of the peasantry broke its ties to the government in power and began to express its independence and new identity with great assertiveness. This transformation had clear leadership from the Aymara sectors and had, from the beginning, strong cultural components, including language.

The referent of this movement is, above all, rural, but along with this orientation the influence of ex-peasants who are established in the city has been important (Hurtado 1986). The activities of the peasants, moreover, have had an important impact on life in the city. For example, the workers' marches on May 1 now have a notable Aymara presence with all of their cultural symbols of communication: the men with their *ponchos*, horns (*pututus*), and flutes; the women in traditional dress, making their slings crack loudly.

Aymara Politics

Even more significant is the role of the urban Aymara in the appearance of new parties and political movements focused, in large part, on the recovery of ethnic and cultural identity. Even though they aspire to impact the politics of the nation, there is no doubt that they have more of an organizing and rallying function at this point in Aymara circles, both urban and provincial. Since 1978, in each electoral contest there have been one or more parties along these lines, and they always promote Aymara candidates.

The first political parties of this kind were known, generically, as *kataristas* in reference to the celebrated anticolonial leader, Tupaj Katari, whom I referred to above. Among these parties are MRTKL, FULKA, MITKA, the Indian party, and others. Initially, they represented a variety of positions within the new movement, even though the leadership and organizational bases were clearly urban in nature.

Their rare electoral successes do not reflect the transitional nature of these developments, given the effect of intervening factors such as the difficulty of generating large economic resources and problems having to do with internal organization and divisions. But what is important, and almost unique on the continent, is that these organizations have been able to break the practice, as well as public sentiment, concerning a key taboo: namely, that politics is the exclusive prerogative of the non-Indian "others."

Since 1989, a new political current of a populist nature has come together with great vigor and efficiency that is much more identified with the cultural (and political) ambiguity of the urban Aymara. We refer specifically to CONDEPA (Conscience of the Country), founded by *compadre* Carlos Palenque, a popular radio and television impresario and a pioneer in the use of Aymara in the latter medium. His discourse and attraction stems in a large part from his ability to bring the previously marginalized urban Aymara out of the shadows and make them into protagonists. It is, for example, significant that a gathering to close his campaign began with a traditional offering to *Pacha Mama* (Mother Earth), and speeches at the ceremony shifted back and forth between Spanish and Aymara. For the first time, a *cholita* in traditional dress was put up for (and won) the seat of representative for the Department of La Paz. This new group, subsequently called "the Palenque Phenomenon," and the subject of many sociopolitical analyses, has orchestrated surprising electoral victories in the last two elections: crushing victories in El Alto; less overwhelming (but nonetheless, clear) on the edges of La Paz.

Promotional Centers of Aymara Culture

These are many different kinds of centers. Linguistically, the most important is the Institute of Aymara Language and Culture (ILCA), founded by Juan de Dios Yapita. At an official level there is the National Institute of Linguistic Studies (INEL), which has had various Aymara directors and has put much of its emphasis on the Aymara language. In the field of history, the Andean Oral History Workshop (THOA) has created an aperture for the Aymara themselves to investigate their own history. The Aymara Center for Agricultural Development (CADA) advocates Andean productive techniques and technologies. At a more global level there is the Center of Formation and Investigation of Indian Cultures *Chitakolla*, which is not limited to Aymara but nevertheless is clearly dominated by urban Aymara. This and various other groups have typically maintained ties to the political organizations cited above and, on occasion, participate in international indigenous movements.

The situation concerning traditional medicine is somewhat unusual. In contrast to the previous cultural institutions, here it is much clearer that beyond an ideological end and the reassertion of identity that was previously hidden, there are also practical and economic ends as well. We cite, apart from many other indications of a more personal nature, the Society of Traditional Medicine (SOBOMETRA) and the Association of *Kallawayas* (Quechuas who utilize the dead language of *pukina*; see Girault 1989).

Another dimension is manifest in the field of entertainment. To try to count the musical, folklorist, and artisan groups would prove an endless task. The majority got their start as clubs among friends or as a dance troupe and afterward became devoted in one of the numerous and concurrent locales of the fiesta of Chukiyawu, or in the fiesta clubs of La Paz, where food and spectacle are combined together. From there, the more successful can produce recordings, act on radio or television, and undertake tours outside the country.

Such cases can be multiplied in other, less institutionalized arenas. For example, a recent car race featuring women drivers generated much commentary because, to the surprise of the spectators posted at the finish line, a *cholita*, dressed to the hilt in traditional clothing, won the contest and left her competitors (from high society, no less!) in the dust. Although her co-driver (another *cholita*) was dressed in a more functional pair of overalls, the former wanted to emphasize with her clothing the fact that, in this previously restricted setting, someone of Aymara ancestry had won.

Religion

Beyond the traditional Aymara practices cited in the previous section, we would like here to refer to other innovations that involve a broadening of the accepted interstices of the Aymara world.

A first advance is the fact that certain Aymara fiestas have come to transcend a particular neighborhood or profession. The most notable case is that of the *Fiesta del Señor de Gran Poder*. This involves what was initially a secret cult. Subsequently, and in the middle of great controversy and conflict, the Señor became the patron of a new neighborhood where, at that time, many of the Aymara immigrants who had businesses resided. The fiesta in this neighborhood during the decade of the 1970s became a huge celebration that affected the entire city and has today become one of the principal ceremonies identified specifically with La Paz.

In a study carried out in 1984 it was discovered that, in spite of this expansion, the direct participants in the *Fiesta del Gran Poder* continue to be the urban Aymara. This includes some 8,000 dancers, organized into 58 troupes or companies, plus some 2,000 additional participants (without even estimating the hundreds of thousands of spectators). Approximately one-half (49 percent) were born outside of the city, but 88 percent knew Aymara; those who only knew Spanish made up only 5 percent. Because of this, when this fiesta began to be limited by its neighborhood boundaries, participants insisted on the right to hold festivities in exclusive, central parts of the city, citing the great interest of tourists and mass media. At this point we can say that Chukiyawu symbolically "took over" La Paz (Albó and Preiswerk 1986).

Taking up another dimension, the Aymara have also won space in terms of the religions officially accepted by the dominant society. This takeover began in terms of very marginalized evangelicals, oriented to the word and the text of the Bible and, because of this, very interested in the linguistic dimension. Even though their pursuit of such activities was carried out primarily in the provinces, religious centers–which conducted their affairs in Aymara, or on a bilingual basis–very rapidly began to spring up in marginalized parts of the city, as did preachers in both languages that began to be heard on the radio and in some of the popular and crowded plazas. All of this activity came accompanied by extensive religious efforts directed specifically at Aymara speakers. In a number of these Protestant religious groups, such as the Methodists, Adventists, Lutherans, and Baptists, a good part of the leadership has now fallen to people of Aymara background.

In terms of Catholicism, the penetration of Aymara culture has been more recent and limited primarily to the rural sector. The stimulus was the Vatican Council II that ended the monopoly of Latin, favoring instead the use of vernacular languages for the liturgy, as well as other very minor changes–for example, in liturgical ornaments and in musical rhythms. But in spite of a very rich heritage of indigenous ritual, the church continues to present an essentially Roman liturgy in Aymara. This partial change, generated in the provinces, encounters more difficulties in Chukiyawu, in part because church leadership remains more firmly in the hands of a clerical class that is foreign or that is seldom of

Aymara descent.

Among Protestant groups the penetration of the Aymara world is primarily in terms of language. In given urban Aymara groups, conversion to some form of Protestantism is usually associated with Aymaras' desire for "modernization" by breaking old beliefs and traditional social ties. Their model seems to be one of maintaining an Aymara identity but with a "gringo" appearance, to be "Indians with white skin," as is suggested by the title of a recent book by Stroebele-Gregor (1989) about an Adventist community of urban Aymara.

What is both new and significant over the last decade is the rise of a new ecumenical movement on the part of some of these Aymara religious leaders–above all, Methodists, Catholics, and Lutherans–who have taken a further step, and seek to bring out into the open Aymara beliefs and rites. For those involved, the latter are not either superstitions or simple "customs" but rather an authentic religion that does not have to be destroyed in order for adherents to become or be Christian. Once again, the leadership of this movement is, to a great extent, in the hands of urban Aymara (Centro de Teología Popular 1986, 1987).

MEANS OF COMMUNICATION

Aymara advances in the area of mass and social communications, deserve their own treatment because of their achievements, and because they involve a new form of rural-urban articulation in many cases. These have been spectacular in the world of radio; they are present, although in a much more attenuated form, in other media.

Radio

The city of La Paz has some twenty-two transmitters. The primary broadcast language is Spanish, by a large margin. But especially since the 1960s, with the advent of the transistor radio, transmission in Aymara has made notable advances, to the point that it is the exclusive language used on some of the urban stations. Only a minority of stations do not use Aymara at all. This situation has also been aided by recent legislation that privileges the use of programs in the appropriate language of each region.

On the basis of their linguistic and cultural deportment, I can classify the radio stations of La Paz into four groups. The following comes from a study carried out in 1979 that we complete in the following text by noting the most significant changes that have occurred in the 1980s.

a. Aymara Stations

In 1979 there were three such stations. One of them, Radio San Gabriel, is run by the Catholic Church and had a primarily educational and informative function in rural areas where it has, by far, the largest audience. In the city, the recent immigrants are the ones who tune in above all. The four other stations are commercial (two of them almost primarily for artisans) and have a much smaller broadcasting range. Because of this, and because of their general orientation, they have audiences of primarily urban Aymara. The most recent of these stations (Radio Abaroa), the first to opt specifically for an audience in El Alto, was not included in this census of 1979. Later, however, ownership changed and this station became a type "c" station, described below.

b. Bilingual Stations

In 1979 there were two such stations: Radio Méndez and Radio Progreso, both of which transmitted locally. In the 1980s two stations were added to the list. One of these was Radio Metropolitana, with a primarily urban range, featuring the announcer-turned politician-Carlos Palenque, to whom we referred above. The three stations are primarily commercial and are described briefly below. Each station is characterized by the frequent use of both languages. In the beginning, these were presented in clearly differentiated programs and time slots. The third station had recourse to bilingualism throughout all of its programming.

The bilingual dimension of the Méndez and Progreso stations came about as a result of the revitalization of key Aymara organizations. The Méndez station began with an Aymara folkloric festival as a result of which, despite the intentions of the owner, the Cultural Center Tupaj Katari was created in 1971. This organization evolved over the course of time into a new peasant unionization movement and into Aymara political parties referred to above. In 1976 Tupaj Katari, which had always dreamed of having its own radio station, acquired 25 percent of the stock of the Radio Progresso station with money obtained from charging fees to participate in the above-mentioned folkloric festival. As a result, Radio Progresso began to broadcast more frequently in Aymara; apart from other morning programs during the week, the station began to broadcast exclusively in Aymara every Saturday and Sunday, with radio announcers from the cultural center. One of the priorities of the programming had to do with communication between the urban Aymara residents and their communities of origin. Subsequent economic and political disagreements have greatly reduced the importance and the audience of this station.

The eruption of Radio Metropolitana in the 1980s modified the scene. Carlos Palenque, the owner, better known as *el compadre*, initiated a new style, giving the highest broadcast priority to an "open mike" program in which a given participant, generally from the popular sectors, was allowed to speak in either Spanish or Aymara, according to the case, about his or her issues or concerns. This was not a simple matter of philanthropy, given that each participant had to pay before holding forth. But it became evident that, by giving the microphone to these social sectors, an important need that had been previously neglected was being fulfilled. In this fashion, the station and its *compadre* director became part of the voice of the urban popular classes and, at the same time, a kind of "consultancy of the air" that offered solutions to problems–solutions based on a paternalistic pedagogy and a politically populist focus. In recent years this station has come to hold the largest audience in La Paz and has constituted, together with its complementary television station, the political basis of power for its promoter.

c. Spanish Stations (with Early Morning Programming in Aymara)

In 1979 this was the predominant orientation, utilized by eight broadcasters. This was and is the approach of most of the institutional stations, including the official radio station of the Bolivian government (Illimani), two stations run by unions, and two religious stations. The latter have increased their Aymara programming in the 1980s, to such a level that they now approach the type "b" stations. A number of stations broadcast in Aymara in order to have a national audience. The rest of the stations are commercial.

These stations either produce their own programs or, more frequently, sell time during the morning when the Aymara programming is run. The latter generally involves either

Aymara announcers/producers who promote their own ends, or institutions interested in reaching the station's audience.

d. Spanish Stations

In 1979 there were only four such stations, all commercial. Also included here is the station run by the National Army, which is infrequently listened to except for when, on the occasions of a military coup, it becomes one of the only stations authorized to be on the air. In such cases the military station has been obliged, of course, to include messages in Aymara and Quechua.

In the previous decade almost all of the stations that transmitted on the modulated frequency were united (with the exception of one religious station); this involves mostly specialized sections of radio stations that also transmit in the medium wave and/or short wave, possibly also in Aymara, but in terms of other programming. But it is a fact that the new FM mode has been considered an exclusively Spanish medium, utilized and listened to by the dominant urban elites and a new "modernized" generation.

Audience Differentials

Naturally, the radios that broadcast exclusively in Spanish appeal primarily to an audience that speaks the same language, a class that is predominantly middle and upper. The exclusively Aymara stations appeal to the other side of the social spectrum: the intermediate and bilingual sectors, among which are found the majority of the urban Aymara population. But within this group one finds more specialized audiences according to the general style of the programming and the stylistic orientation that a given station makes upon changing the language of orientation in its programming. We will analyze these variations in terms of the more Aymara sector of the city–that is, immigrants from the provinces, or those we call residents.

Figure 7.2 compares the preferred hours by the residents and by their peasant counterparts in the highlands in 1979. Within the close similarity between the beginning and the end of the work day, the residents, who enjoy artificial light and have a different work cycle, extend somewhat their workday, and take much more advantage of the midday break. It is likely that, during the 1980s, when there was a proliferation of television stations, including a bilingual channel, the urban radio audience has suffered a significant drop.

On the other hand, Table 7.3 demonstrates the primary preferences of the residents in 1976 and 1979, before Radio Metropolitana entered the scene. For 1979 we also emphasize, as a reference, the options of the Aymara peasants from the highlands, which is the point of origin of most of the residents.[5]

The first significant fact is that for this sector the exclusively Spanish stations are of almost no significance. There is a decided preference for stations that include some form of Aymara programming. Also, as in indicated in Figure 7.2, the audience is larger in the morning hours, during which there is much programming in Ayamra.

On the other hand, there is a clear change in the stations that are preferred in the provinces as opposed to those in the city. Upon immigrating, however, migrants switch to urban stations that are exclusively broadcast in Aymara and are dedicated to this audience. Part II of Table 7.3 indicates that if we add up the first and second preference, the following of these two Aymara stations is even greater.

FIGURE 7.2 PEAK RADIO AUDIENCE IN THE HIGHLANDS AND AMONG PEASANT MIGRANTS IN LA PAZ

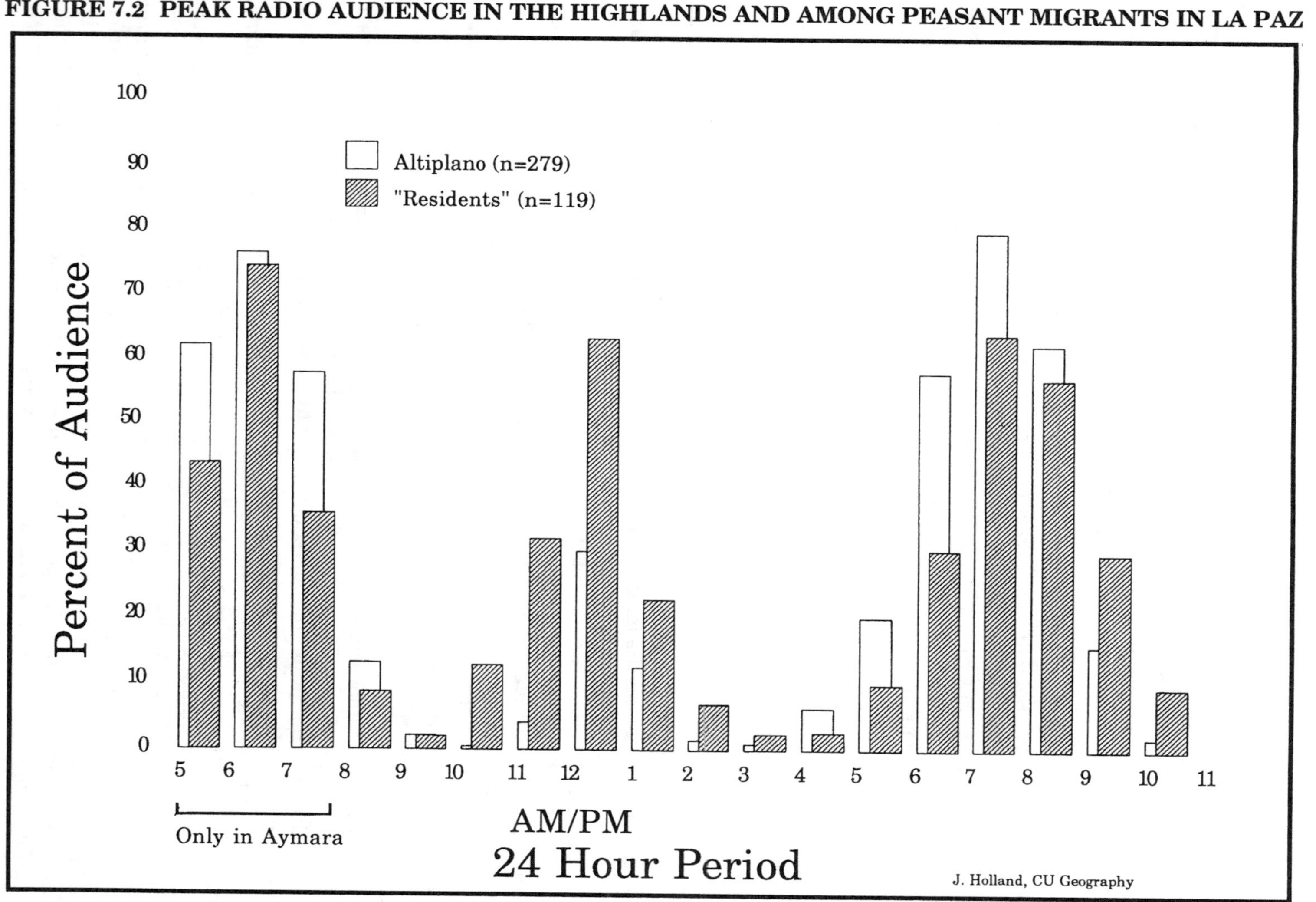

The two preferred radios are located in the heart of Chukiyawu (on the streets Tumusla and Buenos Aires) and function to a large extent as a substitute newspaper and barrio telephone, alternating between Andean music and commercials on the part of an endless number of businesses, and information concerning cultural activities of urban Aymara. Radio soap operas are also produced and often present dramatized vignettes featuring the situations and small tragedies that the residents face.

The preference for Aymara stations is especially notable in the case of women, of whom some 70 percent, in 1979, picked these as their first choice. The preferences of the men is more complicated in that their first choices run the entire range of the stations, including those of group c.

One of the stations that belongs to this group, Radio New America, deserves its own analysis. In the beginning of the 1970s this station had the largest urban audience. It appealed very specifically to the upwardly mobile members of the popular sectors, among whom were many urban Aymara who preferred listening to a Spanish-language station that had a popular style that was more casual and thus more intimate. This preference continued up to 1976 and was one of the reasons why the station director was about to win the mayoral seat.[6] Subsequently, however, the station lost its popular fascination and by the 1980s was displaced in this role by the more sprightly bilingual station of *compadre* Palenque.

Other Media of Communication

In the rest of the means of mass communication the preponderance of Spanish continues to be notable, yet it is not an exclusive trend; there is a general tendency toward the opening of new aperatures, albeit very timidly, for Aymara culture and language. The latter has more or less impact according to the media in question.

Thus, the local recording industry and the local production of films and videos is characterized by its great openness to interculturality. They diffuse, seek, and hum the music and songs of many languages and cultures; on screens both large and small, one can see pictures from around the world and in many languages. Even though it is difficult to compete with the much larger number of available productions in Spanish (Bolivian, Latin American, and Spanish), the practice of making and circulating records and cassettes of Aymara and Quechua music is very much accepted. And in the few but prize-winning Bolivian video and cinematic productions the intercultural theme is very common.

It is very significant that the best-selling record of 1988, by the group Los Kjarkas, is titled *Chukiyawu Marka* and has a totally bilingual texture. Similarly, three full-length Bolivian feature films have focused very specifically on the social and intercultural problematic of La Paz/Chukiyawu: *Yawar Mallku* and *La Nación Clandestina*, by Jorge Sanjinés, and *Chuquiagu,* by Antonio Eguino (both of whom worked with scriptwriter Oscar Soria).

These three productions have made extensive use of sociolinguistic and sociocultural resources in order to demonstrate the urban problematic and its ties to the provinces. The production intentionally named *Chuquiagu* consists of four histories—a recent Aymara immigrant, an urban Aymara, a middle-class native of La Paz, and another native from the upper class—in order to reflect a sociocultural profile of the city. The other two pieces, one of which is by the very genial Bolivian filmmaker Jorge Sanjinés, have integrated to a greater extent the urban problematic with the provincial. The latter film won two

TABLE 7.3   CITY OF LA PAZ. MAIN RADIO STATIONS PREFERRED BY IMMIGRANT AYMARA IN THE CITY BY SEX (CIPCA SURVEY, 1976 AND 1979).

I. Most Popular Radio Station

	1976[a]		1979[b]		1979 Highlands
	Men	Women	Men	Women	Men + Women
a) Aymara Stations					
Splendid	9.3	21.3	8.1	46.3	———
Nacional	12.8	17.4	12.9	22.2	——
San Gabriel	12.2	12.3	6.5	——	52.0
SUBTOTAL	**34.3**	**51.0**	**30.7**	**70.4**	**52.0**
b) Aymara/Spanish Stations					
Progreso	13.5	12.3	3.2	——	3.2
Méndez	9.2	8.8	——	7.4	41.2
SUBTOTAL	**22.7**	**21.1**	**3.2**	**7.4**	**41.2**
c) Spanish Stations					
Nueva América	24.4	12.9	14.3	3.7	——
Cruz del Sur	2.2	3.5	11.3	5.6	3.2
Continental	3.0	0.9	1.6	1.9	——
Illimani	——	——	17.7	7.4	1.4
Altiplano	——	——	6.5	——	——
Panamericana	12.4	9.9	12.9	3.7	1.4
Pides	——	——	1.6	——	——
Others[c]	——	——	3.2	1.9	0.8
SUBTOTAL	**43.0**	**27.2**	**66.1**	**23.0**	**6.8**
TOTAL	**100.0**	**100.0**	**100.0**	**100.0**	**100.0**
	(1003)	**(390)**	**(62)**	**(54)**	**(279)**

II. 1a. + 2a. Most Popular Radio Station - 1979[b]

	Men	Women	TOTAL
1a. Splendid	32.3	72.2	**49.8**
2a. Nacional	17.7	46.3	**34.9 (Aymara)**
3a. Illimani	25.8	18.5	**22.6 (Spanish; Aymara in the mornings)**
4a. Nueva América	24.0	9.3	**18.9 (Spanish; Aymara in the mornings)**
5a. Cruz del Sur	22.6	7.5	**15.7 (Spanish; Aymara in the mornings)**
6a. Panamericana	17.7	9.3	**14.0 (Spanish; Aymara in the mornings)**

Notes: a. The sample is based on residents from five provinces in the highlands
   b. The sample is very limited in terms of residents from any of the provinces established on the Western side.
   c. The Aymara subtotal of 1979 includes 3 respondants who selected Aymara stations "Abaroa" and "Aspiazu" that are low in power. In 1976, Radio Aspiazu remained in the general category "other," and Radio Aboroa was then in Viacha.

international prizes in 1989 and involves the history of an alienated urban Aymara who has rediscovered his communal roots.

Television, which is also a very expensive medium, was restricted to Spanish language programming for a long time and to canned foreign programs with voice-overs. The indigenous presence is limited to occasional performances of folkloric groups, the diffusion of national cinema, and some local news. But the greater accessibility of video programs has stimulated many new local producers whose themes feature the pluricultural reality of the country and of La Paz in particular, as has been the case in cinematic production. These realizations are shown only occasionally on the television, but they have begun to generate alternative networks with the support of mass institutions and organizations.

In addition, the world of the urban Aymara has gained formal access to television with the opening of Channel 4 in 1985, featuring the previously cited *compadre* Palenqe, the owner of radio station Metropolitana. With a basic lack of resources–the show is staged in front of a simple curtain–he repeated for the TV screen his old routine, giving the marginalized social sectors a chance to speak (charging, of course, for this service). He had as much or more success as he had on the radio. In a short time his station began to compete, in terms of audience size, with stations that used much more expensive sets. In 1988, stimulated, perhaps, by the example and taking advantage of the temporary closure of Channel 4 due to a political argument, Channel 2 initiated a half-hour daily news segment in Aymara every morning and soon afterward added a longer and varied weekly program. In a short time the state channel also introduced a similar weekly program. The four other channels in La Paz remained exclusively Spanish.

This involves, as yet, initial steps. Here, competition with expensive programs from the outside supposes a fight between David and Goliath. Nonetheless, it appears that a fresh vein is being discovered, as well as a demand that has been poorly served. The revolution in video and the proliferation of televisions (still absent in almost all of the provinces, which still lack sufficient electricity) can generate a similar revolution that the transistor radio did three decades previously.

At the opposite pole, the press is a medium that more stubbornly maintains the exclusive use of the Spanish language. The fundamental reason for this limitation is another political obstinacy: the exclusivity of Spanish in the scholarly world. In the content of the press, something of the Aymara problematic appears, both in its urban and its provincial manifestations, in a new form in El Alto, called, for variety's sake, *Chukiagu Marka*.

There are, in all, two Aymara attempts at publication in the form of a newspaper but on a much less frequent basis (some four issues per year). These are *Yatiñasawa*, directed by Juan de Dios Yapita of the ILCA, and *Jayma*, which is run by Félix Layme. Still extant, both have life spans of almost ten years. The interesting thing about these papers–run by resident urban Aymara who have university-level training–is that they facilitate the development of language and culture to the point of creating new styles and journalistic themes. Neither, however, has been able to develop a strong circulation level, and both need ongoing financial assistance. Nevertheless, they represent pioneering efforts.

NEW TIES WITH THE PROVINCES

Chukiyawu, the Aymara dimension of the city, also contributes in strengthening and at the same time transforming the entire Aymara countenance of the surrounding countryside, by means of a new system of ties between the urban immigrants and their point of origin. The ties have two related expressions, but each has its own dynamic. One is economic and above all concerns access to communal land. The other is social. Accordingly, social relations transverse a two-way route; they go from the province to the city, as well as from the city to the countryside.

Access to Land in the Community

The principal economic link that residents maintain with their communities of origin is access to one or more pieces of land. Because of this tie, it is very probable that immigrants from the peasant communities continue to be linked to the latter, while those who have come recently from the provinces more easily forget the place of their birth.

This access is quantified in Table 7.4 in accordance with the period during which they emigrated to La Paz. The survey was conducted in 1976 and refers only to peasant migrants who originated in the highlands, who comprise the vast majority of the total. Almost half (42 percent) of those who come to the city own land in the countryside. With the passage of time about a third of them lose this access, possibly because of necessity and the demands of kin, sometimes because they have not complied with the requirements of community service; this also happens because migrants achieve economic stability and lose interest in this complementary resource. More significant is that the other two-thirds retain their land (28 percent of the total residents). Access to and retention of a piece of land, after all, has been made more difficult with the passage of time owing to the growing demographic pressure on the countryside.

The lack of sufficient lands is one of the principal reasons causing out-migration. The effect is that it is relatively normal that families with many children decide to facilitate higher education for some of them so that they can leave the countryside and subsequently look for a better life. If education is not their lot it is still likely that when children reach work age they will try their luck in urban jobs, principally as a bricklayer for men, or as a domestic servant for women.

For this same reason, the fact is even more significant that there are another 40 percent of the migrants who, without even having lands because they are minors, still hope to obtain land in the countryside in the future. This proportion reaches some 55 percent among the recent immigrants (who are, naturally, younger) and diminishes among the long-term elderly migrants, who may not have been able to fulfill their desires. The expectation is only slightly superior in the case of the young men. Even if they do not reach their objective, what is important for our analysis is that, with such hopes, they maintain stronger ties with the community of origin.

The importance of the theme of land is more fully understood in the light of its cultural significance within the Andean theme of reciprocity, especially strong in the Aymara world of the highlands. Even though, after the Agrarian Reform, individual land titles became nearly universal, in practice the control over land reverts in the ultimate instance to the community, whether it involves a community member or a resident of La Paz. A community member (*comunario*) comes to be an actual person (*jaqi*) only when he is married and, as such, achieves stable access to a sufficient number of pieces of land, in the various communal micro-climates, on a regular basis. Thus, only when a man has arrived at a state of *jaqi* is he a full member of the community, with all concomitant rights and obligations.

TABLE 7.4   CITY OF LA PAZ. ACCESS OF THE RESIDENTS TO LAND ACCORDING TO THE PERIOD OF ARRIVAL (CIPCA SURVEY 1976)

			Access to Land		
Living in La Paz since	Never had	Does not have now	Hopes to have	Has now	(N)
0 - 6 years (Bánzar regime)	11.5	7.5	54.6	26.4	(478)
7 - 12 years (Barrientos to Torres)	18.3	15.0	38.9	27.1	(339)
13 to 25 years (MNR)	23.4	18.0	30.4	28.2	(355)
25 or more years (before the agrarian reform)	26.5	17.3	17.9	38.3	(161)
TOTAL (N)	**(243)**	**(151)**	**(530)**	**(380)**	**(1,334)**
PERCENT (%)	**18.2**	**13.6**	**39.7**	**28.5**	**100**

Did not have land when they left provinces: 57.9%
Had land when they left provinces: 42.1%

Parents are the ones who guarantee the fact of access to land (above all, the husband, given that his wife customarily comes from another community), in terms of an "inheritance ceremony" that is carried out at the same time as the church wedding. In a few places there are also occasional intracommunal purchases; land is never sold to outsiders. But the underlying ideology is that, in the final analysis, it is the community that gives this new person/pair access to this indispensable resource in order to survive and reproduce. It is also the community that provides security and handles justice in case of any problem. For this reason, in exchange, the new pair are to be generous in terms of completion of their diverse obligations: paying quotas; participation in assemblies and communal work projects; and in the gradual completion of community posts, both of an administrative and religious nature, that become increasingly important as each post is served.

Such practices generate the strong correlation between access to communal land and the maintenance of social ties with the community. The migrant knows that if he does not fulfill his obligations, sooner or later the community will take away his rights to the land whether or not he has legal title. Perhaps it would be sufficient to delegate an alternative or to pay cash in the case of communal work assignments and routine assemblies, but it is harder to evade the personal service that civil and religious posts require.

In the case of the younger migrants, the hope of obtaining land helps to consolidate stable ties with parents. The former are always helping the latter in every case so that the parents will not forget their children when it is time for them to marry and inherit. Naturally, whether or not this occurs at the moment of truth depends on other additional factors, such as the availability of this resource, the number of children, and the alternative degree of economic success that a migrant has achieved in the city.

Strategies of Mutual Survival

This practice supports a certain stable relationship, involving reciprocity, among urban immigrants and those who remain in the country. Table 7.5 gives us this information, correlating it with the type of access to land in the community of origin. It is likely that these figures are biased in favor of "giving aid to family in the countryside" because it is the urban residents who have been interviewed in this regard.

The data show a notable increment in this type of relation precisely among those who maintain or who hope to procure said access. On the other hand, there is a great drop in reciprocity among those who have lost access: primarily, they complain that their kin and compatriots no longer want to help them, perhaps because the latter have to confront the immigrants in order to take away their right to land that they are no longer working in the community.

Reciprocal relationships consists mainly in "affectionate" exchanges in which each party gives something to which they have greater access to the other: those who remain in the provinces offer agricultural products; those who are in the city provide key manufactured items, as often foodstuffs as clothes and other goods. It should be mentioned that there are other typical forms of aid between the city and the provinces not mentioned in Table 7.5, such as providing shelter to those who come to the city, taking in their relatives and godchildren when they come to study or to work, including aid to the latter in terms of finding them work or offering them jobs in the immigrant's own business.

The flow of exchange, in one or the other sense, is not static. It depends on the given advantages in either the provinces or the urban center. For example, at the time the survey was carried out, in 1976, the city was enjoying a period of relative prosperity, and it is likely that the flow of goods toward the countryside was somewhat larger. Years later, in the beginning of the 1980s, the city suffered the direct impact of a major economic crisis, and the direction of the flow shifted: the number of residents who returned to visit the countryside increased, many of whom wanted to "regularize" access to agricultural products. A bit later, in 1983, one of the worst droughts of the century took place, and the roles were reversed again, although with the burden that the city's economy remained in a grave crisis. Because of this, a third group then entered the scene: the farmers who immigrated from the new areas of colonization in Yungas. In light of all such processes, this type of economic relation between the provinces and La Paz can be considered as part and parcel of the Andean ancestral logic: that of trying to assure access to diverse ecological levels.

Social Ties

The other broad category in which new ties between the city and the countryside are established involves all kinds of social ties, from fiestas to political proselytizing.

In this noneconomic sphere, the province continues to interest those from the city

TABLE 7.5   ACCESS TO LAND IN THE HOME COMMUNITY AND LEVELS OF MUTUAL AID (CIPCA SURVEY, 1976)

Access to Land	% who receive help from back home	% who receive some help from back home			
		In food	In other forms	TOTAL	(N)
Never had	30.6	25.9	10.7	36.5	(243)
Does not have now	18.0	26.6	13.0	39.6	(154)
Hopes to have in the future	56.0	47.2	22.4	69.6	(327)
Has now	54.4	57.3	21.6	78.9	(370)
TOTAL	**46.1**	**43.7**	**18.9**	**63.6**	**(1,294)**

primarily because it is the principal point of reference for their own identity. In many cases, this dimension can have more influence than considerations of a fundamentally economic nature. For example, it is likely that a resident would accept the responsibility of becoming a godparent of a farmer's child, or take an assignment in the community fiesta very seriously, not so much in order to insure access to land but in order to express their achievements in the city. In effect, the great majority of the immigrants have come to the city with the idea of "progressing" and in order to cultivate themselves—for all those who have actually been forced out of the provinces because of the lack of resources and who continue to be poor in the city. In the city, no one pays any attention to their attempts to achieve mobility. On the other hand, in their points of origin, their kin and compatriots are much more aware of whatever gains the immigrant makes. In such a situation, the fulfillment of certain communal obligations, such as the display of generosity toward one's kinfolk, is the immigrant's best path to demonstrate social and economic success.

For those in the countryside, there are many noneconomic reasons that motivate them to solidify their ties with compatriots who are established in the city. One of the most typical instances is to seek the aid of residents in terms of taking petitions to public or private offices in order, for example, to obtain some document, a new item for a school, or some kind of material aid. Another frequent instance, also linked to economic considerations, is the selection of a resident as a godfather. Such a tie assures not only material aid (for example, certain presents) but also, at a more ideological level, parents hope that their child will assimilate the virtues and values of his *padrinos* in the city.

The Activities of a Special Minority of Resident Activists

Beyond these relationships of reciprocity, which are largely restricted to concrete family units, the residents (or at least some of them) fulfill a more general role as social and cultural intermediaries. On one hand, many times, through their daily attitudes, public and private, the residents bring the culture and the problematic of the provinces to the city.

On the other hand, consciously or unconsciously, they are the most effective carriers of new urban values, as often cultural as political, to the countryside. Throughout these pages we have already seen many examples of this general interrelation, as much in the great variety of urban Aymara institutions (unions, political parties, university movements, cultural institutions, etc.) as in the importance of Aymara programs in all the mediums of mass communication, but above all on the radio.

Not all of the residents generate this type of tie or influence of one or the other kind. There will always be a less dynamic and less critical minority that is simply limited to being absorbed by the city, if only in order to join its more infamous sectors. But the history of the last few decades shows the important intermediary role—at once social, cultural, and political—that an active minority of the residents have initiated. These persons are the primary ones responsible for notable advances, in recent years, toward the public acceptance and the democratization of the Aymara—and, at another level of generalization, the rural, the Indian, and oppressed cultures—in the city and throughout Bolivian society.

Still, no one has all of the elements that would allow prediction of the degree of political and ideological influence that this movement will achieve upon other social actors in the provinces, the city and the nation. But what is certain is that there are more and more residents and Aymara peasants who, in a strongly voiced fashion, indicate their firm desire to build a society that will recognize and accept them as they are; where discrimination and exclusion are overcome; and where relationships of solidarity and equality constitute the basis for social relations. A utopia?

CONCLUSION

This overview indicates that, in this city of two names, prevailing social and political practices have generated a clear disequilibrium in favor of the dominant culture. But, in contrast to the situation in the other metropolitan centers of the continent, one cannot speak here of a unilineal or irreversible process. Rather, the subordinate Aymara group shows a unique vitality, and no manifest sense of ambiguity, that is not so expressed in any other Latin American or American indigenous city.

Certainly, we are not speaking of the vigor or creativity extant in other multilingual cities such as Barcelona in Europe. In Bolivia, the economic, political, and even cultural oppression is very brutal. The economic and educational circumstances that face the Aymara in La Paz/Chukiyawu do not permit them to make larger, more ambitious, plans until there is a situation of greater equilibrium. But, within the continent, Bolivia is the setting where there are the greatest possibilities in terms of the process of domination being reversed.

On the other hand, Chukiyawu is clearly the actual capital of the surrounding Aymara world, and, by this means, it also has a notable influence—in many cases hegemonic—over all of the countryside and the diverse languages and cultures therein. La Paz is where many of the changes that are carried out in the provinces are born and, at the same time, the rural problematic gains a certain saliency in the public and state forums. For example, at the political level, the idea that Bolivia should be seen as a multicultural nation has garnered serious consideration in diverse political forums in Chukiyawu; according to a growing number of supporters, Bolivia should thus be *governed* as a multinational country. Here, also, the reality of Chukiyawu/La Paz shows many more possibilities for a reversal of the dominant colonial process than in other nations of the continent.

Whether or not this actually occurs depends, above all, on the organizational capacity of these Aymara, whether urban or rural, along with other sectors and communities of the nation, in order to reconquer ever larger spaces within Bolivian society.

NOTES

1. This paper summarizes data referring to La Paz, including my study of the national census of 1976 (Albó 1980), and those of the study published in four volumes. This study, carried out with my colleagues Thomas Greaves and Godofredo Sandoval, is titled *Chukiyawu, la Cara Aymara de La Paz*. It examines inmigrants from the highlands, who constitute a large majority of the city's population. When necessary, I add complementary information covering the last few years. A related article, with much more emphasis on sociolinguistic data, is forthcoming (Albó, in press). Here, by contrast, I have emphasized the sociocultural organization of Aymara in Chukiyawu/La Paz as well as their ties to the surrounding countryside.

2. Without denying the strong pressure towards the castellanization in the city, we should not forget that, in a census situation, people can be easily swayed into exaggerating their use of the language which carries the most social prestige and to minimize, in contrast, that language that might result in social (and even racial) discrimination.

3. The autobiography of the Aymara woman, Ana María Condori (Condori et al. 1988), who worked for various years in La Paz as a domestic servant, vividly illustrates these contradictions.

4. For more details on this theme in the context of La Paz/Chukiyawu see Albó et al. 1983:Vol. 3, Albó and Preiswerk 1986, and Buchler 1980. For specific information about the residents' centers see Sandoval et al. 1978.

5. The census of 1979 only obtained a random sample in the west side of La Paz, that the previous study of 1976 indicated had the largest concentration of urban Aymara. Interested readers can refer to Albó et al. (1983:Vol. 3) for an analysis of the conditional factors that account for the changes that occurred in these three years.

6. Years earlier, its director, Raúl Salmón, had inspired the Peruvian author Vargas Llosa in the creation of the protagonist, *el escribidor*, or the correspondent, in the novel *La Tía Julia y el Escribidor*.

REFERENCES CITED

Albó, Xavier
    1971   *Social Constraints on Cochabamba Quechua*. Ithaca: Cornell University, Dissertation Series. (Spanish version: *Los mil rostros de Quechua*. Lima: Instituto de Estudios Peruanos, 1974).
    1974   *El futuro de los idiomas oprimidos en los Andes*. Cuadernos de CIPCA (La Paz), 2. [English version in Language and Society series, World Anthropology, pp. 267-288. Mouton: The Hague, 1979.]
    1980   *Lengua y sociedad en Bolivia 1976*. La Paz: Instituto Nacional de Estadística.
    n.d.a. "De la sermonarios Aymaras a la pantalla chica." *Indiana* (Berlin). In press.
    n.d.b. "La Paz/Chukiyawu: The City with Two Names and Cultures." In *The Bilingual City*. Juan Cobarrubias, editor. The Hague: Mouton. In press.
Albó, Xavier, editor
    1988   *Raíces de América: El mundo Aymara*. Madrid: UNESCO y Alianza Editorial.
Albó, Xavier, Thomas Greaves, and Godofredo Sandoval
    1981   *Chukiyawu, la cara Aymara de la Paz*. 4 volumes. La Paz: CIPCA.
Albó, Xavier, and Matías Preiswerk, editors
    1986   *Los señores del gran poder*. (Con la participación del Taller de Observaciones Culturales). La Paz: Centro de Teología Popular.
Briggs, Lucy T.
    1981   "Missionary, Patron, and Radio Aymara." In *The Aymara Language in its Social and Cultural Context*. Martha J. Hardman, editor, pp. 175-185. Gainesville: University Presses of Florida.

Buechler, Hans
   1980   *The Masked Media: Aymara Fiestas and Social Integration in the Bolivian Highlands.* The
          Hague: Mouton.
Cobarrubias, Juan, editor
   n.d.   *The Bilingual City.* The Hague: Mouton. In press.
Condori, Ana María, Ineke Dibbits, and Elizabeth Peredo
   1988   *Nayan Uñatatawi / Mi despertar.* La Paz: HISBOL-TAHIPAMU.
Centro de Teología Popular
   1986   "Religión Aymara y Cristianismo." *Fe y Pueblo* 13. La Paz: Centro de Teología Popular.
   1987   "Religión Aymara liberadora." *Fe y Pueblo* 18. La Paz: Centro de Teología Popular.
Franqueville, André, and Gloria Aguilar
   1988   *El Alto de La Paz: Migraciones y Estrategias Alimentarias en Bolivia.* La Paz: INAN-ORSTOM.
Girault, Louis
   1989   *Kallawaya: El idioma secreto de los Incas.* La Paz: UNICEF-OPS-OMS.
Guardia B., Fernando
   1971   *La evolución de la forma de la ciudad de La Paz.* La Paz: ISAP.
Hardman, Martha J.
   1988   "Jaqi Aru: La lengua humana." In *Raices de América: El mundo Aymara.* Xavier Albó, editor,
          pp. 155-216. Madrid: UNESCO y Alianza Editorial.
Hurtado, Javier
   1986   *El Katarismo.* La Paz: HISBOL.
INE
   1980   *Resultados del censo nacional de población y vivienda 1976.* 12 volumes. La Paz: Instituto
          Nacional de Estadística.
Leonard, Olen
   1948   "La Paz, Bolivia: Its Population and Growth." *American Sociological Review* 13:448-458.
Lindert, Paul van, and Otto Verkoren
   1982   "Segregación residencial y política urbana en La Paz." *Boletín de Estudios Latinoamericanos y
          del Caribe* 33:127-138.
Murra, John V.
   1972   "El control vertical de un máximo de pisos ecológicos en la economía de las sociedades Andinas.
          In *Visita de la provincia de León de Huánuco en 1562.* Inigo Ortiz de Zúñiga, editor, pp. 429-476.
          [Reeditado en *Formaciones económicas del mundo Andino.*] Lima: Instituto de Estudios
          Peruanos, 1975.
Saignes, Thierry
   1978   "Las etnias en el Valle de Chuquiago (La Paz), Siglo XVI." In *II Jornadas Peruano-Bolivianas
          de estudio científico del altiplano Boliviano y del sur del Perú.* La Paz: Casa Municipal de la
          Cultura.
Sandoval, Godofredo, Xavier Albó, and Tomas Greaves
   1978   *Ojje por encima de todo: Historia de un centro de residentes ex-campesinos en la ciudad de La Paz.*
          La Paz: CIPCA.
Sandoval, Godofredo, and M. Fernanda Sostres
   1989   *La ciudad prometida: Pobladores y organizaciones sociales en El Alto.* La Paz: ILDIS-SISTEMA.
Schoop, Wolfgang
   1981   *Ciudades bolivianas.* La Paz: Amigos Del Libro.
Siles, María Eugenia del Valle de
   1980   *Testimonios del cerco de La Paz: El campo contra la ciudad.* La Paz: Ultima Hora.
Stroebele-Gregor, Juliana
   1989   *Indios de piel blanca.* La Paz: HISBOL.
SURPO (Sector Urbano Popular)
   1988   *El Alto desde El Alto.* La Paz: Unión Nacional de Instituciones para el Trabajo de Acción Social.
Yapita, Juan de Dios
   1977   *Discriminación lingüística y conflicto social.* La Paz: Museo Nacional de Etnografía y Folklore.

CHAPTER EIGHT

Borders and Boundaries
of State and Self at the End of Empire

Michael Kearney
University of California, Riverside

Do not ask who I am and do not ask me to remain the same: leave it to our bureaucrats and our police to see that our papers are in order. At least spare us their morality when we write
-Michel Foucault, *The Archaeology of Knowledge*

The geopolitical wound called 'the border' cannot stop the cultural undercurrents. The 'artistic border' is artificial. It shouldn't be there, and it is up to us to erase it
-Guillermo Gómez Peña, "A New Artistic Continent"

INTRODUCTION

This chapter was stimulated by my ethnographic work on the United States/Mexico border. The immediate problem I encountered there was that of representing social and cultural forms of an indigenous people–namely, Mixtecs–who migrated in large and increasing numbers into this border area from their homeland, in the state of Oaxaca in southern Mexico. This task of ethnographic representation is made complex not only by the spatial extension of the Mixtec community into the border area but by the ambiguous nature of the border area itself, which has become a region where the culture, society, and state of the United States encounter the Third World in a zone of contested space, capital, and meanings. Furthermore, the problem of ethnographic representation of this community in this border region is made yet more problematic by a corresponding decomposition of what now, in the late twentieth century, can be seen as the "classic" epistemological relationship between the anthropological Self and the ethnographic Other. In other words, exploration of these themes is prompted by the need not only to make sense of the ethnographic subject that presents itself in this complex field, but also of the changing boundaries and constitution of anthropology itself, that is, its sociology, epistemology, and practice. This is so because anthropology, as an official discipline, is a constituent of the state, and as the boundaries and construction of the nation-state change, so should we expect to find a restructuring of anthropology as a "scientific field."

When I speak of anthropology as a "scientific field," I do so in Bourdieu's sense of scientific field not only as a field of study but also as a field of struggle–a point to which I shall return below (Bourdieu 1981). Also, with respect to terminology, I find it useful to distinguish between "boundaries" as legal spatial delimitations of nations (that is, boundary lines) as opposed to the "borders" of nations, which are geographic and cultural zones or spaces (that is, "border areas" that can vary independently of formal boundaries). The issues with which I am concerned in this chapter have to do with the lack of correspondence between the borders and boundaries of the nation-state.

Let me turn now to the question of changing boundaries and borders of the United States, which, due to the exigencies of exposition, I break into two periods, the first of which I call the modern, and which corresponds to the growth and maturation of the United States as a "colonial" nation-state.

THE COLONIAL NATION-STATE

The nation-state was a necessary form for the development of capitalism in the modern era. As Corrigan and Sayer have shown, the maturation of modern capitalism necessarily entailed the formation of the nation-state as a cultural revolution, which over the course of several centuries put in place not only the bureaucratic and intellectual but also the more general popular forms and practices that in their totality constituted the conditions for the development of capitalist society (Corrigan and Sayer 1985). Apart from these internal conditions, the modern nation-state is the product of two processes of global differentiation, one being the tension with other emergent absolute states, the second being the tension between the nation-state and its dependencies. Here, we are primarily concerned with the latter relationship.[1]

The modern period is thus coterminous with "the Age of Empire," in which the colonial powers, constituted as nation-states, are clearly differentiated from their colonies (Hobsbawm 1987). This external oppositional dimension of the modern nation-state was predicated on distinct spatial separation between it and its colonies, a structural feature that is integral to what elsewhere I call "the Colonial Situation," and that provides the basis for the cognitive distinction between the colonizer and the colonized. Just as the task of the state is to consolidate internal social differentiation as national unity, so must nationalism as a force in modern history effect the differentiation of peoples on a global scale. Globally, the modern age was thus coterminous with the power of capitalism to differentiate the world into developed, underdeveloped, and "de-developed" regions. And in this modern differentiation it is the nation-state that emerges as the supreme unit of order, a social, cultural, and political form that, as Anderson shows, is distinctive in having absolute geopolitical and social boundaries inscribed on territory and on persons, demarcating space and those who are members from those who are not (Anderson 1983). Thus, whereas absolute states achieved the consolidation of absolute power, it remained for the modern nation-state to construct absolute boundaries.

Since its inception, and until boundaries became fixed in the mid-nineteenth century, the United States enjoyed considerable territorial expansion at the expense of Mexico. During its period of territorial growth the United States rolled back Mexican society and sovereignty to its present southwestern border. During a period when passports were devised and required for entry from Europe and Asia, movement across the southwestern boundary was essentially unrestricted. Indeed, this lack of concern with demarcation of the border was a sign of its de facto categorical absoluteness born of military conquest: Anglo was "unitedstatesian" and Mexican was Other.[2]

A firm distinction between Anglo Self and Mexican Other was but one instance of a global system of distinction that was the fundamental structure of what I above refer to as the "Colonial Situation," which reached its apogee in the early twentieth century. This spatial and categorical distinction, this separation of a Western nation from its colonies, provided the poles along which an axis of extraction and accumulation was constructed such that net economic value flows from the latter to the former. It was onto this spatial and economic distinction that social and cultural differences were inscribed. Thus the structuring of the colonial situation depended on the spatial separation of peripheral production and extraction of value and knowledge as raw materials from their consumption and transformation in metropoles such that they could be reinvested back into the colonial project. It was within this systematic asymmetry that anthropology as a distinctive discipline assumed its "classic" modern form as an intellectual enterprise structured by and structuring the lineaments of the colonial situation, such that the collection and consumption of anthropological knowledge became a permutation of the extraction, transformation, and consumption of economic capital.[3]

As absolute boundaries become necessary for the construction of the modern nation-state, so does nationalism,[4] for a nationalism without borders and boundaries that can be defended and enlarged is impossible, as Benedict Anderson might say, "to imagine" (Anderson 1983). It is deemed "natural" therefore, that nationalism is the preeminent totemic sensibility of the modern age. And in no other nation did this distinctly modern sentiment have more power to offset other bases of collective identities than in the United States, with its power to dissolve the ethnicity of its huddled immigrant masses and to reconstruct it as "American" and as, inter alia, race and racism.

A fundamental project of the state–the inward task of the modern nation-state–is to elaborate and resolve the contradiction of differentiation and unity. The disciplinary power of the state must facilitate the reproduction of social and cultural differentiation within the nation while at the same time perpetuating national unity. Thus, beyond the regulation (licensing, censusing, taxing) of the trades of the butcher, the baker, and the candlestick maker as they constitute a Durkheimian organic unity, the state must also ensure the reproduction of difference as social inequality, and this it does in large part by assuming responsibility for public education whereby it establishes a system of "good" and "poor" schools, and then "grades"–in both senses of the term–students such that they come to occupy the same social class position as their parents. We will return to this theme.

THE NATION-STATE AND ITS BORDERS IN THE AGE OF TRANSNATIONALISM

What I propose—and this proposition is suggested by the ethnography of the border area—is that history has passed beyond the "modern age" as I have just described it with reference to boundaries of the nation-state as firm, absolute distinctions between national We and distant They and, by the same token, between anthropological Self and ethnographic Other—between those who write and those who are written about. Whereas the modern phase was socially and culturally predicated on the nation-state, the present state of the nation-state is aptly characterized as "transnational."

"Transnationalism" implies a blurring or, perhaps better said, a reordering of the binary cultural, social, and epistemological distinctions of the modern period—and as I'm using it here, it has two meanings. One is the conventional one having to do with forms of organization and identity that are not constrained by national boundaries, such as the transnational corporation. But I also wish to load onto the term the meaning of transnational as postnational in the sense that history and anthropology have entered a postnational age.

THE BORDER: Scene I

Cañon Zapata is a deep north-south cleft between hills on the U.S.-Mexico Border where it runs along the edge of the city of Tijuana. Most of the canyon is on the California side of the border, but there are no tangible boundary markers except for an old monument and the broken strands of a wire fence on the hills to the east and west of the canyon. Down in the canyon there are no markers or wire at all. Up the canyon, well into the unitedstatesian side are small food stalls made of scrap wood, covered with old sheet metal or boards for a little shade, and equipped with butane or wood stoves. Venders of second hand clothing and shoes have also set up their stalls. The canyon comes to life around three o'clock every afternoon as hundreds of people start to congregate, waiting until the right time to make an attempt to get to 'the other side'. They are of course already on the other side. What they must do, though, is get beyond agents of the Border Patrol that are on the hills overlooking the branches of the canyon above the town of San Ysidro. About a mile to the west of the canyon there is a large unitedstatesian customs facility which sits on the line between San Ysidro and Tijuana. This is the most heavily trafficked official international border crossing in the world. Cañon Zapata is certainly one of the most, possibly the most, heavily trafficked unofficial crossings.

As the afternoon shadows move into the canyon the migrants who have assembled eat their last taco, take a final swig of soda pop or beer, and possibly put on new shoes or a jacket that they have just bought. Then in groups of five or maybe ten or twelve, they start to head out, up the canyon, and into its side branches. They walk in single file, each little group led by its *coyote*, the smuggler that they are paying to lead them to a safe point and to perhaps arrange for transportation to somewhere yet farther north. Or perhaps there are experienced migrants in the group who have made the trip many times and no longer need the expensive services of a smuggler.

When the sun is low, Border Patrol agents, the *Migra*, are silhouetted on the hills above the canyon. They scurry about in jeeps and on motorcycles and horses, responding to the probings of different groups, some of which are serving as diversions to draw the patrols away from others. The *Migra* almost never comes down into the base of the canyon where the migrants congregate, nor does the unitedstatesian government make any attempt to fence off or otherwise close or occupy this staging area.[5]

This same basic scenario is enacted at other sites where the border runs along the edge of Tijuana as well as many other places on its nearly 2,000 mile length between Mexico and the United States.

THE BORDER: Scene II

A few days before Christmas, 1987, several green Border Patrol vehicles filled with agents swoop down into Cañon Zapata. The *ilegales* apprehensively move back towards the boundary line. Border Patrol agents pile out of the vehicles. One is dressed as Santa Claus and has a large bag of presents. The agents spread food and soft drinks on the hoods of their vehicles, and call to the *ilegales* to come and get them. The Santa Claus hands out presents and a 'Christmas party' ensues. Then the *Migra* get back into their vehicles and drive away as the migrants prepare to attempt crossing 'to the other side' by avoiding surveillance and capture.[6]

THE BORDER: Scene III

It is a moonless night. Two sleepy Border Patrol agents sit in an observation post that resembles a gun emplacement. The post is just on the unitedstatesian side of the boundary line where it runs through hills near the Pacific Ocean. Just behind the observation post is a wire mesh fence that runs along the international boundary on the edge of Tijuana. The fence is old, bent, and festooned with rags and scrapes of paper impaled on it by the wind. It has many gaping holes through which 'illegal' border crossers come and go almost as freely as the wind. The Border Patrol agents scan the hills around them and the fields below them with infrared nightscopes. Peering through these devices they see dozens of human forms, bent over, clutching small bags, parcels and sometimes children, silently hurrying along well worn trails through the dry brush. Two days earlier, some eighty miles to the northeast, one of the agents had been sitting on a hilltop with binoculars scanning trails a two day walk from the national boundary line.[7]

The nightscopes are but one component in a sophisticated high-tech surveillance program that also includes motion sensors, search lights, television cameras, helicopters, spotter planes, and patrols in various kinds of boats and ground vehicles, all coordinated by computers and radio communication. The annual budget for this sector of the Border Patrol is millions of dollars, but no money has been allocated in recent years to repair the fence.

The basic thesis concerning transnationalism that I wish to advance is that it corresponds to the political economic and sociocultural ordering of late capitalism (Mandel 1975). Entailed in these new forms is a reordering of the capitalist nation-state. As a global phenomenon the beginning of transnationalism corresponds to a historic moment that might be characterized as "End of Empire."[8] This characterization is most literally apparent for Great Britain at the end of World War II, emerging as it did among the losers, or certainly as having lost its empire. Thus, the middle decades of the twentieth century saw the dismantling of the formal European colonial system and, with it, what had been in effect categorical distinctions between the Western nation-states, and between them and their colonies.

The modern age, the age of imperialism, was driven (according to Lenin, anyway) by the exporting of surplus capital from developed to underdeveloped areas of the world with subsequent destruction of noncapitalist economies and societies, processes that created wage labor, much of which was absorbed in these peripheral areas. The current transnational age is, however, characterized by a gross incapacity of peripheral economies to absorb the labor that is created in the periphery, with the result that it inexorably "flows" to the cores of the global capitalist economy (Kearney 1986). This "peripheralization of the core" is now well advanced in Great Britain, whose colonial chickens have come home to roost, so to speak (Sassen-Koob 1982). The same is also true of former European colonial powers, which are being "overwhelmed" by former colonial subjects who are now "guest workers": Algerians in France, Turks in Germany, Guatemalans and Africans in Spain, and so on.[9]

A similar process is well underway in the decline of the unitedstatesian empire, which is experiencing a comparable dissolution in the spatial and symbolic distinction between itself and its dependencies. Nowhere is this more apparent than in the southwestern border area and in the cities of this zone, which dramatically manifest a transnationalization of identity in the culture, economics, and politics of late capitalism.

In recent years the border area has, after a century of quiescence since the Mexican-American War of 1848, again become contested terrain. Now, however, it is not territory per se that is being contested, but personal identities and movements of persons, and cultural and political hegemony of peoples.[10] A Latino reconquest of much of the northern side has already taken place. But this Latino cultural and demographic ascendancy is not congruent with jural territorial realities that are still shaped by continued unitedstatesian police power. This incongruity of cultural and political spaces makes of the border area, aptly named as such, an ambiguous zone. It is in this border area that identities are assigned and taken, withheld and rejected. The state seeks a monopoly on the power to assign identities to those who enter this space. It stamps or refuses to stamp passports and papers, which are extensions of the person of the traveler who is "required" to pass through official ports of entry and exit. But every day thousands of undocumented persons successfully defy the state's power to control their movement into and through this space and in doing so contest not only space, but also control of their identity.

Within official policy making circles of the state, discussion of transnational subaltern communities is elaborated within a discourse of "immigration policy" whereby the state attempts to regulate international migration. Rhetoric aside, and as noted above, the de facto immigration policy of the unitedstatesian government is *not* to make the U.S.-Mexican border impermeable to the passage of "illegal" entrants but rather to regulate their "flow," while at the same time maintaining the official distinctions between the "sending" and "receiving" nations–that is, between kinds of peoples–to constitute classes of peoples–classes in both the categorical and social sense.[11] Issues concerning "migrant labor" are indeed at the core of the ongoing immigration debate, and here a major contradiction in official immigration policy appears. This situation results from the special nature of labor as a commodity that is embodied in persons and persons with national identities. Foreign labor is desired, but the persons in who it is embodied are not desired. The immigration policies of receiving nations can be seen as expressions of this contradiction and as attempts to resolve it. For the task of effective immigration policy is to separate labor from the jural person within which it is embodied, that is, to disembody the labor from the migrant worker. Capitalism in general effects the alienation of labor from its owner, but immigration policy can be seen as a means to achieve a form of this alienation that increases greatly in the age of transnationalism, namely, the spatial separation of the site of the purchase and expenditure of labor from the sites of its reproduction, such that the loci of production and reproduction lie in two different national spaces. This structure of transnational labor migration distinguishes it from the prevalent modern capitalist mechanisms for the appropriation of labor from subaltern groups: namely, national labor markets, slavery, and internal colonialism. Only in transnational "labor migration" is there national separation of the sites of production and reproduction (see Burawoy 1976; Cohen 1987, Corrigan 1990a).

Modern capitalism has for several centuries relied in various degrees on transnational labor migration. But the point here is that transnational labor migration has now become a major structural feature of communities that have themselves become truly transnational. Official migration theory, informed by and in the service of the nation-state, is disposed to think of the sociology of migration in terms of "sending" and "receiving" communities, each of which is in its own national space. But what the ethnography of transnational migration suggests is that such communities are constituted transnationally and thus challenge the defining power of the nation-states they transcend.

Elsewhere, Carole Nagengast and I characterize the greater Mixtec diaspora and other widely extended subaltern communities as comparable to the transnational corporation, and we accordingly refer to them as transnational communities (see Kearney and Nagengast 1989; cf. Rouse 1991). Both kinds of organizations engage in production orchestrated in two or more national spaces and so reproduce themselves. Thus, just as the transnational corporation in part transcends the Durkheimian power of the nation to impress itself as the basis of corporate identity, so do members of transnational communities similarly escape the power of the nation-state to inform their sense of collective identity.

To the degree that transnational corporations and transnational migrants escape the impress of the nation-state to shape their identity, so must the native, nonethnic "white citizens" avail themselves of the only totemic capital that they have available to form an identity from an inevitable dialectic of opposition with nonnationalist communities that are forming on and within their boundaries. And that totemic capital is, of course, nationalism (with strong dash of racism). In areas of California, European Americans have definitively lost control of much geographic space, of boundaries that have been "invaded" by "foreigners," by "aliens." But having lost control of geographic space in the border area, they have begun to take fallback positions, and we see a shift to defense of social and cultural spaces where the state still has power to legislate identities and practices. Thus, a major part of the discourse on immigration now centers on such issues as English as "the official language," now so legislated in California, Arizona, Colorado, and Florida.

These new forms of discipline correspond to a movement from an offensive jingoist nationalism to a nationalism on the defensive, a shift from a nationalism of expansion and domination to a nationalism concerned with loss of control of its borders. To the degree that the modern nation-state and its associated culture are becoming anachronistic in the age of transnationalism, there should be apparent expression of disease within the body politic—a concern with the integrity of its boundaries. As Gómez Peña aptly notes, "For the North American the border becomes a mythical notion of national security. The border is where the Third World begins. The US media conceives [*sic*] the border as a kind of war zone. A place of conflict, of threat, of invasion" (Gómez Peña, quoted in Fusco 1989:55). The current national obsession with "foreign" drugs and "crime" that are "penetrating" into "our nation" are also forms of transnationalism that also threaten the categorical integrity of the modern nation-state.

> One only need go down to this border just a short distance south of us to see how wildly out of control it is. And when we speak of out of control, we're not just talking about a few folks wanting to come in to get a job, we're talking about a torrent of people flooding in here, bringing all kinds of criminal elements and terrorists and all the rest with them.[12]

Such nativist sentiments as expressed in this quote are symptomatic of the loss of spatial separation between developed and de-developed poles of transnationalism. A major way in which this blurring of the "modern" and the "traditional" is effected is via the spatial relocation of Third World peoples into the core areas of the "modern" capitalist

West.

THE TRANSNATIONAL BODY AND PERSON

THE BORDER: Scene IV

Four Mixtec migrants are sitting around a table in the home of anthropologists having their first meal in several days. For the previous four days they have been walking through the rugged mountains of eastern San Diego County. They are exhausted from cold and lack of sleep and food. Part of their trek was through snow; all of them are wearing light cotton clothing and two of them wear tennis shoes. They are talking with a Paraguayan peasant leader now in political exile, who is living in the house and who is astounded at their manner of entry into the United States. They tell him that when they come through these mountains they try to sleep for part of the day and walk at night when it is too cold to sleep. But one night, they say, they became so cold that they had to stop and build a fire. One of them, the most articulate, says that he was thinking as they were huddled around the small fire, hoping that it would not attract the attention of the M*igra*. He was thinking, he says, that he felt like a criminal, like someone who had to hide because they were doing some bad thing. But, he says, he could not understand what bad thing he was doing for he is an honest man who comes to the United States only to work, to leave his sweat and earn some money. He says he is a father and husband and a good worker, and that is why his *patrones* always hire him. They do not think that he is criminal, but he says that he feels like he is a criminal and he cannot understand why. The other men agree that they feel the same when they are exposed to possible apprehension by the Border Patrol or by other police agents.[13]

As the above sketches reveal, the unitedstatesian-Mexican border is riddled not only with holes, but also contradictions. In this scene the Paraguayan, who is skilled in his own form of a pedagogy of the oppressed, proceeds to explain to the migrants why they feel like criminals, even though they know that they are honest productive workers. He startles them, he grabs their attention by telling them that they run and hide scared from the *Migra* and the police because, as he says to them, "You pay the *Migra* to chase and persecute you." "How is that possible?" they ask. He then proceeds to give them a crash course in the accumulation of surplus value in the California farm labor market. These men will seek work as orange pickers in Riverside. The Paraguayan assists them to calculate the approximate unit wage that they are paid for picking a pound of oranges. He then reminds them of the per pound price of oranges in local markets, which differs greatly from what they are paid. He then explains how the difference is apportioned into costs of production, taxes, and profits that are paid and earned by the grower. He then calls the men's attention to the taxes that the grower pays and how these taxes go toward the maintenance of the Border Patrol. Thus he proves his point that the migrants pay the *Migra* to pursue them like criminals. They of course then ask him why things are arranged this way, and by a Socratic questioning he elicits the answer from them: because they run scared all the time and are desperate to get work before they are apprehended and sent back to Mexico, they accept whatever wage is offered and then work like fiends and otherwise do what they can to satisfy their *patrón*. In short, in a lesson that might have been taken from Foucault, he brings them to understand that the surveillance activities of the Border Patrol are not intended to prevent their entry into the United States to work but instead are part of a number of ways of disciplining them to work hard and to accept low wages.

The contradiction in unitedstatesian immigration policy noted above is inscribed on the social person so constructed, the "alien." This "alien" is desired as a body or, more specifically, as labor power that is embodied in this person by employers and indirectly by all who benefit economically and socially from this cheaply bought "foreign" labor. But this alien as a legal person who might possess rights and prerogatives of a national, of a citizen of the nation, is the dimension of personhood that is denied. The ambiguity of the alien results from policy and policing that inscribe both of these identities—worker and alien—onto his person simultaneously.[14] Being neither fish nor fowl and yet both at the same time, the alien is a highly ambiguous person.

The frontier between the United States and Mexico is formally a line with no width. But it is also a social and cultural zone of indeterminate extent, and some might argue that it runs from deep in Mexico to Canada. It is by passage into but never completely through this transnational zone that the alien is marked as the ambiguous, stigmatized, vulnerable person that he or she is. This border area is a liminal region into which initiates pass via what Van Gennep might punningly have called "*raites* of passage," but from which they never emerge.[15] The alien exists in what appears to be the intersect of one of Edmund Leach's Venn diagrams (Leach 1964; cf. Turner 1964). And as we would expect from the anthropology of liminality, the initiate is reduced to a categorical state of nonhuman—in this case an "alien." In colloquial Mexican Spanish, "illegal" border crossers are *pollos* or *pollitos*, that is, "chickens" or "little chicks." This avian identity can be seen as a symbolism of initiation, of the twice born. Moreover, the *pollos* are also defenseless creatures vulnerable to the predators who prey upon them in the border zone. Indeed, the immediate border area is infested with predators who rob, rape, assault, murder, apprehend, extort, and swindle the vulnerable *pollos,* whose only advantage is their large numbers—most get through alive, although poorer.[16] And, as Leach and Turner might have predicted, the hero of this liminal border is the supremely ambiguous and contradictory trickster and cultural hero of indigenous Mexico and North America, *El Coyote* (Melendez 1982). Ironically, but of necessity, the *pollos* must put themselves in the care of the coyote who may either deliver them or eat them.

We now can return to the Mixtec and ask how they respond to existence in this liminal (transnational) border area. Denied permanent residence in their homeland by economic necessity and denied naturalization by the United States, Mixtec "alien" migrants construct a new identity out of the bricolage of their transnational existence. What form does this transnational identity take? It coalesces as *ethnicity*, as an ethnic consciousness, which is the supremely appropriate form for collective identity to take in the age of transnationalism. In our work we have observed how Mixtec ethnicity rises as an alternative to nationalist consciousness and as a medium to circumscribe not space but collective identity, precisely in those border areas where nationalist boundaries of territory and identity are most contested and ambiguous (Kearney 1988; Nagengast and Kearney 1990). This situation conforms to Varese's analysis of how under "normal" conditions the nation-state is able to suppress other possible nations within it: "Yet, sooner or later, it can no longer mask the development of the existing violent contradiction between the nations (that is the Indian ethnos) and the state" (Varese 1982:35).

As Comaroff notes, "ethnicity has its origins in the asymmetric incorporation of structurally dissimilar groupings into a single political economy" (1987:307). In this case, the single political economy is the transnational milieu of Mexico and the United States, where in both regions the Mixtec are construed as aliens. Denied their patrimony in Mexico, legally prejudiced in the United States, and otherwise used and abused in both nations, the Mixtec are marked as subaltern Other by the nations that reject them so as to exploit them. This transnational structured differentiation obviates the impress of nationalism as a basis for collective consciousness and thus opens the possibility for the ascendance into consciousness of ethnicity as a sign that marks difference, a sign that is recognized as such both by those who are marked, those who mark them.[17] Moreover, those marked persons also remark on and thus collaborate in the construction of this system of difference.[18] The most outwardly visible form of Mixtec self-differentiation is the formation of various kinds of grassroots organizations in the United States and in Mexico that seek to defend their members as workers, migrants, and 'aliens'.

As Mixtecs say, they come to the United States to leave sweat and take home some money. Sweat is a metaphor of *labor* which becomes disembodied from the "alien" and as such contrasts with *work*.[19] Sweating for others in the United States contrasts with sweating for oneself in his or her own community in Oaxaca. There, as it were, one's sweat falls onto their own land and makes it produce *for them*, not for others. The community in Oaxaca is precisely that, a community, which is to say a social body, one that retains, more or less, its own sweat, its own labor in the form of work. To be an "alien" is not only to experience the disembodiment of one's labor, but also to be socially disembodied, that is, to be removed from one's community to the degree that one's sweat, one's labor, and one's identity are soaked up in the United States. The individualized migrant is allowed into the unitedstatesian nation-state not as a citizen but as an "alien," not as someone to be incorporated into the social body but as someone to be devoured by it. Migration policy/policing and resistance to it is thus a struggle for the value contained within the personal and social body of the migrant. The individual migrant resorts to microstrategies invented and reinvented by workers throughout the history of capitalism to retain economic capital embodied in their persons and desired by the *patrón*. The worker seeks to be not just a machine or an "animal," but to be a human being.[20] And as the individual worker seeks to defend his person and its embodied economic capital, so in a parallel manner the community attempts to defend the body social and its collective capital. This it does by converting some of that embodied capital into symbolic capital; specifically, symbolic capital in the form of markers of collective identity, expressions of which are noted by the state and by anthropologists as "ethnicity."

The Mixtec migrants are seemingly paradoxical in that they elaborate what appear to be signs of traditionality under conditions of modernity. But such inconsistency is only a spurious artifact of the discourse of nationalism and its intrinsic component of modernity. In other words, as the borders of the modern nation-state dissolve under conditions of transnationalism so does the opposition between tradition and modernity self-deconstruct and give way, grudgingly, to ethnicity as the primary form of symbolic capital expended in the construction of community in the age of transnationalism.

DISINTEGRATION AND RECONSTRUCTION OF DISCIPLINARY BOUNDARIES

Deterioration of the borders of the nation can be expected to provoke a reconstitution of the state and its components, among which are its disciplines. Among the official academic disciplines anthropology is unusual in the degree to which it has been assigned responsibility for articulating difference, and thus engaging in the intellectual/symbolic reproduction of differentiation, on a global scale, with respect to "less developed peoples" as compared with "us." The fundamental epistemological structure of this classic form of anthropology–classic compared to the baroque anthropology of the present–was its firm categorical separation of anthropological Self from ethnographic Other–of those who undertook to know and those who were to be studied, known and, by implication per Foucault, to be controlled. The modern period, as identified above and that comes to an end after World War II, corresponds with this age of classic ethnography/anthropology.[21]

Anthropology (far from unique among the social sciences) is predicated primarily on the study of the alien Other and has its own distinctive social epistemology of a knowing anthropological Self and a categorically distinct ethnographic Other that is to be known. This epistemological asymmetry of subject-object, of Self-Other, is a reflection of a political asymmetry in which power, like the knowledge being discovered and produced, is unevenly distributed. Moreover, this differential production of knowledge is a differentiating production of power. Within capitalist society the social construction of reality occurs within the structured relations of classes of persons–those who study and consume the knowledge produced and those who are the objects, the raw materials of the knowledge. The dualism of bourgeois epistemology is predicated on this social duality and as such is inherited by all social sciences that acquire it as a basic disposition. But, as noted above, anthropology has its own social basis for epistemological dualism given to it by the ethnographic distinction between Self and Other, which is so structured within the colonial situation and upon which colonial institutions erect parallel distinctions of class. Thus, given the double social origins of anthropology's epistemological dualism, it is, unlike that of, say, sociology, doubly determined.

As noted, the mission of classic (modern) anthropology was contradictory: it had to humanize while it differentiated. We are all human, but we are all different. This is parallel to the contradiction that the nation-state must resolve. We are all one, but we are internally differentiated into classes, genders, and races. In other words, the state states that we are all of one nation and that in this oneness we are all equal, but its policies and practices ensure that we shall remain differentiated along lines of class, race, gender, citizenship, and so on, such that some of us are more equal than others. Similarly, the historical mission of classic anthropology was to humanize while differentiating. In fulfilling this mission anthropology applied the categories given to it by the ordering of official knowledge, especially the categorical distinction between Self and Other. Anthropological categories were established in the modern era, which was associated with a robust nationalism. This classic official anthropology sought to represent an ethnographic Other that was categorically distinct from the national anthropological Self. In the transnational era, this dualistic construction of classic anthropology, in both its positivist and interpretive modes, is inappropriate for the global, transnational differentiation of late capitalism, in which the dualism of the colonial situation has been reconfigured into different spatial relationships. It is not that differentiation at the end of empire lessens, but that it involves a distinctly different spatial and temporal constellation of Self and Other and of the relationship between them. This reordering of anthropological Self and ethnographic Other is most visible spatially when they become interspersed, one in the geography of the other. Classic anthropology was conducted in communities of distinct Others; now, increasingly, the ethnographic Other is constituted in highly dispersed communities that are transnational in form.

With the collapse of the categorical distinction between imperial Self and colonial Other, the basis was laid for the erosion of the social foundation of the modern nationalism of the West and the emergence of new dimensions of global differentiation.[22] The imagining of this transnational condition has been reflected in several innovative "antidisciplines." They are antidisciplinarian in the double sense that they transcend the domains of the standard disciplines and in the sense that they have tended to form themselves outside of the official institutional body of the state and thus have escaped the necessity of official scholarship elaborated as a constituting component of the nation-state. The project of the *Annales* is one such case in point in that it displaced its vantage point outside of national history and transcended historiography seen as the history of nations as actors, to greater contexts and force fields within which the fates of nations are shaped.

It is apparent that the objective reality of transnationalism, in both senses, has called forth a historiography that appears on the stage of history at its appropriate moment to reflect this transnational condition in consciousness: the project of the *Annales*, its global vision, is a reflex of the conditions of the moment of it appearance. And why the *Annales* group and not official scholarship? Bourdieu's (1988) work on the tension between ideas produced by intellectuals institutionalized within the official bureaucracies of the state versus those peripheral to it is instructive and suggests that the *Annales* was disposed to reflect transnational conditions because it was not assigned the task by the state of elaborating a historiography of nationalism, that is, a historiography that is a constituent of the nation-state. It is this sort of antidisciplinary scholarship that has given us the vocabulary to understand transnationalism as global history.

Foucault's project, too, is an exemplar of antidisciplinary and antidisciplinarian scholarship. Foucault is the herald of the "death of man," of the death of the Western subject in the postmodern age, which is to say in the age of transnationalism. The modern subject, the individual "actor" of capitalist society, whose demise Foucault announced, was and is a cultural construction born of two distinctly modern conditions. One of these was the power of commodification to create "individuals" as distinct from the communities from which, by market forces, they were alienated and so formed. The other basis for the cultural construction of the modern individual was the modern distinction between colonial Self and colonized Other. The Western subject/Self only exists in *relationship* to an Other,[23] and thus the collapse of the modern global categorical relationship between anthropological Self and ethnographic Other also occasions the "death of man," of the subject as it was constructed in the modern age. This disappearance of the subject/person of the classic social sciences and humanistic disciplines threatens the constitution of these disciplines as they have been classically constituted. Accordingly, the dissolution of the disciplines that discipline the person/body can be assumed to correspond to a corresponding reconstitution of disciplines.

Foucault does not study the transnational age, focusing as he does on the modern age, but his method–the form of his work–personifies it, based as it is on Marx, whose work was not, as is often observed, interdisciplinary, but transdisciplinary in both senses noted above. Unlike and more than the *Annales* and Foucault, Marx's transdisciplinary method pointed the way to transnationalism, denoted in his discourse as an "internationalism," an idea that informed the subaltern counterpart of the transnational corporation, namely, "The International." *This* internationalism as a vision of global identity is a prescient sentiment that appears in the mid-nineteenth century at the apogee of the modern age and foretells the dissolution of its necessary sociocultural form, the nation-state.

As the "alien" presents a challenge to the integrity of the unitedstatesian nation-state it has responded by developing new disciplines to control its territorial boundaries and the cultural constructions upon which they are predicated. *This* discourse of nations and their borders is manifest, for example, in the current debates on university campuses over

"Western Civilization" and "Ethnic Studies" requirements. One can also note here the recent rise and institutionalization of programs of "Border Studies," which are in some ways the academic counterpart of the Border Patrol. Other homologues of this tension in the boundary of the nation-state are the official language laws noted above and the national debate on immigration policy, which was recently punctuated by the passage of the United States Immigration and Reform Control Act of 1986.

The dialectic of transnational exploitation and resistance takes place on the margins of nations and is both a symptom and cause of the progressive dissolution of the power of these nations to impress themselves as nationalities and as nationalisms on the subaltern peoples within their boundaries. One of the various dimensions of this challenge to the nation-state is the increasing refusal of transnational ethnic minorities to be the objects of study by the disciplines of the nation-state–it might be said that this is but one of a number of ways in which they refuse to be disciplined. As transnational subalterns increasingly penetrate into the cores of the world system, their presence there not only reorganizes the spatial differentiation of development and underdevelopment, but also challenges the epistemological basis of classical anthropology, predicated as it was on the "Colonial Situation" (see above), in which the collection and consumption of anthropological knowledge became a permutation of the extraction, transformation, and consumption of economic capital. One result of this reordering is an increasing refusal of former ethnographic Others to submit to being taken as objects of investigation by the standard disciplines and a corresponding insistence on writing and speaking for themselves.[24]

Just as the borders and boundaries of the modern nation-state have become contested terrain, so increasingly is the power of official anthropology to describe unilaterally peoples and form policies that affect them being challenged. In the case of Mixtecs this sensibility has manifested as a desire and efforts, among various spokespersons and groups, to develop an autochthonous social science that can inform "the community" about itself and its relationships with the powers that encompass it. This informing thus becomes literally part of the process of forming the ethnic community that is informed. In the Mixtec transnational community this indigenous anthropology thus becomes a constituent of that which it seeks to study.[25] Such an anthropology that is brought into being by the conditions of transnationalism, and all that this term implies for the constitution of subaltern communities apart from the impress of national forces and for the dissolution of the traditional disciplining disciplines, is aptly referred to as a "Practical Anthropology" (Kearney n.d.).

On the unitedstatesian side of the border, in California, the differentiating project of the state seems to have gotten "out of control." This is most apparent demographically, with Los Angeles being simultaneously the largest city in California and, as pundits ironically note, the second largest city in Mexico following Mexico City, the largest city in the world. And the second largest city on the Pacific Coast, following Los Angeles, is now Tijuana. Clearly, Latin America does not stop at the border: a Mexican-Latino corridor now extends from Tijuana on the border to deep within unitedstatesian territory, and here and beyond there is a large and growing archipelago of Latino peoples.[26]

Throughout this archipelago practices of differing from below, born of forms of survival and resistance, proceed apace with official differing from above and combine in a dialexis that defies modernism's ideology of the "melting pot" (Corrigan n.d.). For generations, until the late 1970s, one of the main results of this dialexis was "Chicano culture" in its various forms ranging from the more defiant and more or less conscious styles of resistance elaborated by *pachucos*, "low riders," and "home boys" with their distinctive argot to the persistence of more traditional forms of Mexican culture such as Mexican language, music, folk medicine, and cuisine. From the dominant European American perspective all of these "alien" ways were simply Mexican. But to Mexicans–"real Mexicans"–in Mexico, these things Mexican American were *pocho*, that is, ersatz and inferior. But in the late 1970s *el Chicano* was "discovered" by Mexican intellectuals and cultural brokers. No longer seen as a bastard son, the Chicano became an icon of a particular kind of "Mexican" creativity and resistance deep in the belly of the colossus to the north. In Mexican eyes the Chicano has gone from a *pocho* to a cultural hero living in a region of occupied Mexico.[27] The border has thus taken on a different meaning to Mexicans than it has to European Americans.

The dramatic revaluing of the Chicano and of Mexico's relation to the North in general that has taken place in recent years is doubtlessly related to the deep "crisis" that Mexico has been experiencing since the mid 1980s, in which real income of the middle and low sectors has decreased around 50 percent and foreign debt has grown to around $1,500 per capita.[28] Under these conditions there is more pressure than ever for Mexicans to go to the United States to work. Were the Mexicans living and working in the United States to be repatriated into Mexico's supersaturated labor markets, all commentators agree that an impossible situation would result, aggravated by the loss of the sojourners's remittances, which are no doubt Mexico's second or third most important source of foreign exchange. There are thus in Mexico deep structural reasons affecting perception of the border. It has become more of an obstacle, a hindrance in getting to work and back, not unlike commuter problems elsewhere.

With respect to the necessity of the Mexican state to export jobs, a porous border is desirable. But as a modern nation-state, an assault on the integrity of its border is an assault on its power–its power to order and to differ. The border has thus become highly problematic for the Mexican state. And nowhere is this more apparent than in Tijuana, which is, as Gómez Peña notes:

> . . . a place where so-called Mexican identity breaks down–challenging the very myth of national identity. The Mexican government has constructed this myth, which is that we have a univocal identity, one that is monolithic and static, and that all Mexicans from Cancún to Tijuana, from Matamoros to Oaxaca behave, act and think exactly the same. Of course this a very comfortable myth for them to justify their power. By homogenizing all Mexicans and saying that, for example, Mexicans have a hard time entering into modernity, the Mexican state can offer itself as a redemptor of Mexicans, and the one who is going to guide them by the hand into modernity. So Tijuana is a kind of challenge to the Mexican government (quoted from Fusco 1989:70).

Tijuana is in its own way as transnational a city as is Los Angeles, and, indeed, the two are inexorably fusing together into one transnational megopolis spanning the border. Another variant of this transnationalism is the immense demographic, cultural, emotional, and very "illegal" unofficial transnational bridge now in place between urban areas such as Los Angeles and Central America. As a result of unitedstatesian interventions in Central America hundreds of thousands of refugees from that troubled area now live in the liminal world of the "undocumented" who are in the United States but not of the United States. What has become apparent now at the end of the twentieth century is that imperial projects to differentiate the colonized Other promote indigestible differences within the colonizing Self.

CONCLUSION

The border area has become a liminal area where creative energies are released, creating signs and identities that are born outside of the national projects of the two nations which presume to control identities in this zone. This changing configuration of the border challenges the ability of the two nation-states involved to define legal and cultural identities of their border populations which transcend the official spatial and legal bounds. Two forms contributing to decay of the nationalist project are notable: one is inability—an inability born of contradictory desires—of the unitedstatesian state to "document" the "aliens" in its territory; the other is the "crisis of representation" in anthropology about which so much has been said. This is so because the epistemology of modern anthropology has been constructed as part of the dualism in the modern nation-state whereby it differentiates between its "modern" Self and "traditional" Other. In the border area this once spatial, categorical, and very political distinction is becoming increasingly blurred. Whereas the past histories of immigration into the United States have been one of assimilation, the ethnography of the border area suggests that future histories will be one of indigestion as the unity of national totemism gives way to the multiplicity of transnational ethnicity.

NOTES

Acknowledgments. I wish to thank Paul Chace, John Comaroff, Philip Corrigan, Jean Lave, Carole Nagengast, Daniel Nugent, Mary O'Connor, Roger Rouse, and Jonathan Turner for helpful comments on an earlier version of this chapter, which was originally presented in "Ordering Statements and the Order of the State," a session of the annual meetings of the American Anthropological Association, Washington, DC, November 1989. This essay originally appeared in the *Journal of Historical Sociology* 4(1)[March 1991] and is republished here with the kind permission of Basil Blackwell.

1. For an illuminating discussion of the "dialexis" of differentiation and dominance in general, see Corrigan 1990b, n.d.

2. Since 1986, when English became by law the "official language of California," I began to speak a disruptive English. "Unitedstatesian" is drawn from the Spanish *estadounidense* and as such is a (syn)tactical violation of official speech acts. Thus, like Gómez Peña, "I am very interested in subverting English structures, infecting English with Spanish. Finding new possibilities of expression within the English language that English speaking people don't have" (quoted in Fusco 1989:74).

3. Regarding economic capital and its transformations, see Bourdieu 1986.

4. Following Marx's distinction it is useful to see bourgeois society as asserting itself outwardly as nationality and inwardly as state; see Corrigan and Sayer 1985:1.

5. Observations made by the author on various occasions between 1985 and 1988.

6. Description and photos of this event were presented to the author by Jorge Bustamante, President of El Colegio de la Frontera Norte, Tijuana, Baja, California.

7. Observations made by the author on various occasions in recent years.

8. I have taken this term from a recent BBC Television documentary series of the same name.

9. See Mandel (1989) for an illuminating discussion of the cultural politics of ethnicity and difference in the context of foreign labor migration in Europe.

10. Heyman discusses and documents how "the overall trend of U.S. policy from 1940 to 1986 has been increased application of force at the border" (1991:41).

11. Immigration policy is, as Cockcroft (1986) notes, in practice labor policy disguised as immigration policy. This interpretation of unitedstatesian policy regarding the unitedstatesian-Mexican border is supported by research of Bustamante (1983), who has found an inverse relationship between economic

indicators of the health of the unitedstatesian economy and the rate of apprehensions of undocumented Mexican migrants. In other words, as the unitedstatesian economy enters periods of expansion, the "valve" is opened more, allowing a greater "flow" of Mexican labor; when the economy enters a recession associated with rising unemployment in the United States, the valve is partially closed to reduce the "flow."

12. James Turnage, director of the Immigration and Naturalization Service in San Diego, quoted from Daniel Wolf 1988:2.

13. Observed by the author in 1985.

14. "But the body is also directly involved in a political field; power relations have an immediate hold upon it; they invest it, mark it, train it, torture it, force it to carry out tasks, to perform ceremonies, to emit signs. This political investment of the body is bound up, in accordance with complex reciprocal relations, with its economic use; it is largely as a force of production that the body is invested with relations of power and domination; but, on the other hand, its constitution as labour power is possible only if it is caught up in a system of subjection (in which need is also a political instrument meticulously prepared, calculated and used); the body becomes a useful force only if it is both a productive body and a subjected body" (Foucault 1977:25-26).

15. *Raite* is a corruption of "ride" and is pronounced "rye-tay." One of the main services of coyotes is to arrange for *raites*, which are transportation to points north, or informal transportation in general. A person who provides such services is a *raitero*. Migrants sometimes punningly refer to *raiteros* as *rateros* (thieves).

16. Regarding collaboration of police and coyotes, police extortion, and other human rights violations of Mexican migrants in the border area, see Nagengast et al. 1992.

17. Regarding consciousness of the transnational, see Comaroff and Comaroff 1987.

18. John Comaroff comments on this dialectic of ethnic formation: "The emergence of ethnic groups and the awakening of ethnic consciousness are...the product of historic forces which structure relations of inequality between discrete social entities. They are, in other words, the social and cultural correlates of a specific mode of articulation between groupings, in which one extends its dominance over another by some form of coercion, violent or otherwise; situates the latter as a bounded unit in a dependent and unique position within an inclusive division of labor; and, by removing from it final control over the means of production and/or reproduction, regulates the terms upon which value may be extracted from it. By virtue of so [doing], the dominant grouping constitutes both itself and the subordinate population as classes; whatever the prior sociological character of these aggregations, they are, in the process, actualized as groups *an sich*" (Comaroff 1987:308).

19. Regarding the distinction between "work" and "labor," see Comaroff and Comaroff 1987:196-202.

20. A frequent observation of Mixtec migrants in the United States is, "Here we live and work like beasts." And as one Mixtec farmworker recently remarked, "The bosses treat their animals better than they treat us. They give their dogs, horses, and chickens houses to sleep in. But us they leave out in the rain. They even have barns for their tractors, but not for us." The reference here is to the thousands of Mixtecs in California and Oregon who live outdoors in makeshift camps.

21. The "classic" period of anthropology reached its apogee in the interwar period, when the "classic ethnographies" were written—for example, those of Malinowski, Evans-Pritchard, Firth, Radcliffe-Brown, and their Boasian counterparts in the United States.

22. The rise of a differently constituted nationalism, a peripheral nationalism propelled by movements of "national liberation," are an important part of this global shift to transnationalism but cannot be dealt with here; see Chatterji 1986.

23. Regarding the worldview universals of Self, Other, and relationship, see Kearney 1984.

24. See Harlow 1987 and issues No. 70 and 71 (1991), of *Latin American Perspectives*, which are devoted to testimonial literature.

25. Numerous comparable instances exist among other "traditional" groups that have recently assumed and been ascribed ethnicity; regarding the Kayapo, for example, see Terence Turner 1989.

26. This image of Latin America as an archipelago is Gómez Peña's (Fusco 1989:73).

27. Regarding *cholos*, *chavos*, and punks on the border, see Valenzuela 1988.

28. The now chronic nature of the "crisis" has made it a contradiction in terms.

REFERENCES CITED

Anderson, Benedict
    1983   *Imagined Communities: Reflections on the Origin and Spread of Nationalism.* London: Verso.
Bourdieu, Pierre
    1981   "The Specificity of the Scientific Field." In *French Sociology: Rupture and Renewal since 1968.* Charles C. Lemert, editor, pp. 257-292. New York: Columbia University Press.
    1986   "The Forms of Capital." In *Handbook of Theory and Research for the Sociology of Education.* J. B. Richardson, editor, pp. 241-258. New York: Greenwood Press.
    1988   *Homo Academicus.* Stanford: Stanford University Press.
Burawoy, Michael
    1976   "The Functions and Reproduction of Migrant Labor: Comparative Material from Southern Africa and the United States." *American Journal of Sociology* 81:1050-1087.
Bustamante, Jorge A.
    1983   "The Mexicans Are Coming: From Ideology to Labor Relations." *International Migration Review* 17:323-431.
Chatterji, Partha
    1986   *Nationalist Thought and the Colonial World.* London: Zed Press.
Cockcroft, James
    1986   *Outlaws in the Promised Land: Mexican Immigrant Workers and America's Future.* New York: Grove Press.
Cohen, Robin
    1987   *The New Helots: Migrants in the International Division of Labor.* Aldershot Hants, England: Avebury.
Comaroff, Jean, and John L. Comaroff
    1987   "The Madman and the Migrant: Work and Labor in the Historical Consciousness of a South African People." *American Ethnologist* 14(2):191-209.
Comaroff, John L.
    1987   "Of Totemism and Ethnicity: Consciousness, Practice and the Signs of Inequality." *Ethnos* 52:301-323.
Corrigan, Philip
    1990a   "Feudal Relics or Capitalist Monuments? Notes on the Sociology of Unfree Labour." In *Social Forms / Human Capacities: Essays in Authority and Difference.* Philip Corrigan, editor, pp. 54-101. London: Routledge.
    1990b   *Social Forms / Human Capacities: Essays in Authority and Difference.* Philip Corrigan, editor. London: Routledge.
    n.d.   "Power/Difference." Unpublished manuscript, University of Exeter.
Corrigan, Philip, and Derek Sayer
    1985   *The Great Arch: English State Formation as Cultural Revolution.* London: Basil Blackwell.
Foucault, Michel
    1972   *The Archaeology of Knowledge.* New York: Harper.
    1977   *Discipline and Punish.* New York: Vintage
Fusco, Coco
    1989   "The Border Art Workshop/*Taller de Arte Fronterizo*: Interview with Guillermo Gómez Peña and Emily Hicks." *Third Text* 7:53-76.
Gómez Peña, Guillermo
    1986   "A New Artistic Continent." *High Performance* 35:24-31.
Harlow, Barbara
    1987   *Resistance Literature.* New York: Methuen.
Heyman, Josiah
    1991   *Life and Labor on the Border: Working People of Northeastern Sonora, Mexico, 1886-1986.* Tucson: University of Arizona Press.
Hobsbawm, Eric
    1987   *The Age of Empire: 1875-1914.* New York: Pantheon.
Kearney, Michael
    1984   *World View.* Novato, CA: Chandler & Sharp.

1986   "From the Invisible Hand to Visible Feet: Anthropological Studies of Migration and Development." *Annual Review of Anthropology* 15:331-361.

1988   "Mixtec Political Consciousness: From Passive to Active Resistance." In *Rural Revolt in Mexico and U.S. Intervention*. Daniel Nugent, editor, pp. 113-124. San Diego: Center for U.S.-Mexican Studies, University of California Monograph Series, 27.

n.d.   "Practical Ethnography/Practical Anthropology." Unpublished manuscript.

Kearney, Michael, and Carole Nagengast

1989   *Anthropological Perspectives on Transnational Communities in Rural California*. Working Group on Farm Labor and Rural Poverty, Working Paper, 3. Davis, CA: California Institute for Rural Studies.

Leach, Edmund R.

1964   "Anthropological Aspects of Language: Animal Categories and Verbal Abuse." In *New Directions in the Study of Language*. E. H. Lenneberg, editor, pp. 23-63. Cambridge, MA: MIT Press.

Mandel, Ernest

1975   *Late Capitalism*. London: New Left Books.

Mandel, Ruth

1989   "Ethnicity and Identity among Migrant Guestworkers in West Berlin." In *Conflict, Migration, and the Expression of Ethnicity*. N. Gonzalez and C. McCommon, editors, pp. 60-74. Boulder, CO: Westview Press.

Melendez, Theresa

1982   "Coyote: Towards a Definition." *Aztlan: International Journal of Chicano Studies Research* 13:295-307.

Nagengast, Carole, and Michael Kearney

1990   "Mixtec Ethnicity: Social Identity, Political Consciousness, and Political Activism." *Latin American Research Review* 25:61-91.

Nagengast, Carole, Rodolfo Stavenhagen, and Michael Kearney

1992   *Human Rights and Indigenous Workers: The Mixtecs in Mexico and the United States*. San Diego: Center for U.S.-Mexican Studies, University of California.

Rouse, Roger

1991   "Mexican Migration and the Social Space of Postmodernism." *Diaspora: A Journal of Transnational Studies* 1(1):8-23.

Sassen-Koob, S.

1982   "Recomposition and Peripheralization at the Core." *Contemporary Marxism* 5:88-100.

Turner, Terrence

1989   "Amazonian Indians Lead Fight to Save Their Forest World." *The Latin American Anthropology Review* 1(1):2-4.

Turner, Victor

1964   "Betwixt and Between: The Liminal Period in Rites of Passage." In *Proceedings of the American Ethnological Society*, pp. 4-20. Seattle: University of Washington Press.

Valenzuela, José Manuel

1988   *La brava ese*. Tijuana: El Colegio de la Frontera Norte.

Varese, Stefano

1982   "Restoring Multiplicity: Indianities and the Civilizing Project in Latin America." *Latin American Perspectives* 9(2):29-41.

Wolf, Daniel

1988   *Undocumented Aliens and Crime: The Case of San Diego County*. San Diego: Center for U.S.-Mexican Studies, University of California.

CHAPTER NINE

Conclusions

Teófilo Altamirano
Pontificia Universidad Católica del Perú

&

Lane Ryo Hirabayashi
University of Colorado, Boulder

AN ANALYTIC QUERY

In this anthology we have taken a conventional approach to defining *region* as a concrete and specific place that is circumscribed by tangible and generally agreed upon physical boundaries. Whether such a space can be taken for granted, especially in terms of its role in providing a basis for social relations among rural-urban migrants, is open to debate. An alternative perspective, for example, is that the "region" is not most effectively conceptualized as a literal, physical entity in its own right, but rather as the basis of and for particular types of "mentally constructed relationships" (Rosenau 1992:69).

This seems to us to be a useful device when considering long-time migrant residents and their progeny in urban Latin America. In this sense it is possible to argue that when migrants reference "the region" as the basis for norms, values, and social relations in urban settings, this is predicated on the reconstruction of imagined territorial boundaries of, and idealized social relations in, their home communities (Jones 1994:6). Rather than trying to focus on a literal regional connection, then, we may need to explore the region as a kind of "social imaginary," or "a constructed landscape of collective aspirations" (Appadurai 1990:5). More specifically, the study of regional identities in urban settings may well revolve around "the impact of deterritorialization on the imaginative resources of lived, local experiences" (Appadurai 1991:196).

We continue to believe, however, that the feat entailed in the creation of regional identities—whether this is carried out by migrants who are physically contiguous in a given urban setting (be it a block, a neighborhood, or ward), or whether the migrants in question are thoroughly dispersed throughout the city—can be viewed and studied effectively as a manifestation of both material "need" and the sociopsychological "desire" for community. In short, although the "region" in urban migrants' regional identities is very much of a construct, and should not be treated as a literal or unproblematic phenomenon, we will demonstrate below how and why we think that it is more than simply a manifestation of an "imaginary."

COMPARATIVE PERSPECTIVES

As Fallers (1967) and others before us have noted, the phenomenon of regional identities and related forms of social organization are not confined solely to migrants in Latin American cities. There is, in fact, a substantial body of work that delineates the role of regional ties, identities, and associations among internal migrants in diverse settings as well as among international migrants in global diaspora. This fact alone indicates that something substantive is occurring when migrants draw on regional and other provincial ties in urban settings.

African cases, much like their Latin American counterparts, have received enormous attention on the part of anthropologists, especially in terms of the migration process. For example, studies by Cohen (1969, 1974), Dike (1982), Eades (1965, 1987, 1994), Hart (1975, as cited in Roberts 1990:33-34), Little (1965, 1970), Lloyd (1979), Meillassoux (1968), Middleton (1969), Mitchell (1966, 1987), Parkin (1974), Smock (1971), and Southall (1975a, 1975b) have demonstrated the importance of ethnic and regional identities, and of social networks, in the formation of migrant associations, ethnic unions, neighborhood associations, and ethnically based political parties.

In the case of India, authors such as Bose (1974), Bulsara (1964), Lewandowski (1980), and Nagpaul (1988) have described the operation of migrant associations as well as their social base in kin and caste relations. Regional sentiments are clearly present in the larger urbanization processes of ethnic and linguistic groups in India from diverse cultural and geographic origins, although the same sentiments sometimes give rise to "nativistic" resistance to new immigrants, often on the basis that the latter are said to be "too competitive" (Weiner 1978).

Studies of regional identities and associations can also be found in Asia and the Pacific Islands. For example, research on regional associations dating back to premodern, preindustrial urban China is subject to a thoughtful overview in English by Gary Hamilton (1979).[1] Hamilton's essay reminds us that we should not be too quick or too confident in making cross-cultural generalizations from too few cases, representing only a narrow geographical or temporal sample (also see Ma 1984). In more recent settings, Hsieh (1985) studied the importance of regional ties for Waichow Hakka migrants in Hong Kong, with an emphasis on the evolving functions of regional ties, while Skeldon (1980) has written about the formation of sports and mutual aid associations among internal migrants who speak the same language in Papua, New Guinea. Migration studies in the Middle East by social scientists and historians alike indicate that similar processes occur there (Abu-Lughod 1961; Karpat 1976:165-195; Suzuki 1960).

There are a plethora of studies on regional and ethnic ties among non-European migrants in Europe (Basgöz and Furniss 1986; Buechler 1987; Castles et al. 1984; Clarke et al. 1990:219-348; Layton-Henry 1990; Rex et al. 1987; Watson 1977; and Werbner 1990), as well as in the United States and its territories. Older and newer research on Asians includes studies on the utilization and modification of provincial Japanese culture and institutions in Hawaii (for example, Embree 1939). Okamura (1983) has studied the formation of ethnic/regional organizations by Filipinos in Hawaii, although the bulk of his analysis focuses on why such organizations have not been especially long-lasting or efficacious. Kimura (1968), on the other hand, has studied the importance of "locality clubs" among the Okinawan migrants from Japan in Hawaii, granting these the status of the "fundamental units of social organization" beyond the immediate family. Similarly, research on Filipinos, Chinese, Japanese, and South Asians on the U.S. mainland (Almirol 1978; Clarke et al. 1990:197-218; Jain 1989; Lai 1987; Miyabara 1988) indicates that regional ties and associations were often of critical importance in these migrants' social and economic adaptations to the New World.

Outstanding research on migrants from the Caribbean and Central and Latin America in the U.S. includes a pioneering study focusing on Dominicans and Columbians in New York (Sassen-Koob 1979) that has been replicated and extended by other scholars (see Foner 1987; Sutton and Chaney 1987). A good number of studies on Cubans, Mexicans, Haitians, and Peruvians in the United States were carried out during the 1980s (see, for example, Abalos 1987; Altamirano 1990; Burns 1989; Fox 1988; Glick-Schiller and Fouron 1990; Moore and Pachon 1985; Portes and Bach 1985; Portes and Böröcz 1989; Portes and Walton 1981; Vélez-Ibañez 1988).

We might add that the manifestations of regional identities among rural-urban migrants in urban settings are not confined only to Third World people.[2] Anthropologists working in Greece, for example, have made notable efforts to document how provincial dynamics operate in the urbanization process there (see Kenna 1983; Sutton 1978, 1983, 1986). Sutton's research indicates that, among the Greek migrants she studied in Athens, a great deal of attention among compatriots is paid to raising funds in order to promote development at the point of origin. Such research amply demonstrates that regional sentiments and organizations are hardly confined to American, African, or Asian indigenous and peasant communities (also see Layton-Henry 1990; Salt 1983; Schmitter-Heisler and Werbner 1987).

The salience of regional identities among European migrants can been seen in terms of the international dimension as well. Research on such migrants overseas, including Greeks in Australia (Price 1963) and Dutch migrant communities in Argentina (Jongkind 1986), documents the play of ethnic and provincial ties in their social and economic organization (see also Zimmer and Aldrich 1987; and selected pieces in Eades 1987 and Jenkins 1988).

In terms of European immigrants in the United States, there are a number of fascinating studies available about the *bygdelag* movement, having to do with regional affiliations and organizations, among the Norwegian American communities of the Pacific Northwest and the Midwest, almost single-handedly documented in English by Lovoll (1972, 1975, 1976). Similarly, recent scholarship has revealed the cultural and political importance of *landsmanschaften* (migrant aid societies based on "home town" ties among compatriots) among the European Jewry in North America (Weisser 1985). This is especially evident in the research by Soyer (1988) on the linkage between Jewish *landsmanschaften* and the American labor movement.

In sum, because of their multidimensional utility to migrants, regional identities have manifested themselves very widely across cultures and through space. We propose that research on rural-urban migrants in Latin America can provide important comparative insights into the nature of "regional identities" in urban settings, as well as a set of viable alternatives concerning how they may best be conceptualized, documented, and analyzed. In this conclusion, we offer our analysis concerning the persistence of regional identities in Latin American cities in the 1990s, and into the twentyfirst century, in the same spirit.

ON THE PERSISTENCE OF REGIONAL IDENTITIES
IN URBAN LATIN AMERICA

In chapter 2 we outlined a general definition of *region*, and delineated four basic reasons why regional identities are useful to rural-urban migrants. Here, we would like to address two corollary questions: *Why have "regional identities" persisted in contemporary Latin American urban settings into the 1990s, and can we expect this trend to continue into the twentyfirst century?*

As we indicated previously, Bryan Roberts proposed in 1974 that distinctive ethnic identities were typically maintained by those migrants who had strong, on-going ties to their indigenous peasant communities of origin (Roberts 1974). This was definitively *not* a matter of primordial sentiment, however, because Roberts and his associates found that the networks that spanned the provinces and Lima were often the medium for the exchange of goods, services, and labor that were crucial for the economic survival of urban migrants, given the importance of migrants' entreprenureal activities in the informal economic sector of Lima's economy (Long and Roberts 1984).

Some twenty years later, Roberts emphasized that, both because of the debt crisis and the restructuring of the global economy, the central role of the informal economic sector in Latin American urban economies was continuing to grow (Roberts 1994). Writing about the Latin American urban poor in general, Roberts also noted that informal sector activities were not solely economic but also "linked inextricably to community organization and welfare." Coining the term "substantive rationalities" in order to account for the logic entailed in this phenomenon, Roberts proposed that social relationships revolving around solidarity and mutual aid were in fact a key resource allowing strategic calculation geared toward maximizing economic stability and flexibility, and minimizing risk (for example, Roberts 1990, 1991, 1992).[3] Roberts noted that, for many urban dwellers, the informal sector provides

> the informational networks that serve to obtain jobs or conduct...business as well as solicit caring and aid in emergency. In this way, the informal sector, based on locality and local labor markets, can reinforce community relationships, and in turn, be reinforced by them (though it is recognized that informal sector entrepreneurial activities can also be divisive of communities) (Roberts 1990:34-35).

According to Roberts, there are two distinct advantages that accrue for those who utilize informal sector economic strategies. First, they are sheltered from competition on the labor market since jobs in the informal sector are recruited primarily through kinship and community networks and are not generally available to outsiders. In this restricted sense, the informal sector is not an "easy-access" sector because entry into it depends on having particular kinds of social relationships. Second, participants have some relief from broader market pressures since mutual aid within the informal sector and its low cost goods and services (for example, housing, transport, child care) allow people access to substitutes for the same goods and services that would be more expensive if purchased in the formal market (Roberts 1990:35-36). In fact, economic activities in the informal sector can be seen as a source of resources for migrants in terms of two broad historical moments: (1) between the end of World War II and 1980, and, (2) from the 1980s to today (Pérez Saínz 1991). Once this heuristic device distinguishing these two historical moments is employed, the following propositions can be advanced.

In the pre-1980s context, we note that indigenous peasant migrants were basically forced into informal sector economic activities because–given their lack of credentials, experience, or marketable skills on the urban job market–this was the only tangible route open to many. This situation also made communally oriented mutual aid and self-help especially critical in the effort to survive. In this context, then, those who were most able to cope were often those who were able to draw from social networks spanning the points of origin and destination. Roberts, Long, and their colleagues have provided abundant examples of how this worked before the 1980s in Lima, especially in terms of entrepreneurial activities and the ability to recruit labor (Long and Roberts 1984).

Again, the importance of informal sector activities in Latin American urban and national economies has grown during the 1980s (Portes and Schauffler 1993). We propose that the flexibility that is demanded on the production side–the ability to respond quickly and/or opportunistically to demands for labor, characteristic of economic survival even for large, corporate enterprise in urban Latin America–provides a competitive niche for city dwellers who can draw from regional ties and relationships. In terms of informal economic pursuits, the cooperative worldview and forms of organization based on regional ties and relationships can be remolded to fit new demands and opportunities in terms of the exigencies of post-Fordist production demands (Roberts 1994).

In addition, the ongoing structural crisis if not the breakdown of the state has generated a number of pressures in Latin American cities (Morse and Hardoy 1992). Concomitantly, while the urban sector is heavily in debt, unable to provide a modicum of services, crisis has impacted the contemporary rural sector of Latin American countries' economies, which are unable to sustain even small farming families (Roberts 1992). Here, again, the value of communally oriented patterns of urban mutual aid and self-help are clear, given the fact that the possibility of return migration as a kind of "safety net" has disappeared for many, including migrants who still hold land "back home."

We have synthesized Roberts' seminal contributions and, in conclusion, advance the following hypothesis. The kinship, ethnic, and regional ties available to indigenous peasant migrants are central to their personal, social, and economic survival in Latin American cities. Given the importance of informal sector activities to the livelihood of such migrants, both before 1980 and during the period of deep crisis since 1980, we propose that there are both subjective (cultural) and objective (economic) dynamics, far more complex than "primordial sentiment," that help to explain how and why indigenous peasant migrants retain regional identities and relationships in Latin American cities.

Arguing that the literal reproduction of "provincial" culture is impossible, we propose that the regional identity formation discussed throughout this text is, in accordance with Roberts's view, "substantive." Regional identities are "substantive" precisely because they are fully embedded within the context of social institutions that have kinship and friendship, religion, ethnicity, and home village affiliations as their bases. As such, regional identities are very real, and often of "considerable importance and value."[4] Thus, we propose that *indigenous peasant migrants in Latin American cities draw from their regional roots in order to fashion norms and relationships because these (1) help sustain informal economic practices, often spanning the provinces and the city, and (2) provide meaning in conditions of increasing urban fragmentation and disintegration.* The utility of regional identities along these lines appears to have increased in the 1990s and may well continue to do so into the twenyfirst century if urban economic and political conditions worsen.

In sum, although they may be predicated on provincial traditions and practices, the regional identities indigenous peasant migrants develop in urban settings are new and distinctive. They entail a fit between the desire for community and meaning, and material conditions, especially vis-à-vis informal sector economic activities. In this sense, the regional identities created by indigenous peasant migrants cannot be reduced to either simple cultural continuity or material/economic exigencies; rather, as the case studies presented in this volume indicate, they reflect a unique response to these conjoined dynamics.

As others have argued, regional identities can provide the basis for social relations that are, at once, moral, life-sustaining, and life-confirming (cf. Quijano 1993:154-155). They can also provide a basis for various kinds and degrees of political empowerment.

All this, in the final analysis, may help to explain why the importance of "the regional" has persisted in urban migrants' lives in Latin America and, indeed, across the globe. Far from having been diminished by political policies of national integration, sociospatial mobility, or even global processes of accumulation, all of these phenomena have intensified the utility and uses of "the regional" in and for the social organization and social relations of urban migrants from indigenous peasant backgrounds. Thus, "the regional" will continue to play a role in Latin American urban life into the twentyfirst century, although with changing conditions we would expect to see regional sentiments continually subject to transformation into "new and subtle guises."[5]

NOTES

1. Lane Hirabayashi would like to thank Professor Susan Buck Sutton for sharing this point and for referring him to Hamilton's research.

2. Some theorists of urban studies are emphatic that, because of the completely different nature of their political and economic bases, "First" and "Third World" cities cannot and should not be compared (for example, Leontidou 1990:37-38). Perhaps, on a similar basis, some colleagues hypothesize that the manifestations and expressions of regional identities are relatively distinct among migrants from the cities of the developed as versus the less developed nations. Their reasoning is that, first of all, the former is the outcome of international migration, while the latter is more typically the product of internal migration. Second, in the cases involving migration to developed countries, regional identities arises in opposition to the host society, which usually represents a different culture, language, political system, and ideology. By contrast, in the former case, regional identities develops *within* a given country, vis-à-vis a dominant culture, language, political system, and ideology.

Nonetheless, it strikes us that, ethnographically speaking, the broad similarities in creation, form, and functions of regional identities found in very distinct urban settings are striking. An important difference, however, manifests itself in the fact that migrants to cities in developed countries are sometimes able to parlay their regional ties into political or economic niches that bring tangible rewards, as opposed to mere survival and satisfaction (for example, Jain 1989; Soyer 1988). This issue is of great interest but clearly deserves in-depth examination; this would involve a project considerably larger than the one we have attempted here.

3. Here, we have highlighted Roberts' efforts to make rational sense of seemingly "irrational" commitments on the part of the urban poor. In demonstrating that investment in social ties and networks can have very real economic benefits, Roberts use of the term *substantive* transcends the older "substantivist versus formalist" debates in economic anthropology.

4. This is one of the glosses of the word *substantive* that appears in *Webster's*.

5. We have borrowed this last phrase from Robinson (1989:175).

REFERENCES

Abalos, David T.
> 1987   *Latinos in the United States: The Sacred and the Political*. Notre Dame, IN: University of Notre Dame Press.

Abu-Lughod, Janet
> 1961   "Migrant Adjustment to City Life: The Egyptian Case." *American Journal of Sociology* 47:22-32.

Almirol, Edwin B.
> 1978   "Filipino Voluntary Associations: Balancing Social Pressures and Ethnic Images." *Ethnic Groups* 2:65-92.

Altamirano, Teófilo
> 1990   *Los que se fueron: Peruanos en Estados Unidos*. Lima, Peru: Pontificia Universidad Católica Del Perú.

Appadurai, Arjun
> 1990   "Disjuncture and Difference in the Global Cultural Economy." *Public Culture* 2:1-24.
> 1991   "Global Ethnoscapes: Notes and Queries for a Transnational Anthropology." In *Recapturing Anthropology: Working in the Present*. Richard G. Fox, editor, pp. 191-210. Santa Fe, NM: School of American Research Press.

Basgöz, Ilhan, and Norman Furniss
> 1986   *Turkish Workers in Europe: An Interdisciplinary Study*. Bloomington: University of Indiana Press.

Bose, A. N.
> 1974   *The Informal Sector in Calcutta's Metropolitan Economy*. Geneva: International Labor Organization.

Buechler, Judith-Marie
> 1987   "A Review—Guest, Intruder, Settler, Ethnic Minority, or Citizen: The Sense and Nonsense of Borders." In *Migrants in Europe: The Role of Family, Labor, and Politics*. Hans C. Buechler and Judith-Marie Buechler, editors, pp. 283-304. New York: Greenwood.

Bulsara, Jal F.
> 1964   *Problems of Rapid Urbanization in India*. Bombay: Popular Prakashen.

Burns, Allan F.
> 1989   "Internal and External Identity Among Kanjobal Mayan Refugees in Florida." In *Conflict, Migration, and the Expression of Ethnicity*. Nancie L. Gonzalez and Carolyn S. McCommon, editors, pp. 46-59. Boulder, CO: Westview.

Castles, Stephen, Heather Booth, and Tina Wallace
> 1984   *Here for Good: Western Europe's New Ethnic Minorities*. London: Pluto Press.

Clarke, Colin, Ceri Peach, and Steven Vertovec, editors
> 1990   *South Asians Overseas: Migration and Ethnicity*. New York: Cambridge University Press.

Cohen, Abner
> 1969   *Custom and Politics in Urban Africa: A Study of Hausa Migrants in Yoruba Towns*. Berkeley: University of California Press.

Cohen, Abner, editor
  1974   *Urban Ethnicity.* London: Tavistock.
Dike, Azuka A.
  1982   "Urban Migrants and Rural Development." *African Studies Review* 25:85-94.
Eades, Jeremy S.
  1965   "The Growth of a Migrant Community: The Yoruba in Northern Ghana." In *Changing Social Structure in Ghana: Essays in the Comparative Sociology of a New State and an Old Tradition.* Jack Goody, editor, pp. 37-57. London: International African Institute.
  1994   *Strangers and Traders: Yoruba Migrants, Markets, and the State in Northern Ghana.* Trenton, NJ: Africa World Press.
Eades, Jeremy S., editor
  1987   *Migrants, Workers, and the Social Order.* New York: Tavistock.
Embree, John F.
  1939   "New and Local Kin Groups among the Japanese Farmers of Kona, Hawaii." *American Anthropologist* 41:400-407.
Fallers, Lloyd, editor
  1967   *Immigrants and Associations.* The Hague: Mouton.
Foner, Nancy, editor
  1987   *New Immigrants in New York.* New York: Columbia University Press.
Fox, Geoffrey
  1988   "Hispanic Communities in the United States." *Latin American Research Review* 23:227-237.
Glick-Schiller, Nina, and Georges Fouron
  1990   "'Everywhere We Go, We Are in Danger': Ti Manno and the Emergence of a Hatian Transnational Identity." *American Ethnologist* 17:329-347.
Hamilton, Gary
  1979   "Regional Associations and the Chinese City: A Comparative Perspective." *Comparative Studies in Society and History* 21:346-361.
Hsieh, Jiann
  1985   "An Old Bottle with a New Brew: The Waichow Hakkas' Associations in Hong Kong." *Human Organization* 44:154-161.
Jain, Usha R.
  1989   *The Gujaratis of San Francisco.* New York: AMS Press.
Jenkins, Shirley
  1988   *Ethnic Associations and the Welfare State.* New York: Columbia University Press.
Jones, Gareth A.
  1994   "The Latin American City as Contested Space: A Manifesto." *Bulletin of Latin American Research* 13:1-12.
Jongkind, Fred
  1986   "Ethnic Solidarity and Social Stratification: Migrant Organizations in Peru and Argentina." *Boletin de Estudios Latinoamericanos y del Caribe* 40:37-48.
Karpat, Kemal H.
  1976   *The Gecekondu: Rural Migration and Urbanization.* New York: Cambridge University Press.
Kenna, Margaret E.
  1983   "Institutional and Transformational Migration and the Politics of Community: Greek Internal Migration and their Migrants' Associations in Athens." *Archives Européennes de Sociologie* 24:263-287.
Kimura, Yukiko
  1968   "Locality Clubs as Basic Units of the Social Organization of the Okinawans in Hawaii." *Phylon* 29:331-338.
Lai, Him Mark
  1987   "Historical Development of the Chinese Consolidated Benevolent Association/*Huiguan* System." *Chinese America: History and Perspectives* 1987:13-51.
Layton-Henry, Zig, editor
  1990   *The Political Rights of Migrant Workers in Western Europe.* Newbury Park: Sage.
Leontidou, Lila
  1990   *The Mediterranean City in Transition: Social Change and Urban Development.* New York: Cambridge University Press.

Lewandowski, Susan
    1980   *Migration and Ethnicity in Urban India.* New Delhi: Manohar.
Little, Kenneth
    1965   "Voluntary Associations in Urban Life: A Case Study of Differential Adaptation." In *Social Organization.* Maurice Freeman, editor, pp. 153-165. Chicago: Aldine.
    1970   *West African Urbanization: A Study of Voluntary Associations in Social Change.* London: Cambridge University Press.
Lloyd, Peter C.
    1979   *Slums of Hope? Shantytowns of the Third World.* New York: St. Martin's Press.
Long, Norman, and Bryan Roberts, editors
    1984   *Peasants, Miners, and Entrepreneurs: Regional Development in the Central Highlands of Peru.* New York: Cambridge University Press.
Lovoll, Odds Sverre
    1972   "The *Bygdelag* Movement." *Norwegian-American Studies* 25:3-26.
    1975   *A Folk Epic: The* Bygdelag *in America.* Boston: Twayne Publishers.
    1976   "A Folk Rally: The *Stevne* of the American *Bydgdelag.*" In *Norwegian Influence on the Upper Midwest.* Harald S. Naess, editor, pp. 117-120. Duluth, MN: University of Minnesota.
Ma, L. Eve Armentrout
    1984   "Fellow-Regional Associations in the Ch'ing Dynasty: Organizations in Flux for Mobile People. A Preliminary Survey." *Modern Asian Studies* 18:307-330.
Meillassoux, Claude
    1968   *Urbanization of an African Community: Voluntary Associations in Bamako.* Seattle: University of Washington Press.
Middleton, John
    1969   "Labour Migration and Associations in Africa: Two Case Studies." *Civilisations* 19:42-50.
Mitchell, J. Clyde
    1966   "Theoretical Orientations in African Urban Studies." In *The Social Anthropology of Complex Societies.* Michael Banton, editor, pp. 37-68. London: Tavistock.
    1987   *Cities, Society, and Social Perception.* Oxford: Clarendon Press.
Miyabara, Yasuharu
    1988   *Hokorite Ari: "Kensei Gijuku" Amerika e Wataru.* Tokyo: Kodansha.
Moore, Joan W., and Harry Pachon
    1985   *Hispanics in the United States.* Englewood Cliffs, NJ: Prentice-Hall.
Morse, Richard M., and Jorge E. Hardoy, editors
    1992   *Rethinking the Latin American City.* Washington, DC, and Baltimore: The Woodrow Wilson Center Press and The Johns Hopkins University Press.
Nagpaul, Hans
    1988   "Delhi." In *The Metropolis Era, Volume 2.* Mattei Dogan, and John D. Kasarda, editors, pp. 184-211. Beverly Hills, CA: Sage.
Okamura, Jonathan Y.
    1983   "Filipino Hometown Associations in Hawaii." *Ethnology* 22:341-353.
Parkin, David
    1974   "Urban Voluntary Associations as Institutions of Adaptation." *Man* 1:90-95.
Pérez Sáinz, Juan Pablo
    1991   *Informalidad urbana en América Latina: Enfoques, problemáticas e interrogantes.* Guatemala: FLASCO, and Editorial Nueva Sociedad.
Portes, Alejandro, and Robert L. Bach
    1985   *Latin Journey: Cubans and Mexicans in the United States.* Berkeley: University of California Press.
Portes, Alejandro, and Józef Böröcz
    1989   "Contemporary Immigration: Theoretical Perspectives on its Determinants and Modes of Incorporation." *International Migration Review* 23:606-630.
Portes, Alejandro, and Richard Schauffler
    1993   "Competing Perspectives on the Latin American Informal Sector." *Population and Development Review* 19:33-60.
Portes, Alejandro, and John Walton
    1981   *Labor, Class, and the International System.* New York: Academic Press.

Price, Charles A.
  1963   *Southern Europeans in Australia*. Melbourne: Oxford University Press.
Quijano, Aníbal
  1993   "Modernity, Identity, and Utopia in Latin America." *Boundary 2* 20:140-155.
Rex, John, Daniele Joly, and Czarina Wilpert
  1987   *Immigrant Associations in Europe*. Aldershot, England: Gower (published in association with the European Science Foundation).
Roberts, Bryan R.
  1974   "The Interrelationships of City and Provinces in Peru and Guatemala." *Latin American Urban Research* 4:207-235.
  1990   "The Informal Sector in Comparative Perspective." In *Perspectives on the Informal Economy*, Monographs in Economic Anthropology, 8. M. Estellie Smith, editor, pp. 23-48. Lanham, MD: University Press of America.
  1991   "Household Coping Strategies and Urban Poverty in Comparative Perspective." In *Urban Life in Transition*. M. Gottdiener and Chris G. Pickvance, editors, pp. 135-168. Newbury Park, CA: Sage.
  1992   "Transitional Cities." In *Rethinking the Latin American City*. Richard M. Morse and Jorge E. Hardoy, editors, pp. 50-65. Washington, DC, and Baltimore: The Woodrow Wilson Center Press and The Johns Hopkins University Press.
  1994   "Informal Economy and Family Strategies." *International Journal of Urban and Regional Research* 18:6-23.
Robinson, David J.
  1989   "The Language and Significance of Place in Latin America." In *The Power of Place: Bringing Together Geographical and Sociological Imaginations*. John A. Agnew and James S. Duncan, editors, pp. 157-184. Boston: Unwin Hyman.
Rosenau, Pauline Marie
  1992   *Post-Modernism and the Social Sciences: Insights, Inroads, and Intrusions*. Princeton: Princeton University Press.
Salt, John
  1983   "High Level Manpower Movements in Western Europe and the Role of Careers: An Explanatory Framework." *International Migration Review* 17:633-652.
Sassen-Koob, Saskia
  1979   "Formal and Informal Associations: Dominicans and Colombians in New York." *International Migration Review* 13:314-332.
Schmitter-Heisler, B, and P. Werbner
  1987   "Sending Countries and the Politics of Emigration and Destination." *International Migration Review* 19:469-484.
Skeldon, Ronald
  1980   "Regional Associations among Urban Migrants in Papua, New Guinea." *Oceania* 50:248-372.
Smock, Audrey C.
  1971   *Ibo Politics: The Role of Ethnic Unions in Eastern Nigeria*. Cambridge, MA: Harvard University Press.
Southall, Aiden
  1975a   "From Segmentary Lineage to Ethnic Association–Luo, Luhya, Ibo, and Others." In *Colonialism and Change: Essays Presented to Lucy Mair*. Maxwell Owusu, editor, pp. 203-229. The Hague: Mouton.
  1975b   "Forms of Ethnic Linkage between Town and Country." In *Town and Country in Central and Eastern Africa*. David Parkin, editor, pp. 265-275. London: International African Institute.
Soyer, Daniel
  1988   "*Landsmanshaften* and the Jewish Labor Movement: Cooperation, Conflict, and the Building of Community." *Journal of American Ethnic History* 7:22-45.
Sutton, Constance R., and Elsa M. Chaney, editors
  1987   *Caribbean Life in New York City: Sociocultural Dimensions*. New York: Center for Migration Studies of New York.
Sutton, Susan Buck
  1978   *Migrant Regional Associations: An Athenian Example and Its Implications*. Ph.D. dissertation,

University of North Carolina.

1983   "Migrant Associations and Regional Disparities." Paper presented at the 1983 meetings of the Society for Applied Anthropology, San Diego, CA, March 17-19.

1986   "Athenian Migrant Associations and the Underdevelopment of Modern Greece." Paper presented at the 1986 meetings of the American Anthropological Association, Washington, DC, December 6.

Suzuki, Peter

1960   "Village Solidarity among Turkish Peasants Undergoing Urbanization." *Science* 132:891.

Vélez-Ibañez, Carlos

1988   "Networks of Exchange among Mexicans in the U.S. and Mexico: Local Level Mediating Responses to National and International Transformations." *Urban Anthropology* 17:27-51.

Watson, James L., editor

1977   *Between Two Worlds: Migrants and Minorities in Britian.* Oxford: Basil Blackwell.

Weiner, Myron

1978   *Sons of the Soil: Migration and Ethnic Conflict in India.* Princeton, NJ: Princeton University Press.

Weisser, Michael R.

1985   *A Brotherhood of Memory: Jewish* Lansmanshaften *in the New World.* New York: Basic Books.

Werbner, Pnina

1990   *The Migration Process: Capital, Gifts and Offerings among British Pakistanis.* New York: Berg.

Zimmer, C., and H. Aldrich

1987   "Resource Mobilization through Ethnic Networks: Kinship and Friendship Ties of Shopkeepers in England." *Sociological Perspectives* 30:422-445.

NOTES ON CONTRIBUTORS

Xavier Albó is currently a researcher with the Centro de Investigación y Promoción del Campesinado in La Paz, Bolivia. For many years Dr. Albó has been carrying out a study of the rural-urban movement of Aymara-speaking migrants to the cities of Bolivia and Peru, a long-term interest that has resulted in the publication of many books, including *Ojje por encima de todo: Historia de un centro de residentes excampesinos en La Paz*, with Godofredo Sandoval (CIPCA 1978), and *Chukiyawu: La cara Aymara de La Paz*, Volumes 1-4, with Godofredo Sandoval and Thomas Greaves (CIPCA 1981-1987). Dr. Albó has also participated in research on similar themes in Argentina.

Teófilo Altamirano is Professor of Anthropology and also chair of the Anthropology Department at the Catholic University, Lima, Peru. He has carried out extensive field research on Quechua and Aymara migration to Lima, the results of which are reported in his books *Presencia andina en Lima metropolitana* (Universidad Católica del Perú, 1984) and *Cultura Andina y pobreza urbana: Aymaras en Lima metropolitana* (Universidad Católica del Perú, 1988) as well as numerous essays and articles. Professor Altamirano has also carried out research on Peruvian migrants in the United States, reported in his latest books *Los que se fueron: Los Peruanos en Estados Unidos* (Universidad Católica del Perú, 1990) and *Exodo: Peruanos en el exterior* (Universidad Católica del Perú, 1992).

Hernán Carrasco is an Ecuadorian anthropologist working at the Instituto de Estudios Ecuatorianos (IEE). Dr. Carrasco studied economics at the Catholic University of Chile and anthropology at the Catholic University of Quito. His fieldwork, focusing on rural-urban migration and urban adaptation, has resulted in numerous publications, including *Migrantes campesinos de Licto y Flores*, with Carola Lentz (*Ediciones abya-yala*, 1985), and *Caminantes y retornos*, with Gilda Farrel and Simón Pachano (Instituto de Estudios Ecuatorianos, 1988). Dr. Carrasco has been doing research in Ecuador for the past ten years, primarily with the Instituto de Estudios Ecuatorianos, where he also teaches a course, "Formación de Investigadores en Ciencias Sociales," funded by the Consejo Latinoamericano de Ciencias Sociales (CLACSO).

Paul L. Doughty is Distinguished Service Professor of Anthropology and Latin American Studies at the University of Florida. He received his Ph.D. from Cornell University in 1963. Since 1960 he has worked in Peru as a member of the Cornell-Peru Project at Vicos. He has also researched Peace Corps impact and has studied and worked on redevelopment after Peru's 1970 earthquake. Since 1961 he has been studying various aspects of Peru's internal migration process and urban life. Professor Doughty is past president of the Latin American Studies Association and served as co-president of the Society for Latin American Anthropology. Among his recent publications are "Crossroads for Anthropology: Human Rights in Latin America," in *Anthropology and Human Rights* (Cambridge, MA: Society for Applied Anthropology and Cultural Survival, Inc., Cultural Survival Report No. 24); "Decades of Disaster: Promise and Performance in the Callejon de Huaylas, Peru," in *Natural Disasters and Cultural Responses* (special issue of Studies in Third World Societies, 36, June 1988); "The Food Game in Latin America," in *Anthropology and Food Policy* (University of Georgia Press, 1991); and "Society and Environment," in *Peru: A Country Study* (U.S. Government Printing Office, 1993).

Lane Ryo Hirabayashi is Associate Professor of Anthropology and Ethnic Studies, University of Colorado, Boulder, where he is also coordinator of the Asian American Studies program at the Center for Studies of Ethnicity and Race in America. His book *Cultural Capital: Mountain Zapotec Migrant Associations in Mexico City* (1993) is part of the PROFMEX series published by the University of Arizona Press.

Michael Kearney is Professor of Anthropology at the University of California, Riverside. The author of *The Winds of Ixtepeji: World View and Society in a Zapotec Town* (Holt, Rinehart & Winston, 1972), *World View* (Chandler and Sharp, 1984), and *Reconceptualizing the Peasantry* (Westview, 1996), as well as many articles, Professor Kearney has published extensively on the transnational dimensions of Mixtec identity and political activism.

William P. Mitchell is Freed Professor of Anthropology at Monmouth University in New Jersey, and author of *Peasants on the Edge: Crop, Cult and Crisis in the Andes* (University of Texas Press, 1991), in addition to many articles. He is an authority on rural production systems and recently coedited *Irrigation at High Altitudes: Water Control Systems in the Andes* (Society for Latin American Anthropology publication, Volume 12, 1994). He has been a visiting Fulbright scholar in Peru and has taught at the Catholic University in Lima. He has conducted research among Quechua-speaking migrants in Lima, with a special focus on how their remittances create linkages between the urban and provincial spheres of the Peruvian economy. He was last in Peru in 1996, working with peasants displaced by the Shining Path war.

Bryan Roberts currently holds the C. B. Smith Sr. Centennial Chair in US-Mexico Relations at the University of Texas. An internationally recognized authority on Latin America, Roberts is the author of numerous articles and books, including *Organizing Strangers* (University of Texas, 1973) and *The Making of Citizens: Cities of Peasants Revisited* (Arnold, 1995).